WESTMAR COLLEGE LIBRARY

W9-CDS-091

Conscience: Development and Self-Transcendence

Conscience: Development And Self-Transcendence

WALTER E. CONN

Religious Education Press

Birmingham, Alabama

BV
4615
.C66

Copyright © 1981 by Walter E. Conn
All rights reserved

No part of this publication may be reproduced, stored in a retrieval system,
or transmitted, in any form or by any means, electronic, photocopying,
recording, or otherwise, without the prior written permission of the publisher.

Library of Congress Cataloging in Publication Data

Conn, Walter E
   Conscience-development and self-transcendence.

   Includes bibliographical references and index.
   1. Conscience. 2. Moral development. 3. Authen-
ticity (Philosophy) 4. Transcendence (Philosophy)
I. Title.
BV4615.C66   241'.1   80-24043
ISBN 0-89135-025-X

Religious Education Press, Inc.
1531 Wellington Road
Birmingham, Alabama 35209
10 9 8 7 6 5 4 3 2

Religious Education Press publishes books exclusively in religious education
and in areas closely related to religious education. It is committed to en-
hancing and professionalizing religious education through the publication of
serious, significant, and scholarly works.

PUBLISHER TO THE PROFESSION

FOR JOANN

Contents

Preface

This foundational study in theological ethics interprets conscience as the drive of the personal subject toward the authenticity of self-transcendence that is realized in every instance of creative understanding, critical judgment, responsible decision, and genuine love. As an understanding of conscience in terms of such authentic living, this interpretation, of course, is hardly new. But as an interpretation that *critically* grounds the meaning of authenticity in psychological theories of development and the philosophical reflection of transcendental method, the understanding of conscience proposed in this book *is*, I think, quite novel.

The last century has seen the emergence of authenticity—especially in existentialist thought—as the dominant category in moral reflection. Though more demanding than the ideal of sincerity which it replaced, authenticity is not entirely unambiguous, giving moral authority, on occasion, even to such traditionally condemned realities as violence and unreason. The difficulty, I suggest, is that authenticity is not a criterion of the moral life, as it is often claimed to be, but rather an ideal which stands in need of a criterion.

This difficulty accounts in large part for the contemporary emergence of "responsibility" as a central category in theological ethics. Without repudiating the genuine gains of authenticity, the focus on responsibility attempts to reestablish concern for the "other" as a criterion at the center of moral consciousness. More than a simple return to the ideal of sincerity, responsibility symbolizes the discovery that one can only be true to one's self insofar as one is true to others— insofar, that is, as one responds to the *values* in each human situation in a manner that is at once free and creative, critical and fitting. If the responsible person responds to value, then, his or her authenticity is not arbitrary, but self-transcending.

Moreover, the authenticity of such responsibility must be understood within the context of an interpretation of the personal subject which overcomes the alleged conflict between self-realization and one's obligation to, and love of, others. Such a "conflict" is illusory because *true* self-realization (in contrast to the various forms of narcis-sistic self-aggrandizement which masquerade as self-realization) is not only unopposed to responsible love of others, but, far from conflicting with such a love, *requires* it as a fundamental condition for its own possibility. The thesis of this book, indeed, is that authentic self-realization is found only in genuine self-transcendence.

Basic to my thesis that authentic or fully human conscience is the moral consciousness of the concrete human subject who is at once cognitively, affectively, and morally self-transcending is the argument that self-transcendence is operative—at least implicitly—as a key cri-terion of maturity in the developmental theories of Erik Erikson, Jean Piaget, and Lawrence Kohlberg.

Bernard Lonergan's method of self-appropriation offers a personally verifiable analysis of the cognitive, moral, and affective self-transcendence achieved through critical judgment, responsible deci-sion, and genuine love—particularly of those special instances which constitute fundamental conversions, effecting radical transformations of the subject's basic horizon. In Lonergan's transcendental analysis there are the elements of a normative understanding of conscience as the critically appropriated drive of the self-transcending personal sub-ject for the authentic realization of value.

Though the ground had been well prepared some years earlier at Boston College, where I was expertly guided through the complexities of Piaget and Lonergan by Joseph Flanagan and the late Robert Richard, my reflections on conscience as self-transcending subjectivity first took root in 1969 at Union Theological Seminary and Columbia University. Among the several people who helped me during the dissertation phase of my research and writing in New York, I owe much to J. Alfred Martin, Jr., Deanna Kuhn, and Robert Neale. And I am especially indebted to Beverly Harrison and Roger Shinn for their perceptive and caring guidance during that period.

Since 1973 I have been encouraged by the appreciative response from many readers to the first version of my work, as well as by the interest of the journal editors who allowed me to develop and refine my perspective in their pages. During these years I have been particu-larly grateful for the continuing critical interest and personal support of colleagues like Maurice Duchaine and William M. Thompson, Charles E. Curran and Robert Doran, David Tracy and Donald Gelpi, Bernard Tyrrell and Matthew Lamb, Frederick Crowe and Margaret Gorman, Fred Lawrence and Sandra Schneiders. Of course I am espe-cially happy to include Bernard Lonergan in this group.

Faculty colleagues at Villanova have been a constant source of support and delight over the last two years. And the personal assistance I have received at Villanova from Geraldine Bloemker, M.A. (*Villa.*), Teresa Byrne, Patricia Fry, and Marie Lovera has enabled me to produce this latest version while maintaining some degree of sanity. But with all this help, the editorial interest of James Michael Lee is finally responsible for the appearance of my work in book form.

Clearly, this book on self-transcendence has a history; and ever since the first word of its first version was written several years ago, I have shared that history with Joann Wolski Conn, who has been a constant model of self-transcending love in my life; this is truly her book.

Walter E. Conn
Villanova

1

The Problematic Status of Conscience in Theological Ethics

Few major concepts in Christian life and ethical thought have had as complex and ambiguous histories as "conscience." The problem is not that the term "conscience" has been used without some measure of clarity and distinctness of meaning (although this has often enough been the case); rather, it has been employed in so many ways, with so many meanings, that it seems to defy a commonly accepted definition.

So striking is the lack of consensus on the meaning of "conscience," in fact, that one might seriously question its usefulness in ethical reflection. And yet "conscience" will not go away. Even a cursory historical survey of Christian thought or a rapid check of contemporary Christian vocabulary indicates that "conscience" has become a permanent and central feature on the ethical landscape, and is here to stay and be dealt with. This ethical negotiation of "conscience," with both critical and constructive dimensions, is precisely the purpose of this book.

Is there a fundamental meaning of conscience? What are the role and function of conscience in Christian life? Why does it persist as a constant element in Christian thought? How can its various meanings be distinguished and interrelated? Can formal ethical reflection avoid the term and the moral reality or realities it represents?

This study will offer a distinctive interpretation of conscience in terms of self-transcending subjectivity, and argue for the centrality of conscience thus understood as a foundational reality in contemporary theological ethics. It will not attempt to demonstrate the existence of some particular faculty or power named conscience, nor will it attempt to prove that conscience in the sense of any such reality is necessary in theological ethics. Rather, it will argue that a developmental and transcendental interpretation of personal moral consciousness (conscience) in terms of self-transcending subjectivity is an adequate and most appropriate way of understanding not only what H. Richard Niebuhr has called "human moral life in general," but also specifically religious and Christian moral life. For the term "conscience" does not refer to any power or faculty, but is rather a metaphor pointing to the

1

specifically moral dimension of the human person, to the personal subject as sensitive and responsive to value. "Conscience" will be taken in the broad sense here, then, as personal moral consciousness.

Bernard Häring has distinguished conscience in terms of "power" and "act,"[1] and John Macquarrie has identified a basic threefold distinction of conscience as (1) concrete deliberation on a specific moral question in a particular situation, (2) knowledge of general moral principles, and (3) fundamental mode of self-awareness; to these he adds knowledge of a particular code or set of rules, which mediates between the first and second.[2] Interpreted as the conscious drive toward self-transcendence at the heart of personal subjectivity, "conscience" in this study will be understood in a deep and broad enough fashion to include—and to some degree reinterpret—each of these aspects and dimensions.

After exploring the problematic status of conscience and outlining the book's argument here in chapter one, the first step in the study's strategy for developing a foundational understanding of conscience will be the construction of a model of self-transcending subjectivity based on psychological theories of development (chapter two). Then, after showing how such a developmental model of self-transcending subjectivity can be personally verified through the philosophical method of self-appropriation, the study will argue that this developmental and philosophical understanding of conscience as self-transcending subjectivity involves radical personal conversion as a normative criterion of authenticity (chapter three). Having shown the intrinsic relationship between conversion and conscience, the study will propose a normative definition of conscience, and conclude by indicating some of the major implications of its interpretation of conscience and conversion for theological ethics (chapter four).

Anyone well acquainted with the history of ethical theory knows how absolutely central a role reflection upon "conscience" has always played in that history, from the beginning of Greek philosophy to the present, whether the method was metaphysical or analytic, the approach humanistic or theological. Indeed, even the person uninitiated in ethics realizes well how important a place conscience occupies in the morality of common sense, whether religious or secular.

So it has been throughout history in Greek tragedies, Reformation histories, and contemporary newspapers. There has, it seems, always been an Antigone or a Socrates, a Martin Luther or a Joan of Arc, a Thomas More or an Anne Hutchinson, a Martin Luther King, a Dorothy Day, or an Aleksandr Solzhenitsyn. And there has always been someone, too, who felt obliged to reflect upon, to explain the moral ground of such heroes and heroines of conscience. On this much, perhaps, there is no debate. But agreement seems to end here. Men and women of keen conscience are always controversial. Perhaps there should be little wonder, then, that conscience itself—like other fundamental human realities—is continually being brought before the bar of philosophical reason, or that the case has been argued so differently at different times with such varying outcomes. The fact is that one does not give final solutions to foundational questions, one tries merely to respond honestly to them. So it is with conscience. As one, in life, can only try to come to grips with the demands of conscience, not hope to answer it completely once and for all, so in philosophical reflection one finds conscience a relentless yet most elusive questioner. In this book I will respond once more. My hope is not to answer the question of conscience in a final and complete way, then, but to respond to it in such a manner as to enrich and clarify the meaning of the question, and through this response to illuminate in some small way the structure of theological ethics' foundations.

A. CENTRAL ISSUES OF THE STUDY

As a central concept in ethics, conscience has not suffered from any lack of commentators. Unfortunately, however, rather than clarifying its meaning, discussions of conscience have just as often confused it, by reducing it to a faculty, power, or specific act; by identifying it with the unconscious superego or a vague sense of guilt; or by introducing it uncritically into various psychological and theological contexts. In contrast to the approaches to conscience that rest on essentially compartmentalized or reductionist views of the human person, my approach in this book will place conscience within the context of an interpretation of the personal subject that is at once holistic and emergent. Indeed, I shall argue that conscience must be understood as the dynamic core of conscious subjectivity that constitutes the very being of the personal subject, driving him or her toward an authenticity of self-transcendence, a self-transcendence defined normatively in terms of creative understanding, critical judgment, responsible decision, and genuine love.

1. Authenticity and Self-Transcendence

Although the central subject in this study is conscience, I shall be pursuing it within the cultural and theoretical context of such concepts as authenticity, responsibility, and self-transcendence. Since the meaning of none of these terms is self-evident, fixed, or univocal, we should consider the specific linguistic and conceptual environment in which they function in this study.

Moral language has, like all language, a history, and we must be aware of the various influences which have given the contemporary moral idiom its particular shape. We can briefly examine the background of some of the key elements in contemporary moral language by turning our attention to an important study by Lionel Trilling.

"Now and then," writes Trilling, "it is possible to observe the moral life in process of revising itself, perhaps by reducing the emphasis it formerly placed upon one or another of its elements, perhaps by inventing and adding to itself a new element, some mode of conduct or feeling which hitherto it had not regarded as essential to virtue." The origin and development of two such new elements is the subject of Trilling's 1970 Charles Eliot Norton Lectures, *Sincerity and Authenticity*. "Sincerity," as Trilling means it, "refers primarily to a congruence between avowal and actual feeling." It is, as definitively conceived early in its history by Polonius in what Trilling calls a rare "moment of self-transcendence, of grace and truth," the "avoidance of being false to any man through being true to one's own self. . . ."[3]

Though it ruled the moral imagination in the West for some four hundred years, the concept of sincerity has suffered a "sharp diminution of the authority it once exercised." Even the word itself, as Trilling says, "has lost most of its former high dignity. When we hear it, we are conscious of the anachronism which touches it with quaintness."[4]

If this is true, "if sincerity has lost its former status," says Trilling, "if the word itself has for us a hollow sound and seems almost to negate its meaning, that is because it does not propose being true to one's own self as an end but only as a means." Not only is there no longer moral urgency in "the reason that Polonius gives for being true to one's own self: that if one is, one cannot then be false to any man," but, we can ask, "if one is true to one's own self for the purpose of avoiding falsehood to others, is one being truly true to one's own self?" Further, Trilling argues that sincerity itself is compromised inasmuch as contemporary

> society requires of us that we present ourselves as being sincere, and the most efficacious way of satisfying this demand is to see to it that we really are sincere, that we actually are what we want our community to know we are. In short, we play the role of being ourselves, we sincerely act the part of the sincere person, with the result that a judgment may be passed upon our sincerity that it is not authentic.[5]

To Trilling the word "authenticity" suggests "a more strenuous moral experience than 'sincerity' does, a more exigent conception of the self and of what being true to it consists in, a wider reference to the universe and man's place in it, and a less acceptant and genial view of the social circumstances of life." And it is this concept, according to Trilling, that has arisen both to "suggest the deficiencies of sincerity and to usurp its place in our esteem."[6]

"A very considerable originative power had once been claimed for sincerity," Trilling tells us, "but nothing to match the marvelous generative force that our modern judgment assigns to authenticity, which implies the downward movement through all the cultural superstructures to some place where all movement ends, and begins." And that "some place," he says, is none other than the heart of darkness, Yeats' "foul rag-and-bone shop of the heart."[7]

If, however, authenticity offers the moral imagination a more rigorous ideal than sincerity did, it is not without its own problematic ambiguity. For, as Trilling points out, "at the behest of the criterion of authenticity, much that was once thought to make up the very fabric of culture has come to seem of little account, mere fantasy or ritual, or downright falsification. Conversely, much that culture traditionally condemned and sought to exclude is accorded a considerable moral authority by reason of the authenticity claimed for it, for example, disorder, violence, unreason."[8]

The difficulty here, I suggest, is that authenticity itself is not a criterion, as Trilling says it is, but rather an ideal which stands in need of a criterion. This difficulty accounts in large part for the contemporary emergence of "responsibility" as a dominant concept in philosophical and theological considerations of the moral life. For, without repudiating or rejecting the positive gains connected with the ideal of authenticity, the focus on responsibility attempts to reestablish concern for the "other" as a criterion at the center of moral consciousness. The stress on responsibility by recent ethical thinkers is, in other words, a retrieval of one of the key moral elements that drifted to the background of ethical thinking with the introduction of the ideal of authenticity as a replacement for sincerity.

The turn to responsibility is not simply a return to sincerity, however. It is, instead, a significant twist on the profound but fundamentally normless and therefore arbitrary ideal of authenticity. As such, responsibility is rooted in, and symbolizes, the discovery that (while one cannot truly be true to one's own self simply as a means to, and for the purpose of, avoiding falsehood to others) one can only be true to one's own self insofar—and just insofar—as one is true to others—

insofar, that is, as one responds to the *values* in each human situation in a manner that is at once free and creative, critical and fitting. If the responsible person responds to value, then, authenticity is not arbitrary, without norms. The thesis of this book, indeed, is precisely that the *criterion* of human authenticity, of the responsible person, is the self-transcendence that is effected through sensitive and creative understanding, critical judgment, responsible decision, loyal commitment, and genuine love. Put most simply, my thesis is that authentic self-realization is to be found in nothing else than such self-transcendence.

The term "self-transcendence" has many meanings, some of them quite vague and mysterious. As we have just seen, however, in this study the meaning of "self-transcendence," though not univocal, is quite direct and concrete: it refers primarily to the threefold achievement of "moving beyond one's own self" that is effected in every instance of correct understanding (cognitive), responsible decision (moral), and genuine love (affective). Each of these aspects will be examined in detail when we consider the developmental theories of Erikson, Piaget, and Kohlberg, and then the transcendental analysis of Lonergan.

2. The Personal Subject: Radical Moral Consciousness

In *Sincerity and Authenticity*, Trilling suggests that while a "ready recognition of change in the moral life is implicit in our modern way of thinking about literature," it is sometimes precisely "our experience of literature that leads us to resist the idea of moral mutation, to question whether the observed shifts in moral assumption deserve the credence we are impelled to give them." For, as he says, we all know moments when the differences between the values and moral assumptions of our culture and those of another, "as literature attests to them, seem to make no difference, seem scarcely to exist." Though our awareness of these differences is generally "so developed and so active that we find it hard to believe there is any such thing as an essential human nature," says Trilling, still, "we read the *Iliad* or the plays of Sophocles or Shakespeare and they come so close to our hearts and minds that they put to rout, or into abeyance, our instructed consciousness of the moral life as it is conditioned by a particular culture—they persuade us that human nature never varies, that the moral life is unitary and its terms perennial, and that only a busy intruding pedantry could ever have suggested otherwise."[9]

Trilling admits to an ambivalence on the question, however, inasmuch as he finds his judgment revising itself as soon as he turns to and begins "noting with eager attention all the details of assumption, thought, and behavior that distinguish the morality of one age from that of another...." Then, he says, "it seems to us that a quick and informed awareness of the differences among moral idioms is of the very essence of a proper response to literature." And, also, I would add, of the very essence of a proper ethical response to the moral life. For ethical theory must take serious account of historical change as well as personal development.[10]

Trilling's ambivalence on the character of the moral life seems well founded, for if moral idioms, assumptions, and values change, as he argues in the case of sincerity and authenticity, and as I have noted in the most recent instance of responsibility, still, there is something— namely, moral life, moral consciousness, or, as he says, "essential human nature"—that undergoes the change. And ethical reflection must take this perduring moral consciousness that is subject to historical change and personal development into account, along with its historical and developmental differences. And if historical-literary analysis such as Trilling's, on the one hand, and developmental psychology, on the other, provide appropriate means of interpreting moral life in its courses of historical change and personal development, the transcendental method of philosophy, I propose, is an especially suitable way of reflecting upon the essential character of what has been recognized throughout history as moral consciousness—in a word, conscience.

This book, then, will bring the transcendental method (as developed by Bernard Lonergan) to bear on the perennial question of conscience within the contemporary framework of authenticity and responsibility. Further, because the great advances in developmental psychology of the last half century have demonstrated conclusively that moral consciousness cannot be considered in any univocal fashion, it will proceed with the transcendental reflection on conscience only after having established a context of personal moral development based on the theories of Erik Erikson, Jean Piaget, and Lawrence Kohlberg. In this way it will be possible to demonstrate the validity of a course drawn between the extremes of an obedience-oriented legalism that is at once absolutist and minimalist, on the one hand, and an arbitrary, normless situationalism on the other. Such a course is not new (Aristotle and Aquinas, for example, had some valuable things to say about it), but the explanatory power of contemporary psychological theories such as those of Erikson, Piaget, and Kohlberg, together with the phenomenological and transcendental analyses of thinkers like H. R. Niebuhr and Bernard Lonergan, illuminate it in a new way and give it a persuasiveness it has never before had.

Insofar as authenticity is a central concept in existential thought, this study can be understood as an attempt to bring the theoretical power of developmental psychology and the critical edge of transcendental philosophy to a revision of the existential theme of self-creating subjectivity.

My purpose here, then, is neither to present a historical overview of the various approaches to conscience, nor to survey several contemporary analyses of conscience, nor to consider the significance of conscience from diverse practical and methodological perspectives.[11] Each of these angles will be incorporated in a minor way, of course. But the major approach and primary purpose here will be to bring together into an incipient synthesis the contributions of several thinkers from various disciplines who each supply different but important elements to the construction of an interpretation of conscience as the most profound expression of the concrete personal subject in his or her drive for self-transcendence.

3. Conscience: The Whole Person

In his interesting and helpful study of *Conscience and Responsibility*, Eric Mount suggests that "F. D. Maurice gets to the heart of the matter when he makes the understanding of the meaning of *person* inseparable from the meaning of *conscience.*"[12] Discussing ethical method, Maurice wrote, "first make it clear what you mean by a Person; that you will do when you make it clear what you mean by a Conscience."[13] On the same note, Helmut Thielicke has said that the "differences in the understanding of conscience clearly arise out of differences in the understanding of man. My view of conscience," he continues, "is determined by my understanding of what is the normative factor determining human existence . . . ." Further, according to Thielicke, inasmuch as an interpretation of conscience is "always indicative of a specific self-understanding of human existence," the "ambiguity of the concept [of conscience] is in fact a sign that the unifying center has been lost, and that there is now a wild and panic-stricken search for substitutes."[14]

Because I agree with Maurice and Thielicke on this fundamental point, my basic strategy in this study will be the development (drawing from several perspectives) of an interpretation of the person in the concrete terms of conscious subjectivity, rooted in a "self-understanding of human existence" as determined by the "normative factor" of self-transcendence. Within this anthropological interpretation of the "unifying center" we shall be able to discern the radical meaning of conscience. For such an understanding of the personal subject reveals that conscience is the very core of conscious subjectivity. It reveals, indeed, that, in the most radical sense, as Eric Mount puts it, "man does not have a conscience; he is a conscience."[15] We shall understand, then, through an interpretation of person in terms of self-transcending subjectivity, not only what Gerhard Ebeling means when he says that conscience is both a "question mark branded irradicably on man" as well as a "coming to expression of man himself," but also his statement that "man is a matter of conscience in two senses: he is ultimately conscience, and he ultimately concerns the conscience."[16] Further, because we shall be interpreting the personal subject who reaches for self-transcendence in a developmental fashion as a being in the process of becoming (principally through the dynamic thrust of questioning), we will be able to appreciate Gordon Allport's distinction between "must" and "ought," and thus conscience in a fully human sense as *emergent.*[17]

Because our interpretation of conscience will be developed within the context of psychological theory, it is important that we understand the rather dubious place the term "conscience" holds in the view of many psychologists. While Erich Fromm distinguishes (in much the same way as Allport) between "authoritarian" conscience and a "humanistic" conscience—frowning upon the former as primitive and destructive while approving the latter as mature and healthy—many psychologists understand the conscience simply as the product of social conditioning, indistinguishable from the "moral" phenomena Freudians identify under the rubric of the "superego."[18] A good example of this pattern, and an important illustration because of its valuable contribution to ethical reflection, is the work of the Jungian psychologist Erich Neumann. In *Depth Psychology and a New Ethic,* Neumann operates in terms of a basic distinction between "conscience," "the representative of the collective norm," and what he names the "Voice," "which is the individual expression of psychic truth":

> Conscience, as the representative of the collective superego, is a heteronomous influence which comes from the outside, quite irrespective of whether this influence encourages the development of consciousness or not. The external authority of the superego, which possesses the character

of givenness, stability, fixity and unbending tradition, is opposed by the "Voice," in its capacity as an ordaining and determining factor, the expression of an inner revelation of a new and progressively unfolding development—of that which is to come, in fact.[19]

The "new ethic," according to Neumann, roots itself in, and takes its orientation from the "Voice," that expresses not the ego, but the "Self, which appears as the inner center of the [total] personality." This "new ethic rejects the hegemony of a partial structure of the personality, and postulates the total personality as the basis of ethical conduct." The aim of the new ethic, says Neumann, is "the achievement of wholeness." Its "principal requirement" is "not that the individual should be 'good,' but that he should be psychologically autonomous—that is to say, healthy and productive . . . ."[20]

According to Neumann, "ethical autonomy and an ethic of wholeness require that each one of us should, himself, consciously undertake the management of his own shadow" and "live and suffer the evil which falls to [his] lot in a spirit of freely accepted responsibility." Still, it remains true, as Neumann says, that

> In the psychological development of the individual, we are again and again confronted by the problem that the "Voice," in contradistinction to conscience, demands that what appears to the ego to be "evil" should be done, and that the inner and outer conflict which arises out of this situation should be accepted, with all its difficulties. Surprisingly often, the avoidance of evil and of the conflict which evil brings in its train turns out to be "unethical" from the standpoint of the "Voice."[21]

The essential point to be noted here is that the moral phenomenon called "conscience" by Neumann (and many others of various viewpoints) is *not* the conscience we shall be concerned with in this study. On the contrary, while I shall not be following Neumann's approach, my interpretation of conscience will be in many respects— e.g., in its emphasis on autonomy and wholeness of the total personality, with special attention to the unconscious—similar to Neumann's interpretation of the "Voice." The emphasis throughout the entire book, then, to repeat, will be on conscience as the deepest expression of the autonomy and wholeness of the personal subject in his or her drive for self-transcendence.

Many distinctions within the reality of the personal subject will be necessary, however, for, though one, the person is not simple. And in the past much confusion has arisen when the many aspects of the personal subject have not merely been distinguished in order to be united, but separated to be set at odds with one another. Fundamental in this regard is the distinction between knowing and deciding, and their role in moral action.

Along with Camus's narrator in *The Plague*, I shall place much weight on the moral function of intelligence:

> The evil that is in the world always comes of ignorance [he says], and good intentions may do as much harm as malevolence, if they lack understanding. On the whole, men are more good than bad; that, however, isn't the real point. But they are more or less ignorant, and it is this that we call vice or virtue; the most incorrigible vice being that of an ignorance that fancies it knows everything and therefore claims for itself the right to kill. The soul of the murderer is blind; and there can be no true goodness nor true love without the utmost clear-sightedness.[22]

Good intentions, of course, are not enough, but they are necessary, and the understanding that illuminates them must be truly clear-sighted, able to grasp the complexities and various dimensions of each human situation in a manner that is at once critically realistic and sensitively creative. But even such finely-tuned, humanly sympathetic understanding constitutes only one part of the moral life, important as that is.

Thus I will argue, as Sidney Hook has, that "though there is no substitute for intelligence, it is not enough," even when matched with good intentions. "There are human beings who have intelligence but do not have the moral courage to act on it," says Hook. *Both* sensitive understanding and moral courage are necessary, and if understanding without courage is ineffectual, it is also true, as Hook says, that "moral courage without intelligence is dangerous. It leads to fanaticism." I will try to show that an interpretation of conscience as self-transcending subjectivity places equal emphasis on both creative, critical knowing and courageous, reponsible deciding as the two key "moments" of moral consciousness, and thus points to Hook's conclusion that "education should develop both intelligence *and* courage."[23]

This interpretation of conscience as the radical thrust of the personal subject for the authenticity of self-transcendence—grounded as it is in both developmental psychology and a critical philosophical position—is not just another description of conscience, but an explanatory anthropological theory that is a key to some of the fundamental questions in theological ethics. After establishing the basic argument, therefore, we shall have the opportunity to see how such an interpretation of conscience and its conversions illuminates such basic issues as the nature of moral knowing, the relationship between creativity and structure in moral life, and the perennial attempt to understand the way facts relate to values. By way of a few anticipatory words on the last point, for example, I will attempt to show that beneath all the discussions about deriving values from facts, the "ought" from the "is," is the fundamental fact that the human person is characterized by a drive toward and a demand for the realization of value—that the radical "is" of the human person is an "ought."

Abraham Maslow has used the notion of "physical health" as an example of a prescriptive ideal derived from observation and description in order to show that ideals of "psychological health" and "self-actualization" need not be based on implicit value judgments, but can be derived from observed facts.[24] I shall be arguing that a genuine understanding of the *fact* of what the human person fundamentally *is* includes the realization of what he or she *ought to be,* a responsible originator of *value.* In other words, if we understand Schiller's "archetype" not as a lifeless form but as the radical dynamism of the human spirit, we can agree with him that

> Every individual human being . . . carries within him, potentially and prescriptively, an ideal man, the archetype of a human being, and it is his life's task to be, through all his changing manifestations, in harmony with the unchanging unity of this ideal.[25]

B. CHRISTIAN CONSCIENCE: DECLINE AND FALL

If the meaning of conscience has suffered from ambiguous and multiple understandings in the world of ordinary language as well as in the general domains of psychology and philosophy, its fate within Christian thought has not been noticeably better. And, of course, whenever a fundamental reality in any particular field is poorly understood or in some way distorted, the entire discipline suffers—as the poverty of contemporary theological ethics clearly indicates. The work of Paul Lehmann provides a striking example of the kind of ethical difficulty that arises when an explanatory theory of conscience in the fundamental sense of a radical drive of the personal subject for self-transcendence is neglected.

"Ethical theory must either dispose of the conscience altogether or completely transform the interpretation of its ethical nature, function, and significance." Such is the conviction permeating Lehmann's 1963 *Ethics in a Christian Context.* After some three hundred pages of historical analysis in Lehmann's study, conscience emerges as the central question for a contemporary ethic. Lehmann's diagnosis and prescription are as fully documented as they are abrupt:

> The semantic, philosophical, and theological pilgrimage of conscience begins with the Greek tragedians of the fifth century before Christ and ends with Sigmund Freud. It is a moving, tortuous record of decline and fall which forces upon us in our time the frankest possible facing of a sharp alternative: either "do the conscience over" or "do the conscience in "![26]

This is not the place for a full historical survey of conscience's pilgrimage. However, since Lehmann's negative view of conscience is representative of a major stream in contemporary theological ethics, and since his "contextual ethics" has had significant influence in the field, it will be instructive to consider Lehmann's interpretation of some key turning points in this pilgrimage. Although Lehmann's interpretation can in no way be taken for the last word on conscience as it has been understood at any particular point of its history, it does indicate very clearly the highly problematic status of conscience in much of contemporary theological ethics.

In its original semantic environment, conscience, as Lehmann understands it, was the "enemy of humanization." In this Greek context conscience denoted "the moral quality of the self's own acts or behavior, as in such variant phrases as 'to be a witness for or against oneself,' 'to hug a secret to oneself,' usually a guilty secret." In this Greek moral usage, Lehmann discerns something of a structure in which conscience, an order intrinsic to human nature, is also connected with the fixed order of things as they are (ultimately God as the orderer of the universe). Functioning as pain, conscience also refers to specific past acts. Quite simply, then, conscience means that human nature is such that men and women will suffer the pain of self-knowledge if they transgress the moral limits of their nature. Above all, Lehmann stresses that, according to its original semantic environment, "the ethical significance of conscience is not that it is a teacher of morals. Its ethical significance is that it resides in human nature as the bearer of ethical negation and futility in the relations between man and the order of things in which he lives."[27]

From the classical Greek perspective Lehmann moves to the next key phase in the development of conscience, a phase which he considers the apex of conscience's cultural journey: the "domestication of conscience" in the writings of Thomas Aquinas. Here "the first principles of moral action are known to all men without deliberation. But the behavioral implementation of this knowledge requires a kind of

liaison between the principle and any given action"—that is, conscience. "What a man knows together with himself is that this or that
particular, freely chosen action is in accordance with natural law.
Conscience is, thus, the bond between law and responsibility."[28] But,
for Lehmann, the significant transformation in the ethical meaning of
conscience that Aquinas brought about was in its assignment to a
twofold task:

> ... Insofar as knowledge is applied to an act, as directive of that act,
> conscience is said to prod or urge or bind. But, insofar as knowledge is
> applied to an act, by way of examining things which already have taken
> place, conscience is said to *accuse or cause remorse* when that which has
> been done is found to be out of harmony with the knowledge according to
> which it is examined; or to *defend or excuse* when that which has been done
> is found to have proceeded according to the form of the knowledge.[29]

Here, then, conscience, which in its original context had been un-
bearable with its single negative function, has become bearable
through the acquisition of a second positive function. The uneasy
conscience has been joined by an easy partner. Originally, says
Lehmann, "conscience was that in a man which above all things else
he could not endure. Now conscience can be lived with; the knowledge which a man has together with himself could be counted upon as
still against him, but sometimes also—and this is the important
change—as on his side."[30]

From the classic Thomist view Lehmann shifts his focus to the
philosophical perspective of Kant, in which conscience is seen as
"duty's inner citadel." After noting the similarities which constitute
the continuity between the two positions, Lehmann explains that
whereas Aquinas understood conscience principally as a faculty of
judgment, Kant adds to this judgmental aspect an important emphasis
on conscience as juridical. By this shift Kant "displaced the human
significance of conscience as the link between the internal nature of
man and the order in which his life is sustained." In its place he
substituted "the legal significance of conscience as an internal voice of
an external authority." Because "it is this authoritarian conscience
which has so conspicuously lost its ethical persuasiveness and force
today," it may be said that Kant, by directly preparing the ground for
its fall, was "the principal architect of the decline of conscience."[31]

But, if in Lehmann's view Aquinas and especially Kant are responsible for the decline of conscience, the credit for its fall must go to
Sigmund Freud.

The career of conscience, as Lehmann sees it, comes full circle with Freud; the ethical futility of conscience dramatically scored in Euripides' tragedies is now underlined with clinical evidence by Freud. "Conscience did not, as Kant had claimed, express and facilitate the moralization of man. On the contrary, the net effect of the Kantian account of conscience was the dehumanization of man."[32] Freud stated this pessimism quite forcefully in his *New Introductory Lectures:*

> The philosopher Kant once declared that nothing proved to him the greatness of God more convincingly than the starry heavens and the moral conscience within us. The stars are unquestionably superb, but where conscience is concerned God has been guilty of an uneven and careless piece of work, for a great many men have only a limited share of it or scarcely enough to be worth mentioning.... It is a very remarkable experience to observe morality, which was once ostensibly conferred on us by God and planted deep in our hearts, functioning as a periodical phenomenon. For after a certain number of months the whole moral fuss is at an end, the critical voice of the superego is silent, the ego is reinstated, and enjoys once more all the rights of man until another attack.[33]

Lehmann's analysis points up a certain ambivalence in Freud's attempt to explain the origin and formation of conscience. There appears to be a certain fluctuation between internal psychic responses and external social pressures in Freud's use of the term "conscience." What is clear, however, is the identification of conscience with the superego, in which Lehmann sees both the neurotic and the societal aspects of conscience meeting.

Clear also is the conscience's decisive function as a negative censor, judging and condemning. So aggressive and so thoroughgoing is this censoring function that in the end, according to Lehmann, "conscience has exchanged its ethical role and function for a psychoanalytic one."[34]

As Lehmann understands it, then, Freud's documentation of the fall of conscience is "the rejection of the hostile conscience through the demonstration of its ethical impotence and uselessness. Such a fall could be the prelude to a rise of conscience if the loosing of conscience from its barren ethical moorings should prove to be a way of loosing it for a context within which its potential ethical role and significance could acquire ethical reality." For Lehmann, of course, the new context for which conscience's fall has prepared it is—or should be—the context of the *koinonia,* for here a "transformation of the nature and function of conscience occurs in terms of which conscience acquires both ethical reality and the power to shape behavior."[35]

...It is the conscience which explains how and why man discerns in the knowledge of good and evil the conditions for and the behavior appropriate to what it takes to make and to keep human life human. It is the conscience—theonomously understood—which forges the link between what God is doing in the world and man's free obedience to that activity. Conscience is neither libertarian nor legalistic, neither antinomian nor nomian, but whole, i.e., unified and sensitized in the freedom wherewith Christ has set us free.[36]

In briefest fashion, then, we have Lehmann's answer to the dilemma of conscience—its theonomous transformation within the context of the *koinonia*. And this, for Lehmann, is the central and critical question in ethics, for "the question of conscience is the point of no return for the methodology of ethics." The methodological differentiation of the theonomous conscience is only part of his story, however, for Lehmann feels that he must "try also to show how it comes about that a *koinonia* ethic provides the conscience with its proper ethical function and significance." He suggests that the roots of such a possibility might lie in "the biblical way of looking at human responsibility in a world being governed and guided by the politics of God." Noting how conspicuous is the semantic silence of the Bible with respect to conscience, Lehmann reminds us how the "Old Testament insists that it is the *heart*, not the *conscience*, which is the nexus of human responsibility."[37]

This silence about conscience and stress on the heart also characterizes the speech of Jesus. Conscience does not come into its own in the scriptures, really, until the Pauline epistles. In fact, because of the originality and frequency of Paul's use of the term, Lehmann suggests that "his conception of conscience may be regarded as normative for New Testament thought." By appropriating the commonly understood Greek and Stoic meaning of conscience for Christian purposes, Lehmann argues, Paul brought about a "notable shift of semantic perspective which not only drew the conscience into the orbit of the Old Testament understanding of *heart* but made the conscience instrumental to the dynamics and direction of God's humanizing activity in the world in Jesus Christ."[38] "The behavioral consequences of this transformation of the context of conscience are," in Lehmann's mind, "tantamount to a revolution in the ethical role and significance of conscience."[39]

During the long history of the decline and fall of conscience, the Reformation stands out in Lehmann's mind as especially important for the understanding of *koinonia* and therefore of the ethical revolution brought about through Paul's bonding of conscience to *koinonia*. Like

Paul before him, Luther "broke across the frontier of the tragic conscience into a fresh sensitivity to the nexus of human responsibility in the intimate confrontation between God and man."[40]

Calvin, too, recognized that a correct understanding of Christian liberty depends on an adequate grasp of conscience. And like Paul and Luther, he not only perceived the *koinonia* as the validating context for conscience, but concretized this understanding of conscience in terms of the Old Testament *heart:* "Therefore, just as works express respect for men, so conscience is referred to God; *thus a good conscience is nothing other than inward integrity of heart.*"[41]

So, concludes Lehmann, "in marked contrast to behavior done out of respect for men, conscience is referred to God. Loosed from its dehumanizing context, the conscience is joined instead to the knowledge of good and evil as the environment of humanization. In this context, conscience is nothing other than a good conscience, and a good conscience is nothing other than inward integrity of heart."[42]

No such brief summary could possibly hope to do full justice to the richness of Professor Lehmann's analysis of the historical development and contemporary status of conscience. However, even so sketchy a survey of the highlights of such a powerful study should reveal two important points: first, the reality of conscience stands at the living center of Christian life and therefore of Christian ethics; secondly, despite the strength and subtlety of his argument for the centrality of conscience and its need of transformation in the new context of the Christian *koinonia,* Lehmann leaves us with a radically inadequate understanding of the very reality of conscience that stands in need of a transforming context.

The problem is that Lehmann never advances beyond a *descriptive* approach to the phenomenon of conscience. After his analysis of the many historical views of conscience, we are still left with no satisfactory positive account of the central reality. We still want to ask: But what is the nature of this conscience for which we seek a context? It is a helpful beginning to associate conscience with the Old Testament *heart,* but it is only a beginning, a direction. For once the spell of its affective coloring and poetic overtones fades, we want to know what, precisely, is the nature of this heart that "knows by a kind of sensitivity at once central and total which marks the person as a whole," this "pivotal personal center of man's total response to the dynamics, direction, and personal thrust of the divine claim upon him."[43]

Lehmann's footnoted response tells us that "the heart is the organ of thinking and knowing in the cognitive sense of 'mind' or 'intelligence' and also in the reflexive or intensive sense of the involvement of the self in the act of thinking and knowing. Cognition and the response of the self are thus conjoined in the act of knowing." Following hard upon a description of conscience as knowing "by a kind of internal sight, a cognitive seeing which condemns the knower," the foregoing "definition" of heart itself cries out for an explanatory context, but it is left standing alone in a peculiar kind of descriptive nakedness. What, we wonder, for example, would be a noncognitive sense of thinking and knowing, or, again, how should we understand an act of thinking and knowing in which the self is not involved? We need a meaningful context in which to answer these questions constructively—and not only these questions. For without a context of cognitional theory, terms like "internal sight" contribute very little if anything to our understanding; and what should we think of a "cognitive seeing which condemns the knower?" Likewise, we would want to know how the heart, the "personal center of man's total response," can render an "external judgment." We need a context, then, in which we can reach a precise, explanatory understanding of conscience in its relation to the full human subject.[44]

So, by all means, let us have a new context for conscience; Lehmann has made his point well. But in our enthusiasm for giving conscience a Christian context of *koinonia*, let us remember that we need a conscience for our new context!

In short, it is my contention—though Lehmann would likely not agree—that conscience needs a *philosophical* interpretation as well as a theological context. Lehmann has gone far toward clarifying the Christian *koinonia* as a theological context for conscience. The necessary construction of an adequate philosophical interpretation remains. Such an explanatory understanding will not only supply a Christian consideration of conscience with a firm foundation, but will also make dialogue with non-Christian and nontheological understandings of conscience more productive. The remainder of this work, then, will be devoted to this prior philosophical task of attempting to construct such an explanatory foundational interpretation of conscience.

C. CONSCIENCE AND RESPONSIBILITY

Perhaps the most important contemporary attempt to develop a foundational interpretation of moral consciousness is H. Richard Niebuhr's analysis of responsibility in *The Responsible Self*, which can accurately be described as seminal for much of the work done in theological ethics since its publication in 1963.[45] A careful consideration of Niebuhr's analysis will indicate the nature and extent of the basic contribution that contemporary theological ethics has made toward an adequate interpretation of personal moral consciousness. It will also indicate the limitations of that contribution.

Niebuhr proposes the new symbolism of responsibility as an important alternative or additional way (along with the traditional images of "man-the-maker" and "man-the-citizen") of understanding ourselves in our quest for true existence. For Niebuhr, "what is implicit in the idea of responsibility is the image of man-the-answerer, man engaged in dialogue, man acting in response to action upon him." As we analyze our activities, we understand what it means "to be engaged in dialogue, to answer questions addressed to us, to defend ourselves against attacks, to reply to injunctions, to meet challenges—this is common experience." Now, Niebuhr suggests, we should "think of all our actions as having this character of being responses, answers, to actions upon us."[46]

In an attempt to give a systematic definition to the symbol of responsibility, Niebuhr specifies four major elements. The first of these, appropriately, is *response*. Moral action is action in response to interpreted action upon us. We affirm our moral character inasmuch as we affirm that "we are characterized by awareness and that this awareness is more or less that of an intelligence which identifies, compares, analyzes, and relates events so that they come to us not as brute actions, but as understood and as having meaning." As we interpret the meaning of actions upon us, so we respond. This interpretation is performed, of course, not only in our rational consciousness, but also in the deepest feelings and intuitions of our psyche. A second element of responsibility, then, is that it is not only responsive action, "but responsive action in accordance with our *interpretation* of the question to which answer is being given."[47]

Accountability is the third element in Niebuhr's delineation of responsibility. Though often defined in terms of legal discourse, Niebuhr's specific meaning is based on the fact that "our actions are responsible not only insofar as they are reactions to interpreted actions upon us but also insofar as they are made in anticipation of answers to our answers." Responsible action "looks forward as well as backward; it anticipates objections, confirmations, and corrections. It is made as part of a total conversation that leads forward and is to have meaning as a whole."[48]

Further, it seems that our action is responsible only when it is "response to action upon us in a continuing discourse or interaction among beings forming a continuing society." A fourth element in responsibility, then, is named *social solidarity*. These four elements of responsibility are summed up in admittedly abstract form by Niebuhr as "the idea of an agent's action as response to an action upon him in accordance with his interpretation of the latter action and his expectation of response to his response; and all of this is in a continuing community of agents."[49]

The last of these four elements, social solidarity, is clearly central to an understanding of the moral self and properly receives much attention from Niebuhr. To be sure, the older images took the social nature of human reality into account, but the major emphasis was elsewhere—the objects of reason for "man-the-maker," the law for "man-the-citizen." Niebuhr, however, wants to emphasize that view of self-existence which, without obscuring the fact that the self exists in the presence of ideas and laws, focuses sharply on the radically social character of selfhood. "To be a self in the presence of other selves is not a derivative experience but primordial. To be able to say that I am I is not an inference from the statement that I think thoughts nor from the statement that I have a law-acknowledging conscience. It is, rather, the acknowledgment of my existence as the counterpart of another self." To be a self—a being that is an object to itself—is possible only as one takes upon oneself the perspective of other selves. Niebuhr quotes G. H. Mead: "The self as that which can be an object to itself is essentially a social structure, and it arises in social experience. After a self has arisen, it in a certain sense provides for itself its social experiences, and so we can conceive of an absolutely solitary self. But it is impossible to conceive of a self arising outside of social experience."[50]

While modern sociology, cultural anthropology, and social psychology have made much of the social nature of human existence, "the understanding of the self as social, living in response-relations to other selves, has been current in the realm of moral philosophy for a longer time.... The strange duality in man which manifests itself in the phenomenon of conscience had of course long been remarked by philosophers." Niebuhr quotes Kant in his legal archetype imagery: "Every man has a conscience, and finds himself observed by an inward judge which threatens and keeps him in awe ... and this power which watches over the laws within him is not something which he himself (arbitrarily) *makes,* but it is incorporated into his being.... Now this original intellectual and moral capacity, called *conscience,* has this peculiarity in it, that although its business is a business of man with himself, yet he finds himself compelled by his reason to transact it *as if* at the command of *another person.*" Yes, says Niebuhr, but "isolated

reason does not... invent another person. The experience of conscience is not *like* being judged by another person; it is indeed being
judged by another, though the other is not immediately or symboli-
cally and physically present to sense-experiencing man. Conscience is
a function of my existence as a social being, always aware of the
approvals and disapprovals of my action by my fellow men." Whatever
the merits of the debate between the social analysts and the rationalist
view of the phenomenon of conscience, we may rule out the "as ifs,"
says Niebuhr; "when we judge our actions, approve or disapprove of
ourselves, value and disvalue our evaluations, the situation is the same
social situation in which we transcend ourselves by knowing ourselves
as knowers. All this reflective life is life in relation to companions; it is
I-Thou, I-You, existence. It is existence in response to action upon us
by other selves."[51]

The social self responds neither to generalized nor to atomic others,
but to Thou's who are members of a group possessing interactional
constancies upon which action can be both interpreted and anticipated. For Neibuhr, then, conscience represents an awareness not so
much of the "approvals and disapprovals of other individuals in isolation as of the ethos of...society, that is, of its mode of interpersonal
interactions."[52]

Niebuhr pushes his analysis of the social self as responsive and
responsible to what he calls the *third*—revealing the triadic form of our
life in response. The encounter of I and Thou always takes place in
"the presence of a third, from which I and Thou are distinguished and
to which they also respond," whether this third is the complex of
natural events or the cause which evokes one's loyalty. "When we
reflect about this third reality that is present to us in all our responses
to our companions we note that it always has a double character. On
the one hand it is something personal; on the other it contains within
itself again a reference to something that transcends it or to which it
refers." For example, "the law to which I refer in all questions of legal
responsibility means both the administrators of my society's justice and
the justice to which my society refers as lying beyond it." And for
Niebuhr, this "process of self-transcendence or of reference to the
third beyond each third does not come to rest until the total community of being has been involved." Thus, not unlike the more traditional ethical images, an ethics rooted in the symbolism of responsibility moves toward the universal—toward an understanding of self as
necessarily responding in and responsible to no less than a universal
community.[53]

Also, when the question of the total human context of interpretation and response is raised, we need to stress that the self is not only social in its existence, but also time-full and historical—a consideration to which legal and artistic images give little attention. Here Niebuhr sees the drive for universality in the self's demand for a new understanding of its ultimate historical context, for a transformation of the past and future in its present through reinterpretation. Beyond every personal and social reinterpretation of past and future, however, there remains, stubbornly resistant, the mythology of death in all its many forms. It is in this context, according to Niebuhr, that Christianity and the other great religions assume their peculiar significance as the ultimate reinterpretation, the total transformation of the mythology of death and destructiveness into a history of life and being.[54]

On the basis of this brief sketch of Niebuhr's interpersonal understanding of responsibility and conscience, I will now raise some critical questions, with the aim of further clarifying theological ethics' need of an interpretation of conscience based on a critical understanding of the personal subject.

We may begin by asking if the symbol which Niebuhr presents to us is really one of responsibility, or if it is more properly a symbol of *responsiveness*? While agreeing that Niebuhr's analysis of responsibility admirably stresses the interactional character of human life, can we also say that—as an analysis of "human moral life in general"—it adequately unpacks the fundamental reality of responsibility? I think not. Response, interpretation, accountability, and social solidarity are all key elements in properly human activity. But, in the context of common moral experience, none of them—nor all of them taken together—seem to come to grips with what I take to be the radically *moral* reality: the *experienced imperative to realize value*. Response seems to characterize *all* seriously human activities—some of which we might want to name *irresponsible*. The same is true, I think, of interpretation. Interpretation is presupposed by responsible deed—it does not guarantee it; reasonable judgment invites responsible decision—it does not produce it. The marriage of accurate understanding and ready willingness is not a universal phenomenon. At first glance, accountability seems to point in a more radical direction, but Niebuhr's account never takes it beyond the inverse of response; it ends up as merely an anticipator of further responses—and not fundamentally linked with value. As valuable as the analysis of the social self is in clarifying the interpersonal character of the objective pole of personal horizon, it reveals directly nothing of the radical thrust for value at the *subjective* pole of personal horizon. As helpful a tool as

Niebuhr's symbol of responsibility is, then, can it really be considered as an adequate *moral* symbol unless it also includes something like a pattern of obligation, command, imperative, demand? Should we not expect a moral symbol to be characterized by what Paul Tillich is pointing to when he says that "the moral imperative is the command to become what one potentially is, a *person* within a community of persons, . . . respond[ing] 'responsibly,' namely, after deliberation and decision rather than through a determined compulsion. This is [a person's] greatness, but also his danger: it enables him to act *against* the moral demand."[55] In a similar vein, Austin Farrar points out that the moral self-judgment involved in responsibility is essentially the "habit of imposing on one's conduct the law of one's mind. . . . The ultimate responsibility acknowledged and enforced by conscience is that of acting in accordance with our serious valuations."[56]

The analysis of conscience as social in the second chapter of *The Responsible Self*, "Responsibility in Society," is highly valuable, but in it conscience appears as merely derivative—the censor or judge, approving or condemning actions. G. H. Mead's social self—the self-as-object of reflection—is taken as ultimate and normative; Niebuhr never explicitly moves back into the depths of subjectivity, the source of moral activity, the reflecting self-as-subject. Clearly, conscience emerges and develops only in community—a particular community; conscience is both social and historical. Only through critical dialectic with others in the community of persons is personhood and thus conscience realized. And this point cannot be overemphasized. But nowhere in *The Responsible Self* do I find Niebuhr analyzing and critically grounding the fundamental imperative which is operative in every person demanding that value be effected—an imperative that can be ignored only at the cost of personal wholeness. It is this personal exigence for the pursuit of value—whether recognized as religious or not—that grounds any further notion of responsibility or conscience.

Obviously, my difference with Niebuhr on this point is finally methodological rather than substantive. If every response is made in the presence of a third, is finally a response to God, as it is for Niebuhr, then the question of value is indeed present, for God is the center-of-value. In "The Center of Value" Niebuhr makes it eminently clear that he understands every human act as a response to *some* center of value—not necessarily a divine one.[57] It is this kind of consideration, perhaps, that is needed in his analysis of responsibility. Without it, in the context of "human moral life in general," responsibility remains no more than responsiveness. But even this kind of

consideration does not indicate clearly enough the intimate connection between responsibility, conscience, and value at the personal,
subjective pole. For this God is ultimately reached at the end of an
analysis that pushes *out* beyond every third to the total context, to the
community of being. It clearly establishes the universality of the Cause
to which loyalty responds. But response to cause involves more than
the cause itself. The very notion of cause implies a sensitive subject
capable of interpreting reality precisely as cause and of responding to it
precisely as value. Ethical analysis of cause, in other words, demands
reflection on the moral subject as source of loyalty. In criticizing
previous contributions to the analysis of responsibility, Niebuhr refers
to W. Fales' *Wisdom and Responsibility*, which, he says, "tries to account for the *feeling* of responsibility but never analyzes that feeling
itself."[58] But, finally, this is his own problem. Niebuhr characterizes
responsible action for us very ably, but he never presses his analysis to
the radically personal source of that responsible action.

It is the failure to develop a satisfactory *theoretical* account of the
personal subject that constitutes the central weakness in Niebuhr's
reflections on responsibility (more generally, his anthropology). Thus,
the key to my criticism lies in the very significant differences between
our understandings of fundamental personal realities such as experience, consciousness, and the self. While Niebuhr himself does not
offer any lengthy development of these phenomena, his explicit reliance on the thought of G. H. Mead is clear. And for Mead, who
understands the self as essentially a social process going on within the
two distinguishable phases of an "I" and a "me," the self has experience of itself only as an object, never as a subject.[59] According to
Mead, the "I" is not experienced, but hypothesized. Hence, both
consciousness and self-consciousness are objectified, and one is left
without any theoretical handle on the radical subjectivity of the self.

My point here is not to equate or identify the positions of Niebuhr
and Mead on the subject of selfhood. For Niebuhr's reliance on Mead
is neither total nor exclusive; he also makes explicit reference to
Buber's theory of interpersonal subjectivity. Indeed, Niebuhr's entire
work does presuppose the *existential experience* of the self as subject, of
the "I". But because Niebuhr does not himself offer a *theoretical* interpretation of this experience, the result is an understanding of conscience as a function of the social "me" along the lines of Mead's
theory, rather than as the core of the primordial "I" that comes into
full being in interpersonal relationships. This latter understanding of
conscience (and the theory of experience, consciousness, and selfhood

upon which it stands) will be the central concern of the following chapters.

However, in order to clarify the perspective from which I am evaluating Niebuhr, and to anticipate the later constructive sections of this study, perhaps a few preliminary remarks on the personal source of responsible action can be sketched out here—taking the above quotations from Tillich and Farrar as points of departure. Tillich speaks of "respond[ing] 'responsibly'...after deliberation and decision"; Farrar speaks of acting "in accordance with our serious valuations." Both, I think, are pointing to an inescapable fact of "human moral life in general," a fact with which any basic ethical reflection must deal. This radically personal moral fact—that is yet common to everyone—is the demand which we all experience in our innermost selves to respond in every instance in a way fully consistent with our best judgment of a situation.

In experiencing any situation, any action upon us, we do not merely react, we try to understand, to interpret, to find *meaning in the experience*. And this search for meaning does not occur apart from a pattern of values that has grown into the texture of our consciousness over many years. But just as we are not satisfied with mere experience, and seek to understand it, so the same dynamism for transcendence is revealed in our demand for evidence, for a verified answer to the question, "Is my interpretation of the situation adequate, correct?" The answer may not always be as straightforward and unambiguous as we would like, but in our experience we do recognize instances of satisfactory answers, answers grounded in evidence sufficient to warrant assent.

In practical affairs, the same processes of understanding and critically reflecting upon our understanding are operative as we try to discern fitting responses, to work out appropriate courses of action. And in every case the same unrelenting drive that moves us from experiencing to understanding, and from understanding to judging, now manifests itself in the further dimension of moral consciousness as conscience in its most radical form—the imperious demand that I decide to respond in the way I have reasonably judged best, the always present exigence to realize the value that I have recognized in understanding and affirmed in judgment. This imperative is the root of moral consciousness, the possibility of ethics, and, I am maintaining, the very core of any notion of responsibility.

A turn to the personal subject and an analysis of conscience in this transcendental sense is necessary in order to do full justice to the contribution Niebuhr has made to ethics through his emphasis on the symbolism of responsibility. For only in this way can ethics—even from a Christian perspective—seriously take "human moral life in general" as its point of departure. As Bernard Häring puts it in *The Law of Christ*, "conscience must be studied as a moral phenomenon, for the simple reason of its universal presence. Even those who have no realization of its religious depth recognize its existence. Here we have a point of contact with those who are not religious-minded at all. The greater the dimension of moral depth within conscience, the more significant its religious foundation appears. Inevitably the religious must reveal itself as the ethical deepens and develops, for conscience is in the very roots of its being a religious phenomenon with its ultimate origin in man's likeness to God."[60] Yes, but the very roots and ultimate origin which must reveal themselves must just as certainly not be presupposed in ethical analysis, if one wishes to speak of common moral experience.

Even Christians—or especially Christians—while recognizing God at the center of their personal moral lives, in the depths of their consciences' demand for response to real value, must realize that at his death the "God of the gaps" ceased functioning as part of the explanatory process. They should appreciate that it is now incumbent upon all theoreticians—including ethicists—to proceed with relative autonomy. There is no reason why the Christian—recognizing that God is better understood as the ultimate ground of the possibility of explanation than as a part of any explanation—cannot engage in *fundamental* ethical reflection on common moral experience without reference to God. Such a strategy not only entails ecumenical advantages, it guarantees that, because God is not introduced prematurely at any proximate stage of explanation, the ethicist will be forced to penetrate as far as possible into the depths of the personal subject for the grounds of morality. If God is ultimately discovered here as the absolute ground, the discovery is as it should be—ultimate, and one also has some assurance that within authentic morality it is indeed God, the One beyond the many.

D. NATURE AND OUTLINE OF ARGUMENT

The nature or character of this study can be best described, perhaps, as an exploratory, critical, and constructive essay in foundational ethics. In it I will consider from a philosophical perspective a basic

issue in the epistemology of theological ethics that is at once methodological, metaethical, and normative.

Most generally, the issue I intend to explore is the peculiarly
modern philosophical one concerned with the demonstration of first
moral principles, that is, the key question of an ethics conscious of its
problematic status attempting to ground or justify itself by uncovering
its foundations. What I shall call "foundational ethics," then, can be
understood as an attempt to disclose the "conditions for the possibility" of moral consciousness. From the Kantian perspective, foundational ethics is an attempt to come to grips with the same critical
issue Kant dealt with in his *Foundations of the Metaphysics of Morals*
and *Critique of Practical Reason*. Within the limits of this Kantian
analogy, however, my approach can be understood most accurately as
an extension of a revised *Critique of Pure Reason* into the realm of
ethics, that is to say, an attempt to ground the categorical imperative
in speculative intelligence and reason.

My approach to this epistemological question is not restricted to
formal a priori demonstration, however; my response to Kant's foundational issue is an approach that can be described as a broadly
phenomenological analysis of and transcendental reflection upon
moral experience. While recognizing that there is no single method
peculiar to theological ethics, I will show that there is a properly
ethical subject matter, and that this common human experience of
moral phenomena is open to critical examination by various methods
of inquiry, especially a philosophical one when the question is foundational. So my project is first of all the critical one of trying to
uncover the foundations of moral consciousness and attempting to
justify these presuppositions of the ethical enterprise as both meaningful and true. My strategy will be to work out a model of *self-
transcending subjectivity* by way of phenomenological and psychological
approaches, and then to show how the method of transcendental
reflection can offer personal verification for that model. (The nature
of transcendental method will be described in detail in chapter three.)
The book's central issue, then, is establishing the foundation of
theological ethics—and the basic category is self-transcending subjectivity. Fundamental to my argument will be the radical identity of
genuine objectivity and authentic subjectivity, that is, that *subjectivity
is objective insofar as it transcends itself*.

Clearly, I will not be attempting to give a full presentation of the
work of the various authors I consider. Nor will I imply that their
contribution to my project is the central aspect of their own work.

Rather, I will only claim that my appropriation of certain facets of their work in this study constitutes a valid interpretation in terms of their own full contexts.

The burden of the book's fundamental argument in chapters two and three, then, will be to set forth a model of self-transcendence as one capable of explaining and critically justifying the reality of personal subjectivity as at once the principal meaning of conscience/responsibility and the foundation of ethics.

Chapter two will show that the developmental psychologies of Erik Erikson, Jean Piaget, and Lawrence Kohlberg make fundamental contributions to an empirically based model of self-transcendence. Rooted in clinical and experimental data, these theories place the developing subject in a radically social context across many different cultures. I will emphasize the concreteness and detail they can bring to a philosophical notion of self-transcending subjectivity. It is not my intention, however, to employ these theories as a ground for the strictly philosophical transcendental reflection in chapter three. Rather than a foundation, they are meant to form a concrete context for the philosophical analysis. The clinical and experimental evidence supporting the developmental theories is not intended, therefore, to *verify* the substantive philosophical argument presented in chapter three, even though the empirical psychological data do in fact point in the same direction as the philosophical analysis. In other words, the developmental theories are presented because of the especially illuminating fashion in which they concretely and critically establish the *meaning* of self-transcending subjectivity; the consequent persuasiveness that their convergence with the philosophical argument adds to that argument is significant, I think, but not necessary in the sense that the philosophical position, which has its own personal manner of *verification,* depends on them.

The thesis of chapter two will be advanced within a sequential correlation of the developmental patterns of Piaget and Kohlberg with Erikson's psychosocial epigenesis.

In particular, I will emphasize the extrapolation of Piaget's various dialectics of *egocentrism* and *decentration* (greater subjectivity equals greater objectivity) into an overall dialectical pairing of *egocentrism* and *self-transcendence* (which, in chapter three, will extend to intellectual and moral conversion).

With Erikson, in relation to subjectivity, I will stress the centrality of the concept of *identity*—as well as his rather clear explication of the relationship between "I", ego, and self. Also to be highlighted, of course, is the self-transcending dynamism of his developmental structure, which progresses normatively toward intimacy, generativity, and integrity—with their strengths or virtues of love, care, and wisdom. Another important point to be noted is Erikson's developmental differentiation of childhood morality, adolescent ideology, and adult ethics.

Kohlberg's moral stages (like Piaget's) also move in the direction of self-transcendence—from egocentric hedonism toward true conscience and personal principles (which may transcend even a morality of social contract). I will utilize the fact that few people reach Kohlberg's highest level of principled conscience as a key point on which to turn to a strictly philosophical analysis of moral reality—especially the phenomenon of moral conversion.

Chapter three will develop a philosophical argument for self-transcending subjectivity as a model for conscience (and the foundation of ethics). Central here will be an analysis of the notions of horizon, consciousness, and self-transcendence itself—particularly those special instances of self-transcendence named conversions: intellectual (self-affirmation) and moral (self-appropriation).

Literally, the horizon is a "maximum field of vision from a determinate standpoint." It is specified by two poles, one objective and the other subjective, and each conditions the other. From the viewpoint of methodological reflection on ethics, the subject-pole is the conscious subject and the manner in which he or she evaluates the data relevant to any particular moral question; the object-pole is then constituted by the total complex of data so evaluated (from the humanities, the natural and human sciences, personal and communal experience, philosophical and theological interpretations). Foundational ethics is primarily concerned with the subject-pole, that is, clarifying the manner in which an authentic subject would evaluate given data, and uncovering the conditions and presuppositions of such evaluation.[61]

More generally, and substantively, horizon can be understood as a hermeneutic tool for analyzing the reality and development of the concrete conscious subject; here the poles are the subject and his or her various worlds of meaning (or, in Piaget's framework, operations and their objects). In this way the visual image of horizon is extrapolated into a general model of consciousness. As it is precisely on this point of consciousness that the fate of any understanding of subjectivity is decided, chapter three will develop a detailed explanation of consciousness as the personal subject's nonreflexive self-presence.

Chapter three will then detail the dynamic exigence toward self-transcendence intrinsic to this interpretation of conscious subjectivity. Here the key will be the differentiation of conscious intentionality in terms of the basic operations revealed in the reflection of transcendental method: experiencing, understanding, judging, and deciding. Of special concern will be those peculiarly reflexive instances of knowing and deciding: self-affirmation (intellectual conversion) and self-appropriation (moral conversion). Here the subject not only affirms his understanding of himself as an experiencer, understander, judger, and decider, but, on the highest, existential level of consciousness where conscience reveals itself in the exigence to conform decision to judgment, also chooses himself as a free and responsible agent committed to the realization of value.

In the context of intellectual conversion I will discuss the "virtually unconditioned" of judgment as the proximate criterion of reality—the key in my attempt to establish the radical identity of genuine objectivity and authentic subjectivity. This point will then be transposed to the level of decision where I will show that the subject is objective and authentic in his or her decisions insofar as they are consistent with reasonable judgment and thus transcend themselves in the realization of true value (which is not arbitrarily created, and thus "merely subjective," but is normatively objective in a heuristic way).

Just as each individual decision, to be responsible, must be rooted in and consistent with critical, realistic judgment, I will show how full moral conversion also presupposes at least an implicit intellectual conversion. In other words, while moral conversion in the sense of a "turn toward value" may be effected on almost any intellectual basis, I will argue that full moral conversion—in which the self-creating subject realizes that it is up to herself to decide what she is to make of herself—must include the subject's critical realization of herself in her own judgment's "virtually unconditioned" as the criterion of the real and thus of the truly good, however implicit this realization may be.

Having developed this basic argument on self-transcending subjectivity and moral conversion, a consideration of moral impotence will turn our attention to the meaning and possibility of affective and religious conversion. Finally, chapter four will show how a notion of converted self-transcending subjectivity affords not only a critical grounding for ethics, but also an understanding of conscience as creative, and therefore an ethical perspective which focuses upon positive ideals rather than minimally negative rules.

With such a brief summary of where we are going, then, we must get underway. The tiny capsule we have just seen should give some indication of the kind of implicit compass that will be guiding us throughout. Although it will not be fully explicit until the third chapter, this viewpoint has been operative as a critical norm from the beginning. To the extent that I have "presuppositions" as we discuss various positions, then, they are the convictions that the consideration of a fundamental human reality such as conscience must be grounded in an adequate philosophical analysis (therefore, theological ethics, for example, must also be philosophical); that such philosophical analysis must be explanatory and not merely descriptive; and that for an analysis of conscience to be such an explanatory theory, it must successfully confront two key issues: the radically subjective reality of the concrete person, and the critical, realistic nature of judgment (i.e., human knowing). These convictions, now explicitly stated, are not hidden standards; and, as analyzed in chapter three, are not uncritical presuppositions. As critical norms, I want to emphasize that these convictions are standards for my study; I do not mean to impose them unfairly on others. Thus, in pointing out what I consider to be shortcomings in the valuable work of the authors discussed in this chapter, I am not suggesting that they should have done what I am trying to do, nor do I mean to judge them harshly for not doing what they never intended to do (especially inasmuch as in many instances they did not share my convictions). On the contrary, I mean simply to indicate the differences between their valuable contributions (which must be built on) and what I think is necessary (and therefore am trying to do).

Notes

1. Bernard Häring, *The Law of Christ*, trans. Edwin Kaiser, 3 vols. (Westminster, MD: Newman Press, 1961), 1:139.
2. John Macquarrie, *Three Issues in Ethics* (New York: Harper & Row, 1970), pp. 111–112.
3. Lionel Trilling, *Sincerity and Authenticity* (Cambridge: Harvard University Press, 1972), pp. 1, 2, 3, 5.
4. Ibid., p. 6.
5. Ibid., pp. 9, 11.
6. Ibid., p. 12.
7. Ibid., pp. 11–12.
8. Ibid., p. 11.
9. Ibid., pp. 1–2.
10. Ibid., p. 2.
11. On these issues, see respectively: Curatorium of the C. G. Jung Institute, Zurich (ed.), *Conscience*, trans. R. F. C. Hull and Ruth Horine (Evanston, IL: Northwestern University Press, 1970); Eric Mount, Jr., *Conscience and Responsibility* (Richmond, VA: John Knox Press, 1969); William C. Bier (ed.), *Conscience: Its Freedom and Limitations* (New York: Fordham University Press, 1971).
12. Mount, *Conscience and Responsibility*, p. 22.
13. Quoted in ibid., from F. D. Maurice, *Conscience* (London: Macmillan, 1883), p. 174.

14. Quoted in Mount, *Conscience and Responsibility*, p. 23, from Helmut Thielicke, *Theological Ethics*, trans. William H. Lazareth, 2 vols. (Philadelphia: Fortress Press, 1966), 1:298.

15. Mount, *Conscience and Responsibility*, pp. 60, 34.

16. Quoted in ibid., pp. 60–61, from Gerhard Ebeling, *Word and Faith*, trans. James W. Leith (Philadelphia: Fortress Press, 1963), pp. 420, 417, 412.

17. See Mount, *Conscience and Responsibility*, p. 32; see also Gordon Allport, *Becoming* (New Haven: Yale University Press, 1955), pp. 71-72.

18. See Erich Fromm, *Man for Himself* (New York: Fawcett, 1967), pp. 145-175.

19. Erich Neumann, *Depth Psychology and a New Ethic*, trans. Eugene Rolfe (New York: G. P. Putnam's Sons for the C. G. Jung Foundation for Analytical Psychology, 1969), pp. 122, 35-36.

20. Ibid., pp. 123, 92, 102.

21. Ibid., pp. 103-104, 105.

22. Albert Camus, *The Plague*, trans. Stuart Gilbert (New York: Modern Library, 1948), pp. 120-121.

23. Quoted in "Professor Out of Step," *Time* (January 1, 1973), p. 39.

24. Abraham Maslow, "Reply to Professor Weisskopf" in A. Maslow (ed.), *New Knowledge in Human Values* (Chicago: Henry Regnery, 1970), pp. 245-246, at 246.

25. Quoted in Trilling, *Sincerity and Authenticity*, p. 5, from F. Schiller, *On the Aesthetic Education of Man*, trans. and ed. E. M. Wilkinson and L. A. Willoughby (Oxford: Clarendon Press, 1967), p. 17.

26. Paul Lehmann, *Ethics in a Christian Context* (New York: Harper & Row, 1963), p. 327.

27. Ibid., pp. 328-330.

28. Ibid.

29. Quoted in ibid., pp. 331-332, from *De Veritate*, Q. 17, art. 1, Reply; Lehmann's italics.

30. Lehmann, *Ethics*, p. 332.

31. Ibid., p. 336.

32. Ibid., p. 337.

33. Quoted in ibid., from Sigmund Freud, *New Introductory Lectures on Psychoanalysis*, trans. W. J. H. Sprott (New York: Norton, 1938), p. 88.

34. Lehmann, *Ethics*, p. 342.

35. Ibid., pp. 343-344.

36. Ibid., p. 350.

37. Ibid., pp. 352-353.

38. Ibid., pp. 355, 357

39. Ibid., p. 357.

40. Quoted in ibid., p. 363, from Martin Luther, *Lectures on the Psalms*, WA, 3, 593, 28-29.

41. Quoted in Lehmann, *Ethics*, p. 366, from John Calvin, *Institutes of the Christian Religion* (Philadelphia: Westminster Press, 1936), Chap. 19.16; Lehmann's translation and italics.

42. Lehmann, *Ethics*, p. 366.

43. Ibid., pp. 353-354.

44. Ibid., p. 353.

45. H. Richard Niebuhr, *The Responsible Self* (New York: Harper & Row, 1963).

46. Ibid., p. 54.

47. Ibid., pp. 61, 63.

48. Ibid., p. 64.

49. Ibid., p. 65.

50. Ibid., pp. 71-72.

51. Ibid., pp. 74-76.

52. Ibid., p. 79.
53. Ibid., pp. 79, 84, 87.
54. Ibid., pp. 106–107.
55. Paul Tillich, *Morality and Beyond* (New York: Harper Torchbook, 1963), p. 19.
56. Austin Farrar, *Freedom of Will* (New York: Charles Scribner's Sons, 1958), pp. 236, 278.
57. Supplementary Essay in H. Richard Niebuhr, *Radical Monotheism and Western Culture* (New York: Harper Torchbook, 1970), pp. 100–113.
58. Niebuhr, *Responsible Self*, p. 57.
59. George Herbert Mead, *On Social Psychology*, ed. Anselm Strauss (2nd ed.; Chicago: The University of Chicago Press, 1964), pp. 233, 244.
60. Häring, *The Law of Christ*, p. 146.
61. See Donald Johnson, "Lonergan and the Redoing of Ethics," *Continuum* 5 (Summer 1967): 211–220.

2

Self-Transcendence in Developmental Psychology

This chapter focuses on the work of three developmental psychologists, Erik Erikson, Jean Piaget, and Lawrence Kohlberg. It is important that what is and what is not intended—and therefore to be expected—in this chapter be clear from the beginning. I intend to show through an examination of key aspects of the work of Erikson, Piaget, and Kohlberg that self-transcendence is implicitly operative as a fundamental criterion in their theories of development: that human maturity is clinically and experimentally defined in terms of a person's realization of objective knowing (Piaget) and genuine love and care (Erikson) in universal, inclusive, and consistent judgments of conscience based on objective, ideal, and impersonal grounds (Kohlberg).

This means that I will be making a selective, but critical, use of their work in terms of my overall strategy. I do not in any way intend to present a comprehensive view of the total contribution made by these men to psychological theory; that would be the work of many volumes. I do claim, however, that my interpretive use of central themes from the works of Erikson, Piaget, and Kohlberg is justified in terms of the overall context and intention of each author. And because I am convinced that self-transcendence can be *discovered* as a criterion in the work of Erikson, Piaget, and Kohlberg, my presentation of their theories will be—as far as space allows—in their own words. I will not merely assert that self-transcendence is operative as a criterion in their work, then, but, by having the theorists speak for themselves, help the reader to verify my argument for herself or himself in critically selected passages. Finally, my concern is not with the verification of these psychological theories in themselves; I use these prominent examples of developmental theory not as a foundation but as a context for my philosophical analysis. [1]

Having clarified the limited intentions of this chapter, we can now proceed to determine in some detail what self-transcending subjectivity can mean in terms of developmental psychology. My strategy here will be to place Piaget's general theory of cognitive development and Kohlberg's theory of the development of moral judgment within the overall life cycle framework of Erikson's eight stages of psychosocial epigenesis, and this in order to emphasize the specific stage-by-stage positive correlations among these different theories.

One might naturally expect that a consideration of conscience in terms of the psychoanalytic perspective of a psychologist such as Erik Erikson would concentrate on that period of development in the child known as the phallic or Oedipal. Indeed, the classical literature of psychoanalysis has consistently understood conscience in terms of the emergence of the superego.

My approach in this chapter will be significantly different, however. For, agreeing with Erikson that ethical capacity is the criterion of identity, I will focus on the psychosocial crises of identity and intimacy in adolescence and young adulthood, thus locating the emergence of true conscience in the successful resolution of the identity crisis. Thus, while I shall review all eight stages of Erikson's life cycle, indicating how each is a moment in a fundamental process of self-transcendence, I intend to do it with an eye always cast toward the problem of identity as the center and critical focus of the process.

Coincidental with—and complementary to—this emphasis on the crisis of identity in Erikson's scheme will be my concentration on the highest degree of cognitive development in Piaget's genetic epistemology—the formal operations of adolescence. Indeed, I will indicate the complementarity of these two schemes along the entire range of development. With Piaget my emphasis will be primarily epistemological, for his explanation of cognitive development offers an excellent context for the later discussion of cognitive self-transcendence and objectivity in chapter three. It will be necessary to introduce a certain degree of complexity into the discussion of Piaget's genetic epistemology, for it is impossible to communicate the great explanatory (in contrast to merely descriptive) power of Piaget's theory in any simple set of conclusions such as the usual summaries of Piaget give. In much the same way, an adequate grasp of the significance of Erikson's theory for our study requires—over and above summary statements—at least a minimum amount of the descriptive detail of his concrete analysis.

Further, because Lawrence Kohlberg deals explicitly with the formal aspects of moral judgment in his refinement of Piaget's original studies on the moral development of the child, I will also incorporate his theory on the levels of moral judgment into an integrated understanding of psychosocial, cognitive, and moral development. The highest common denominator in this integrated interpretation of normative personal development will be the movement towards self-transcendence which I will argue is operative at least implicitly as a criterion in the theories of Erikson, Piaget, and Kohlberg (with Kohlberg's analysis of the form of moral judgment bringing together the cognitive and affective elements of its content).

In order to achieve some degree of clarity in examining the various stages and levels peculiar to each of these schemes, it will be helpful to think of the developmental process as dividing into the following four basic periods in terms of which all the theories can be discussed: (1) preoperational (prelatency), (2) concrete operational (latency), (3) formal operational (adolescence), and (4) postadolescent (see diagram). This fourfold breakdown—employing terminology from Erikson as well as Piaget—is merely a tactical move for clarity and convenience. It implies no necessary presuppositions about the substantive issues involved in the respective theories. With this much said as a preface, then, we can begin the implementation of this plan for demonstrating the implicit norm of self-transcendence in developmental theory by reviewing the first stage of the Eriksonian scheme. In this, as in all the Eriksonian stages, I shall consider three factors: (1) the *crisis* which defines the stage, (2) the stage's potential psychosocial strength or *virtue*, and (3) the stage's relationship to the overall question of *identity*.

A. INFANCY AND EARLY CHILDHOOD

1. Erikson: Trust in Infancy

It seems particularly illuminating in relation to our theme of self-transcendence that the first psychosocial crisis of Erikson's life cycle—the infant's struggle to work out a balance favoring basic trust over against mistrust—brings forth, if successfully resolved, the fundamental strength or virtue of hope. For more than anything else it is the rudimentary trust or hope resulting from this first critical stage that forms the bedrock for adult faith, in many ways the epitome of self-transcendence. But an incipient self-transcendence is already manifest in the favorable resolution of this first psychosocial crisis, which is primarily a function of the quality of maternal care. Erikson tells us that

ERIKSON	PIAGET	KOHLBERG
(8) OLD AGE (Wisdom) Integrity/Despair		(6) UNIVERSAL ETHICAL PRINCIPLES OF CONSCIENCE, JUSTICE
(7) ADULTHOOD (Care) Generativity/Stagnation		(5) SOCIAL CONTRACT UTILITY, INDIVIDUAL RIGHTS, DEMOCRATIC LAW
(6) YOUNG ADULTHOOD (Love) Intimacy/Isolation		(4½) RELATIVIST
(5) ADOLESCENCE (Fidelity) Identity/Confusion	FORMAL OPERATIONS	(4) SOCIAL SYSTEM, AUTHORITY MAINTAINING
		(3) INTERPERSONAL EXPECTATIONS, RELATIONS, CONFORMITY, APPROVAL
(4) SCHOOL AGE (Competence) Industry/Inferiority	CONCRETE OPERATIONS	(2) INSTRUMENTAL PURPOSE AND EXCHANGE
(3) PLAY AGE (Purpose) Initiative/Guilt		(1) PUNISHMENT — OBEDIENCE
(2) EARLY CHILDHOOD (Will) Autonomy/Shame, Doubt	PREOPERATIONAL (INTUITIVE (SYMBOLIC	
(1) INFANCY (Hope) Basic Trust/Mistrust	SENSORIMOTOR	

Mothers create a sense of trust in their children by that kind of administra-
tion which in its quality combines sensitive care of the baby's individual
needs and a firm sense of personal trustworthiness within the trusted
framework of their culture's life style. This forms the basis in the child for a
sense of identity which will later combine a sense of being "all right," of
being oneself, and of becoming what other people trust one will become.[2]

By "sense of trust," then, Erikson means a "pervasive attitude toward oneself and the world derived from the experiences of the first
year of life, . . . an essential trustfulness of others as well as a fundamental sense of one's own trustworthiness."[3] From this point of view,
therefore, a "mother must represent to the child an almost somatic
conviction that she (his first 'world') is trustworthy enough"[4] to satis-
factorily respond to his "need for *intake* and *contact* with warm and
calming envelopment and provide food both pleasurable to ingest and
easy to digest."[5] According to Erikson, the baby, "in thus getting what
is given, and in learning to get somebody to do for him what he wishes
to have done, . . . also develops the necessary groundwork 'to get to be'
the giver—that is, to identify with [the mother] and eventually to
become a giving person."[6]

I must stress at this point, however, that the resolution of this crisis
of trust—like those of all the following crises—is never a case of all or
nothing, once and for all. A successful resolution means a favorable
balance of trust over mistrust, not the total victory of what would be
an inappropriately pure, that is, naive, trust. In fact, says Erikson,
unavoidable pain, delay of satisfaction, and "inexorable weaning"
make this first stage "prototypical for a sense of abandonment and
helpless rage."[7] Even under the most favorable circumstances, he
adds,

> this stage seems to introduce into psychic life . . . a sense of inner division
> and universal nostalgia for a paradise forfeited. It is against this powerful
> combination of a sense of having been deprived, of having been divided,
> and of having been abandoned—that basic trust must maintain itself
> throughout life.[8]

Although Erikson explains this primary infantile crisis in terms of
the struggle between trust and mistrust, he refers to the virtue related
to this stage as hope. Here, as at other stages, the strength or virtue
proper to infancy is not only closely related but very similar (though
not necessarily identical) to the positive member of the opposing pair
in the crisis. As a strength to be brought forth and developed in

infancy, Erikson understands hope as "the enduring belief in the attainability of fervent wishes, in spite of the dark urges and rages which mark the beginning of existence."[9] Hope is not only the earliest, but the "most indispensable virtue inherent in the state of being alive," says Erikson. ". . . If life is to be sustained hope must remain, even where confidence is wounded, trust impaired."[10] For the adult, serious loss of hope means regression into a state of virtual lifelessness. But even mature hope, Erikson suggests, is of all the ego-qualities the most childlike, and the "most dependent for its verification on the charity of fate." In Erikson's view, hope, though independent of the verifiability of "hopes" once it is established as a basic quality of experience, is no exception to the fundamental rule that "nothing in human life . . . is secured in its origin unless it is verified in the intimate meeting of partners in favorable social settings."[11]

It is precisely from this intimacy in the encounter between the mother and small infant that the earliest and most undifferentiated sense of identity arises. This encounter of mutual trustworthiness and mutual recognition, says Erikson, "in all its infantile simplicity, is the first experience of what in later reoccurrences in love and admiration can only be called a sense of 'hallowed presence,' the need for which remains basic in man." In the language of hope, "the shortest formulation of the identity gain of earliest childhood," says Erikson, "may well be: I am what hope I have and give."[12]

In summary, then, we can say with Erikson that "hope is verified by a combination of experiences in the individual's 'prehistoric' era, the time before speech and verbal memory." But, as Erikson indicates in the following passage, we have so far considered only one dimension of the development that occurs during this early stage.

> Both psychoanalysis and genetic psychology consider central in that period of growth the secure apperception of an "object." The psychologists mean by this the ability to perceive the *enduring quality* of the *thing world* while psychoanalysts speak loosely of a first love-object, i.e., the experience of the care-taking person as a *coherent being,* who reciprocates one's physical and emotional needs in expectable ways and therefore deserves to be endowed with trust, and whose face is recognized as it recognizes. These two kinds of object are the first knowledge, the first verification, and thus the basis of hope.[13]

For a consideration of the development of the "permanent object" in the infant's world we shall now turn to Jean Piaget's study of the sensorimotor intelligence that characterizes this early stage of cognition.

2. Piaget: Sensorimotor Intelligence

The titles of the two volumes by Piaget which will occupy our attention in considering his study of early cognitive development— *The Origins of Intelligence in Children*[14] and *The Construction of Reality in the Child*[15]—very clearly describe the shape of our present subject matter and, further, reveal the fundamental structure of Piaget's entire cognitional analysis. For in Piaget's thought cognition is always a bipolar phenomenon: we may say that *reality* is an "objective correlative" constructed in function of and isomorphic to the development of intelligence at the subject-pole. Thus *The Origins of Intelligence in Children*, focusing on the subject-pole, describes the genesis of the activities of intelligence at the sensorimotor stage, while *The Construction of Reality in the Child* explains the formation of the correlative categories of object, causality, space, and time, and their organization into a world at the object-pole.

This bipolar structure that Piaget finds in the earliest stage of cognition is characteristic of his understanding of the entire development of the cognitional process—it is, indeed, the defining element of his genetic epistemology. It is important, then, that before beginning a specific consideration of the sensorimotor stage, we review quite briefly the general orientation and character of Piaget's overall perspective.

In essence, Piaget understands the invariant functional features of intelligence as assimilating and accommodating activities moving dialectically toward adaptational equilibrium, and in so doing constantly creating and re-creating both organized structures of intelligence and, as we shall see, the shape of the world. This movement toward equilibrium falls under a "law of evolution,"[16] according to which cognitive development, through a differentiation between assimilation and accommodation, proceeds from an initial state of profound egocentrism to a final state of objective equilibrium.

We shall begin our consideration with the profound egocentrism of the young infant, therefore, as we attempt to trace the gradual erosion of egocentrism (and thus the establishment of an ever more stable equilibrium and, therefore, objectivity) through the succeeding stages of cognitive growth—stages that mark new heights of self-transcending subjectivity.

Piaget has described the cognitive development of the first two years of life as a "miniature Copernican revolution": at first the infant grasps everything to his or her own body, but towards the end of this period, as language and thought begin to appear, he or she has become one entity among others in a gradually constructed universe, now expressed as external to the self. Piaget has summarized in capsule form the central theme and main conclusion of his analysis of this earliest form of cognition:

> The successive study of concepts of object, space, causality, and time has led us to [these] conclusions: the elaboration of the universe by sensorimotor intelligence constitutes the transition from a state in which objects are centered about a self which believes it directs them, although completely unaware of itself as subject, to a state in which the self is placed, at least practically, in a stable world conceived as independent of personal activity. How is this evolution possible?[17]

Piaget's answer to this question—a development of intelligence in terms of an ever more complex differentiation of activities—will be the subject of the following pages.

In *The Origins of Intelligence in Children,* his most detailed analysis of cognitive growth during these first two years, Piaget has designated six different stages through which the development of this period proceeds—each marking the emergence of a "qualitatively new" interaction between the child and the environment.[18] It would distract us from rather than further our purpose to consider each of these stages at any length here. However, because the development from stage to stage during this sensorimotor period does reveal in its earliest form the movement toward ever increasing self-transcendence that is operative throughout later periods of the developmental process, we should—before going on to view the period as a whole—briefly consider Peter Wolff's specification of the stages in terms of the key transitional factors which not only highlight the shift from one stage to the next but indeed constitute the very transformation of intelligent activity:

> The transition from inborn to acquired behavior patterns characterizes the shift from the *first* to the *second* stage; the transition from body-centered to object-centered motor activity initiates the *third* stage; the emergence of intentional means-ends relationships marks the transition from the third to the *fourth* stage; the *fifth* stage is characterized by the intentional motor exploration of unfamiliar objects and events; finally, the transition from empirical motor explorations to mental invention characterizes the *sixth* stage and completes the sensorimotor phase of intelligence development.[19]

In summary fashion, then, these are the stages through which Piaget has traced the development of sensorimotor intelligence—from the use of reflex in the first stage (characterized above all by the complete absence of genuine intelligent behavior), through the acquisition and coordination of habits, to the threshold of the new world of intelligence with the development of intentionality, exploration, and invention, i.e., various facets of the self's cognitive drive to reach out, to move beyond itself.

The intelligence of this sensorimotor period is, of course, "an entirely practical intelligence based on the manipulation of objects; in place of words and concepts it uses percepts and movements organized into 'action schemata.'"[20] As an example of this practical intelligence Piaget cites (at about the eighteenth month) the use of a stick in order to draw up a remote object.[21]

We must now view these gains from the angle of the "Copernican revolution," and consider their precise effect on the infant's original and radical egocentrism. In the following paragraph Piaget summarizes in an exceptionally clear fashion his view on both the nature of egocentrism and its fate in the course of the development of intelligence:

> The result of this intellectual development is in effect to transform the representation of things to the point of completely changing or inverting the subject's initial position with respect to them. At the outset of mental evolution there is no definite differentiation between the self and the external world, i.e., impressions that are experienced and perceived are not attached to a personal consciousness sensed as a "self," nor to objects conceived as external to the self. They simply exist in a dissociated block or are spread out on the same plane, which is neither internal nor external but midway between these two poles. These opposing poles will only gradually become differentiated. It follows that, because of this primitive lack of dissociation, everything that is perceived is centered on the subject's own activity. The self is at the center of reality to begin with for the very reason that it is not aware of itself, while the external world will become objectified to the degree that the self builds itself as a function of subjective or internal activity. In other words, consciousness starts with an unconscious and integral egocentricity, whereas the progress of sensorimotor intelligence leads to the construction of an objective universe in which the subject's own body is an element among others and with which the internal life, localized in the subject's own body, is contrasted.[22]

In assessing the developing differentiation and equilibrium of assimilatory and accommodating activities, a relationship which begins as one of chaos and antagonism, John Flavell characterizes the movement from radical egocentrism to increasing self-transcendence as constituting "simultaneously a centrifugal process of gradual objectification of external reality and a centripetal process of burgeoning self-awareness—the self comes to be seen as an object among objects."[23] The result of these simultaneous centrifugal and centripetal movements, according to Piaget, is, as we have seen already, the dual structure of cognition: knowledge of self and knowledge of other objects.

Indeed, "it is this process of forming relationships between a universe constantly becoming more external to the self and an intellectual activity progressing internally which explains the evolution of the real categories, that is, of the concepts of object, space, causality, and time."[24] Now, it is the construction of these four categories, of course, which at the object-pole constitutes the very intellectual revolution of the first two years. The object concept, or the belief that what is seen continues to exist even when not perceived (i.e., conservation), is not only the most fundamental category and thus presupposed by the concepts of space, time, and causality, but, as we shall soon see, is of particular interest for our study as it relates closely to a fundamental transformation of affective life at this stage.

In summary, Piaget's basic thesis is that "the subject's perspective of the universe is transformed" in the course of sensorimotor development, and that a movement "from integral egocentrism to objectivity is the law of that evolution."[25] At this point, we should consider not only how this notion of objectivity is central in Piaget's own epistemology, but also how crucial an issue the general question of objectivity is for the fundamental problem of self-transcendence and thus of conscience. We should pay careful attention to Piaget's stress on the activity of the subject, then, as he states his position on objectivity:

> In conclusion, not only does experience become more active and comprehensive as intelligence matures, but also the "things" on which it proceeds can never be conceived independently of the subject's activity. . . . It is, in effect, to the extent that the subject is active that experience is objectified. Objectivity does not therefore mean independence in relation to the assimilatory activity of intelligence, but simply dissociation from the self and from egocentric subjectivity. The objectivity of experience is an achievement of accommodation and assimilation combined, that is to say, of the intellectual activity of the subject, and not a primary datum imposed on him from without.
> . . . To put it still differently, the object only exists, with regard to knowledge, in its relations with the subject and, if the mind always advances more toward the conquest of things, this is because it organizes experience more and more actively, instead of mimicking, from without, a ready-made

reality. The object is not a "known quantity" but the result of a construction.[26]

It is difficult to conceive of a view which would place active subjectivity more at the core of objectivity than that expressed in the above passages. Piaget seems to be in no way under the spell of the "myth of the given." The subject's world as already "given" out there to be passively observed is completely demythologized.[27]

I have devoted a good many pages to a consideration of the general features of Piaget's psychology of cognition, his epistemological stance, and in particular, now, the issue of objectivity. For our purposes a careful consideration of these questions is unavoidable, and the discussion of sensorimotor intelligence seemed an especially appropriate occasion for it, since the most important issues are so clearly manifest in this period, where Piaget has discovered what he calls a Copernican revolution, the transition from an egocentric chaos to a structured cosmos.[28]

However, we must not simply identify the objectivity achieved by this Copernican revolution of the sensorimotor period with the entirety of Piaget's epistemological thesis on objectivity. We must, it seems, take the phrase "Copernican revolution" in a fuller historical sense than the obvious "turning things upside down—or inside out" suggested by a cursory glance or facile Kantian analogy. For while that understanding may do justice to the great advance made during the sensorimotor period, we must not forget that it, as only the first of many decentering stages, must be put into developmental perspective in much the same way as the revolution of Copernicus must now be put into the historical perspective of our contemporary understanding of the universe. Piaget helps us to put the cognitive advances of the sensorimotor period into their appropriate developmental and epistemological contexts by suggesting that they "resemble Newton's achievements as compared to the egocentrism of Aristotelian physics," but, restricted as they are to only one perspective, remain themselves egocentric, as do Newton's absolute space and time from the viewpoint of Einstein's relativity.[29] Despite the almost incredible importance of the infant's Copernican revolution, then, it remains no more than Copernican. Later cognitional development, demanded by the disequilibrium inherent in the representative abilities that crown and signal the end of the sensorimotor period, will, as we shall see, include a significant relativization of the advances made during this period of sensorimotor intelligence.

All this, however, must not lead us to minimize the importance of sensorimotor gains. Indeed, so convincing is the objectification achieved during this time that it becomes practically absolutized into an "already-out-there-now-real," taken for granted implicitly and totally by the person of so-called "common sense," and enthroned in the palace of theory by the various "copy" theories of knowledge. And never has it wanted for loyal subjects. Indeed, so totally taken for granted by "common sense" is the "objectivity" of the "already-out-there-now-real" world that even my "broken record" repetition of Piaget's objectivity of a world that is actively constructed by and inseparable from a subject seems thoroughly justified. And thus far we have heard only the first bar of a song whose constant refrain will be "critical objectivity."

The difficulties involved in correlating independent theories of development cannot be overemphasized.[30] Piaget, himself, however, has remarked on the possibility of establishing a correlation between his understanding of the object concept's formation and the appearance of the "object choice" in psychoanalytic theory. For his own part, of course, Piaget sees affectivity developing parallel to, and as the dynamic side of, cognitional structures. Thus, correlated with the "elaboration of an external universe and especially with the construction of the schema of the 'object,'" there occurs a similar transformation of the infant's primitive affective life.[31] This transformation, says Piaget, "is epitomized, in the language of psychoanalysis, by the 'object choice,' i.e., by the objectification of the emotions and by their projection onto activities other than those of the self alone." The mechanics of this affective transformation involve the differentiated "subject" as well as the "object" of the infant's cognitive revolution. It is important to note here again, then, that the construction of the "object"—in the affective dimension as well as the cognitive—is only one half of a twofold process: the awareness of "self" is its necessary subjective correlative. Piaget reminds us that the "narcissism" of psychoanalysis is a "narcissism without Narcissus, i.e., without any sense of personal awareness as such."[32] We should, therefore, switch our attention back to a consideration of the psychosocial development exhibited in the young child's growing sense of autonomy, the central feature of Erikson's second stage, in order to specify in some concreteness the dynamics of the young child's emerging awareness of "self."

3. Erikson: Autonomy of Early Childhood

As Erikson's first stage is the psychosocial analogue of Freud's oral period, his second stage parallels the classical psychoanalytic period of anality, which is characterized by "the particular pleasurableness and willfulness which are often attached to the eliminative organs in early childhood." As Erikson explains it,

> The overall significance of this second stage of early childhood lies in the rapid gains in muscular maturation, in verbalization, and in discrimination and the consequent ability—and doubly felt inability—to coordinate a number of highly conflicting action patterns characterized by the tendencies of "*holding on*" and "*letting go.*" In this and in many other ways, the still highly dependent child begins to experience his *autonomous will*. [33]

While the anal zone is especially expressive of "stubborn insistence on conflicting impulses" inasmuch as it is "the model zone for two contradictory modes which must become alternating, namely, retention and elimination," still, "the sphinctus are only a part of the muscle system with its general ambiguity of rigidity and relaxation, of flexion and extension." In fact, says Erikson, "all basic modalities... lend themselves to both hostile and benign expectations and attitudes. Thus, 'to hold' can become a destructive and cruel retaining or restraining, and it can become a pattern of care: 'to have and to hold.' To 'let go,' too, can turn into an inimical letting loose of destructive forces, or it can become a relaxed 'to let pass' and 'to let be.' "[34]

As the young child begins to stand firmly on its feet, then, he or she not only learns to distinguish between an "I" and a "you," but also begins to face "limits in the form of spatial restrictions and of categorical divisions between 'yes and no,' 'good and bad,' 'right and wrong,' and 'yours and mine.' "[35] This entire stage, then, becomes what Erikson has called a "*battle for autonomy,*" in which the issue of "mutual regulation between adult and child now faces its severest test."[36]

A correct understanding of the epigenetic principle operative in Erikson's differentiation of the various stages in the life cycle involves a recognition that the stages are in no sense closed off from each other or mutually exclusive in their concerns, and therefore that no crisis is solved "once and for all" at any point in the cycle. Crises look back on and presuppose each other inasmuch as the issue of any particular crisis, while highlighted in a critical way during a given stage, is a permanent concern of human development and perdures throughout the entire life cycle. This interaction and overlapping between stages is concretized by Erikson as he discusses how autonomy has its roots in stage one:

> To develop autonomy, a firmly developed and a convincingly continued stage of early trust is necessary. The infant must come to feel that basic faith in himself and in the world (which is the lasting treasure saved from

the conflicts of the oral stage) will not be jeopardized by this sudden violent wish to have a choice, to appropriate demandingly, and to eliminate stubbornly. *Firmness* must protect him against the potential anarchy of his as yet untrained sense of discrimination, his inability to hold on and to let go with circumspection. Yet his environment must back him up in his wish to "stand on his own feet" lest he be overcome by that sense of having exposed himself prematurely and foolishly which we call shame, or that secondary mistrust, that "double-take," which we call doubt.[37]

This stage of autonomy, says Erikson, "becomes decisive for the ratio between loving good will and hateful self-insistence, between cooperation and willfulness, and between self-expression and compulsive self-restraint or meek compliance. A sense of self-control without loss of self-esteem is the ontogenetic source of a sense of *free will.*"[38] In thus summarizing the essential issues at stake during this second stage, Erikson has also pinpointed what he considers the characteristic virtue of this stage—will, "*the unbroken determination to exercise free choice as well as self-restraint, in spite of the unavoidable experience of shame and doubt in infancy.* Will is the basis for the acceptance of law and necessity, and it is rooted in the judiciousness of parents guided by the spirit of law."[39]

In concluding our brief consideration of this second stage of the life cycle, we may note with Erikson that its "overall contribution to an eventual identity formation is the very courage to be an independent individual who can choose and guide his own future." We will recall that, for Erikson, the earliest stage of infancy "leaves a residue in the growing being which, on many hierarchic levels and especially in the individual's sense of identity, will echo something of the conviction 'I am what hope I have and give.' The analogous residue of the stage of autonomy," says Erikson, "appears to be 'I am what I can will freely.'"[40] We shall have an opportunity in the next chapter to recognize the radical importance of the emergence of this autonomous will inasmuch as it constitutes the ontogenetic basis for the mature adult's *responsible* decisions and choices, and thus for the realization of real self-transcendence.

4. Piaget: Preoperational Period

The period of early childhood between two and seven years is essentially one of transition in Piaget's scheme of the development of intelligence. More precisely, this transitional period is best understood as a period of preparation for the logical thought that is to follow it. Since logical thought, which functions as the normative standard in Piaget's system, is characterized by "operations," Piaget has called this preparatory period "preoperational." Our consideration of this period will be brief, and focused principally upon its transitional and preparatory nature.

In order to account for such a long period of difficult transition Piaget has isolated two factors introduced by conceptual thought which place it in opposition to sensorimotor intelligence: first, whereas sensorimotor intelligence aims only at practical adaptation, conceptual thought seeks knowledge as such, and "therefore yields to norms of truth"; second, this search for knowledge depends on a structural transformation of thought effected by socialization.[41]

It is very difficult to single out one of the preoperational stage's many features as characteristic of its fundamental development, but perhaps David Elkind's suggestion that we give close attention to the role of the symbol in this period will be most helpful for our present purpose. As the conquest of the object was at the top of the infant's cognitive agenda, says Elkind, so, he suggests,

> During the preschool period the symbolic function becomes fully active, as evidenced by the rapid growth in the acquisition and utilization of language, by the appearance of symbolic play, and by the first reports of dreams. Yet this new capacity for representation, which loosed the infant from his egocentrism with respect to objects, now ensnares the preschool child in a new egocentrism with respect to symbols.[42]

Thus, the preschool child's major cognitive task, says Elkind, can be understood as the *"conquest of the symbol."*[43]

The "most reality-oriented" kind of thinking found in this early childhood period characterized by egocentric finalism, animism, and artificialism is, according to Piaget, intuition. "In some measure the logic of early childhood," intuition is "sensorimotor experience and coordination that can be reconstituted or anticipated thanks to the ability to use representation." In discussing this intuitive form of thought, Piaget introduces the social factor while making this important point:

> One quality stands out in the thinking of the young child: he constantly makes assertions without trying to support them with facts. This lack of attempts at proof stems from the character of the child's social behavior at this age, i.e., from his egocentricity conceived as a lack of differentiation between his own point of view and that of others. It is only vis-à-vis others that we are led to seek evidence for our statements. We always believe ourselves without further ado until we learn to consider the objections of

others and to internalize such discussions in the form of reflection. In questioning children under seven years one is struck by the poverty of their proofs, by their incapacity to find grounds for their statements, and even by the difficulty they experience in recapitulating through retrospection how they reached their conclusions.[44]

The central feature of intuition, which is no more than a "simple internalization of percepts and movements in the form of representational images,"[45] and thus of the egocentrism of early childhood in general, is the absence of reversibility, the defining quality of true "operations." None of the tests of conservation—an earmark of reversibility—is positive at this stage, says Piaget: "... If ten blue tokens are lined up opposite a row of ten red tokens, the child will think that the number or quantity changes if you spread out or push together one of the rows. Again, if you give him two similar balls of Plasticine and then reshape one as a sausage or as a pancake, he will think that the quantity has changed." The same nonconservation characterizes length, distance, surfaces, volumes.

"The necessary condition for operational development at this age," says Piaget, "is a decentering from the child's own actions and own point of view." The symbolic plane, which enabled sensorimotor intelligence to reach some stability, must now effect a new equilibrium for itself. The "Copernican revolution [of the sensorimotor stage], as it were, must be effected all over again in the realm of representational thought and in social relations; another decentering is necessary to liberate the child from his own point of view." As we have already noticed above, a central factor in this further cognitive revolution is the socialization of intelligence.[46] Thus, having indicated the emergence of symbolic-conceptual thought in early childhood, and having noted its significantly increased potential for cognitive self-transcendence as well as its essential egocentric limitations, we will now switch back to Erikson, first to see the importance of this cognitive development in the psychosocial realm, and then to consider the psychosocial development that Piaget sees as a necessary element in the child's liberation from the symbolic egocentrism of the preoperational period.

5. Erikson: Initiative in the Play Age

"Having found a firm solution of his problem of autonomy," says Erikson, "the child of four or five is faced with the next step—and with the next crisis. Being firmly convinced that he *is* a person, the child must now find out *what kind* of person he is going to be."[47] The child's immediate and, indeed, virtually exclusive models are, of course, his or her parents, who are, as Erikson puts it, at once both powerful and beautiful and yet "unreasonably dangerous." Erikson sets out the context for his next crisis by summarizing under three headings the motor and cognitive gains which he sees as both supporting the development of this stage and at the same time instigating its crisis:

> (1) The child learns to move around more freely and more violently and therefore establishes a wider and, to him, unlimited radius of goals; (2) his sense of language becomes perfected to the point where he understands and can ask incessantly about innumerable things, often hearing just enough to misunderstand them thoroughly; and (3) both language and locomotion permit him to expand his imagination to so many roles that he cannot avoid frightening himself with what he himself has dreamed and thought up. Nevertheless, out of all this he must emerge with a *sense of initiative* as a basis for a realistic sense of ambition and purpose.[48]

A necessary part of all human activity, "initiative adds to autonomy the quality of undertaking, planning and 'attacking' a task for the sake of being active and on the move, where before self-will, more often than not, inspired acts of defiance or, at any rate, protested independence." This initiative that moves autonomy beyond itself manifests itself most characteristically in an intrusive mode, whether physical or psychological, the most significant form of which lends its name to this stage which the theory of infantile sexuality calls phallic. There is no need to repeat here the details of the sexual orientation that the child's relationship to parents is said to take at this time—nor the related Oedipal complex and the fear of castration. More generally, though, and in tension with initiative, "the danger of this stage is a sense of guilt over the goals contemplated and the acts initiated in one's exuberant enjoyment of new locomotor and mental power: acts of aggressive manipulation and coercion which soon go far beyond the executive capacity of organism and mind and therefore call for an energetic halt on one's contemplated initiative."[49]

It is at this stage, says Erikson, "that the great governor of initiative, namely *conscience*, becomes firmly established. Only as a dependent," Erikson continues, "does man develop conscience, that dependence on himself which makes him, in turn, dependable; and only when thoroughly dependable with regard to a number of fundamental values can he become independent and teach and develop tradition."[50] I think we should underline the fact here that Erikson's use of the term "conscience" at this stage of development is, as will soon be apparent, indistinguishable from "superego." As already noted in our reference to guilt, the full and hard truth about this stage of development is that the emergence and establishment of "conscience/superego" is not simply the positive and undiluted good that the above quote alone might lead us to suspect. The complexity of the situation is more adequately conveyed by Erikson in the following passage:

> Infantile sexuality and incest taboo, castration complex and superego all unite here to bring about that specifically human crisis during which the child must turn from an exclusive, pregenital attachment to his parents to the slow process of becoming a parent, a carrier of tradition. Here the most fateful split and transformation in the emotional powerhouse occurs, a split between potential human glory and potential total destruction. For here the child becomes forever divided in himself. The instinct fragments which before had enhanced the growth of his infantile body and mind now become divided into an infantile set which perpetuates the exuberance of growth potentials, and a parental set which supports and increases self-observation, self-guidance, and self-punishment.[51]

As Erikson points out, the emergence of an "inner voice" from this radical internal split within the child is "the ontogenetic cornerstone of morality. But from the point of view of human vitality," he says, "we must point out that if this great achievement is overburdened by all too eager adults, it can be bad for the spirit and for morality itself."[52] For, as Erikson has well put it, "the superego of the child can be primitive, cruel, and uncompromising, as may be observed in instances where children overcontrol and overconstrict themselves to the point of self-obliteration; where they develop an over-obedience more literal than the one the parent has wished to exact; or where they develop deep regressions and lasting resentments because the parents themselves do not seem to live up to the new conscience." And this kind of maiming, of course, remains as a significant part of childhood's psychic legacy. Erikson could not be stronger nor more clear in his judgment: "The fact that human conscience remains partially infantile throughout life is the core of human tragedy."[53]

Beyond the personal tragedy, moreover, there are consequences of maldevelopment at this stage which bear upon the very quality of the human community. Erikson explains this societal tragedy in terms of infantile moralism:

> One of the deepest conflicts in life is the hate for a parent who served as the model and the executor of the conscience but who (in some form) was

found trying to "get away with" the very transgressions which the child can
no longer tolerate in himself. These transgressions often are the natural
outcome of the existing inequality between parent and child. Often, however, they represent a thoughtless exploitation of such inequality; with the
result that the child comes to feel that the whole matter is not one of
universal goodness but of arbitrary power. The suspiciousness and evasive-
ness which is thus mixed in with the all-or-nothing quality of the superego,
that organ of tradition, makes moralistic man a great potential danger to
himself and to his fellow man. It is as if morality, to him, became
synonymous with vindictiveness and with the suppression of others.[54]

In this context Erikson's estimation of the importance of the quality
of family life should be obvious. As a "counter-force to those hidden
hatreds based on differences in mere size or age," it is difficult to
overestimate the value of the "experience of essential equality in
worth, in spite of the inequality in developmental schedule," which is
communicated to children in the companionship between a father or
mother and son or daughter rooted in the concreteness of shared work
and play.[55]

Erikson also makes it clear how imperative is marital and familial
loyalty for "inner unity in the child's conscience at the very time when
he can and must envisage goals beyond the family"—an inner unity
that depends on the internalization of noncontradictory adult voices.
"The play age relies on the existence of the *family in one of its
exemplary forms*, which must gradually delineate where play ends and
irreversible purpose begins, where fantasy is no longer permissible and
to-be-learned reality all-demanding: only thus," says Erikson, "is conscience integrated."[56] And "only thus are guilt feelings integrated in a
strong but not severe conscience," in such a way that "the 'Oedipal'
stage . . . eventually results not only in a moral sense constricting the
horizon of the permissible," but "also sets the direction toward the
possible and the tangible which attaches infantile dreams to the varied
goals of technology and culture."[57]

We may say, then, that *purpose*, the virtue that normatively
emerges from the child's development at this stage, is "the courage to
envisage and pursue valued and tangible goals guided by conscience,"[58] but "uninhibited by the defeat of infantile fantasies, by
guilt and by the foiling fear of punishment." Purpose "invests ideals of
action and is derived from the example of the basic family. It is the
strength of aim-direction fed by fantasy yet not fantastic, limited by
guilt and yet not inhibited, morally restrained yet ethically active."[59]

In the following passage, Erikson, by highlighting the role of imagination as he explains the function of the play age in the larger picture

of identity formation, reinforces for us the intimate interrelation that
exists between the cognitive and psychosocial schedules of development:

> The indispensable contribution of the initiative stage to later identity
> development, then, obviously is that of freeing the child's initiative and
> sense of purpose for adult tasks which promise (but cannot guarantee) a
> fulfillment of one's range of capacities. This is prepared in the firmly
> established, steadily growing conviction, undaunted by guilt, that "I am
> what I can imagine I will be." It is equally obvious, however, that a
> widespread disappointment of this conviction by a discrepancy between
> infantile ideals and adolescent reality can only lead to an unleashing of the
> guilt-and-violence cycle so characteristic of man and yet so dangerous to
> his very existence.[60]

Having noted the definite influence of the symbolic or imaginative
powers on psychosocial development during the play age, and consequently the increased ability of the young child to reach beyond
itself and expand its world, we can now turn in the following section
on middle childhood, and specifically Erikson's school age, to consider how the cooperative nature of the psychosocial tasks of this stage
supports the cognitive transition from the symbolic and imaginative
egocentrism of the young child's intelligence to the greater objectivity
of concrete operational thought.

B. MIDDLE CHILDHOOD AND CONCRETE
OPERATIONS

1. Erikson: School Age Industry and Competence

"Such is the wisdom of the ground plan" of human development,
says Erikson, "that at no time is the child more ready to learn quickly
and avidly, to become big in the sense of sharing obligation, discipline, and performance than at the end of the period of expansive
imagination. He is also eager to make things together, to share in
constructing and planning, instead of trying to coerce other children
or provoke restriction."[61] At the same time, it is also true that the
larger plan of "evolution has brought it to pass that man, when he
approaches the age of instruction in the basic elements of his culture's
technology, is the most unspecialized of all animals. The rudiments of
hope, will, and purpose anticipate a future of only dimly anticipated

tasks. Now the child needs to be shown basic methods leading to the identity of a technical way of life."[62] Such, then, is the ontogenetic and, indeed, phylogenetic context for the next identifiable psychosocial stage that Erikson names the school age, the period during which "the child develops a sense of industriousness, i.e., he begins to comprehend the tool world of his culture, and he can become an eager and absorbed member of that productive situation called 'school,' which gradually supersedes the whims of play. In all cultures, at this stage," Erikson reminds us, "children receive systematic instruction of some kind and learn eagerly from older children."[63]

> Without this [sense of industry, says Erikson], even the best entertained child soon acts exploited. It is as if he knows and his society knows that now that he is psychologically already a rudimentary parent, he must begin to be something of a worker and potential provider before becoming a biological parent. With the oncoming latency period, then, the advancing child forgets, or rather quietly "sublimates"—that is, applies to concrete pursuits and approved goals—the drives which have made him dream and play. He now learns to win recognition by producing things.[64]

From this perspective, also, the genetic wisdom of the human psychological ground plan confronts us. For, inasmuch as "infantile sexuality lacks any chance of competence," it is not difficult to agree with Erikson that it makes eminently good sense "that a period of psychosexual latency should permit the human to develop the tool possibilities of body, mind, and thing-world and to postpone further progress along sexual and sensual lines until they become part of a larger area of social responsibility."[65]

If a sense of industry is the positive quality that must be established during this period, a sense of inferiority or inadequacy is the dangerous negative characteristic over against which a favorable balance must be won. "If the child despairs of his skill or his status among his tool partners," writes Erikson, "he may be discouraged from further learning. He may regress to the hopeless rivalry of the oedipal situation. It is at this point that the larger society becomes significant to the child by admitting him to roles preparatory to the actuality of technology and economy."[66]

Inferiority is not the only danger of this period, however. If we may say that inadequacy falls short of the target, there is also the fundamental danger of overshooting it—"namely man's restriction of himself and constriction of his horizons to include only his work to which, so the Book says, he has been sentenced after his expulsion from paradise."[67] For, as Erikson puts it, "if the overly conforming child accepts work as [his only obligation] and the only criterion of worthwhileness, sacrificing imagination and playfulness too readily, he may become ready to submit to what Marx called 'craft-idiocy,' i.e., become a [conformist and thoughtless] slave" not only of his technology but also of its "dominant role typology" and "those who are in a position to exploit it."[68]

In light of our specifically ethical concerns, this danger of excessive—in some cases almost exclusive—attention to work and to "what works" must be heavily underlined, for, as we have heard Erikson state, it means the neglect and thus atrophied existence of play, of imaginative life, and thus of a vital affectivity—the very sources of moral insight.

The virtue that Erikson recognizes as normative for this stage is competence—"*the free exercise of dexterity and intelligence in the completion of tasks, unimpaired by infantile inferiority.* It is the basis for cooperative participation in technologies and relies, in turn, on the logic of tools and skills"[69]—a point which leads quite naturally into the next section on Piaget's logic of concrete operations. But first we can close this section with Erikson as he anticipates the central theme of identity in his concluding reflections on the school age:

> Here we are already in the midst of identity problems, for with the establishment of a firm initial relationship to the world of skills and tools and to those who teach and share them, and with the advent of puberty, childhood proper comes to an end. And since man is not only the learning but also the teaching and above all the working animal, the immediate contribution of the school age to a sense of identity can be expressed in the words "I am what I can learn to make work." It is immediately obvious that for the vast majority of men, in all times, this has been not only the beginning but also the limitation of their identity; or better: the majority of men have always consolidated their identity needs around their technical and occupational capacities, leaving it to special groups (special by birth, by choice or election, and by giftedness) to establish and preserve those "higher" institutions without which man's daily work has always seemed an inadequate self-expression, if not a mere grind or even a kind of curse. It may be for that very reason that the identity problem in our time becomes both psychiatrically and historically relevant. For as man can leave some of the grind and curse to machines, he can visualize a greater freedom of identity for a larger segment of mankind.[70]

2. Piaget: Concrete Operations

From the close interrelationship and complementarity we have already seen between the psychosocial and cognitive dimensions of development, it should not surprise us that the period of latency or school age coincides with the occurrence of what Piaget considers one of the most significant breakthroughs in the child's entire process of cognitive development—the emergence, growth, and stabilization of a *system of concrete operations.* The key to understanding this fundamental cognitive breakthrough is the word "system." "Operational" thought is *systematic.* And in this sense it is not too much of an exaggeration to say that the advance in thought achieved during middle childhood is, indeed, *the* most radical and far-reaching of all. Earlier cognitive activity (immediately, of the "preoperational" period) is flawed precisely by a lack of any kind of systematic approach. It is true, as we have seen, that "in the preoperational period the child does possess . . . representational actions in various states of internalization. But," according to Flavell, "these preoperational actions, which Piaget sometimes labels *intuitions,* are sporadic and isolated cognitive expressions which do not coalesce into the tight ensembles" that are definitive of middle childhood and later thought.[71] It is also true that operational thought will undergo a significant transformation during adolescence, and I do not wish to minimize the importance of that later advance. But the shift from concrete to formal thought that characterizes adolescent cognitive development occurs within the systematic field of "operations," the basic framework that is established during the years of middle childhood.

The concept of an "operation," which is central to an understanding of Piaget's interpretation of the radical transformation of thought that accompanies the industrious activity of the period of psychosexual latency, is defined in relation to a highly complex logical structure. Basically, says Flavell, in Piaget's perspective, an operation is "any representational act which is an integral part of an organized network of related acts." Operations can be logical, arithmetic, geometric, temporal, etc. "A useful rule of thumb, one Piaget has used, is to say that all the actions implied in common mathematical symbols like $+$, $-$, $\times$, $\div$, $=$, $<$, $>$, etc., belong to, but do not exhaust, the domain of what he terms *intellectual operation.*"[72] Genetically, says Piaget, operations are actions with perceptual, intuitive, or motor origins. "The actions which are the starting point for operations are thus rooted in the sensorimotor schemata, i.e., in actual or mental (intuitive) experience. Before becoming operational, they constitute the substance of sensorimotor intelligence, then of intuition."[73]

An essential quality of operations for Piaget is reversibility:

> Intuitions become transformed into operations as soon as they constitute groupings which are both composable and reversible. In other words, actions become operational when two actions of the same kind can be com-

posed into a third action of the same kind and when these various actions can be compensated or annulled. Thus the action of combining (logical or arithmetic addition) is an operation, because several successive combinations are equivalent to a single combination (composition of additions) and because the combinations can be annulled by dissociations (subtractions).[74]

One of Piaget's most famous experiments—in which children are quizzed about the results of pouring a liquid from a short, broad vessel into a narrower and taller one—illustrates many of the qualities of concrete operational thought while highlighting one of the central categories that runs throughout the entirety of his developmental analysis: *conservation,* a concept we met first in our consideration of the sensorimotor schema of the "object." This experiment, like Piaget's other studies of conservation, shows that nonconservation "does not result from a spontaneous tendency toward change (because the child is, on the contrary, above all a conservationist), but from an initial lack of reversible operations."[75]

Piaget has isolated what he considers two "particularly noteworthy" facts about this kind of conservation experiment:

First, the young subjects seem to reason only about states or static configurations, overlooking transformations: the water in B is higher than it was in A; therefore it has increased in quantity, regardless of the fact that it is the same water that has merely been poured from one container to another. Second, the transformation, although the child is perfectly well aware of it, is not conceived as a reversible movement from one state to another, changing the form but leaving the quantity constant. It is viewed as a particular action, a "pouring," situated on a level other than that of physical phenomena and assumed to have results that are literally incalculable, that is, nondeductible in their external application. However, at the level of concrete operations, after seven or eight the child says: "It is the same water," "It has only been poured," "Nothing has been taken away or added" (simple or additive identities); "You can put the water in B back into A where it was before" (reversibility by inversion); or, particularly, "The water is higher, but the glass is narrower, so it's the same amount" (compensation or reversibility by reciprocal relationship). The states are henceforth subordinated to the transformations, and these transformations, being decentered from the action of the subject, become reversible and account both for the changes in their compensated variations and for the constant implied by reversibility.[76]

This experiment, of course, involves only one kind of conservation, one that appears very early during the period of concrete operations and thus plays an important role in distinguishing this period from the preoperational. Other conservations only appear gradually throughout the period—for example, weight at about nine or ten years of age, and volume not until about eleven or twelve.[77] The important point to note for our present purposes, however, is the radical distinction that conservation reveals between operational and preoperational thought, a distinction rooted in the fact that conservatory "reactions are based on identity or reversibility by inversion or reciprocity," while reactions "at the preoperatory levels . . . are centered on perceptual or imagined configurations."[78] Conservation, then, requires reversible thought, and reversibility, in its turn, is dependent on operations, "operations that result in a correction of perceptual intuition—which is always a victim of illusions of the moment—and which 'decenter' egocentricity so as to transform transitory relationships into a coherent system of objective, permanent relations."[79] The advent of operational thought, therefore, marks the key victory in what with Elkind we referred to as the "conquest of the symbol," the preoperational period's central task.

This arrival of concrete operations stands in relation to preoperational thought as the arrival of the symbol stands to sensorimotor activity: the achievements of both the symbol and concrete operations are primary instruments in helping the subject transcend the egocentrism peculiar to the respective period, for, in a way analogous to that of the sensorimotor child, the preoperational child also is egocentric, "not in the sense of a hypertrophy of the self, but in the sense of centration on his own point of view." There is, as Piaget puts it, a "lack of differentiation among points of view," a state that requires "a differentiation by means of *decentration* in order to arrive at objectivity."[80] I must underline this by repeating the basic thesis in Piaget's epistemological perspective: *objectivity through decentration*. This is the key to understanding Piaget's developmental psychology and genetic epistemology as the explication of a fundamental process of increasing cognitive self-transcendence that begins in infancy and continues through adolescence to adulthood. This is also the key to a full understanding of the significance of the transformation brought about by the "operational" breakthrough. For operations, in Piaget's sense, are the central factor that enables the cognitive subject to transcend herself by radically relativizing her own perspective as she places herself in the context of many viewpoints that are interrelated in a coherent, permanent, and objective system.

We can bring our consideration of the cognitive development of this period to an appropriate end by summarizing, with Flavell's help, the key achievements of this stage and, especially as contrasted to the anticipated formal operations, its basic limitations.

One of the most impressive advances made by the concrete operational child is "the fact that his cognitive superstructure consists of systems in equilibrium, i.e., tightly knit ensembles of reversible operations (logical and infralogical groupings, etc.) which enable him to organize and stabilize the surrounding world of objects and events to a degree quite impossible to the younger child."[81] While the cognitive activities of the preoperational child are tied to "phenomenal, before-the-eye reality," the school-age child, with the new powers of his concrete operational structures, begins to extend his thought, in Piaget's words, from "the *actual* in the direction of the *potential.*"[82] For example, the child with concrete operational structures is much more disposed than a preoperational child to anticipate the extension of a given concrete series of seriated elements, such as A < B < C (the actual) to new, as yet unordered, elements D, E, etc. (the potential). In an admittedly homely analogy, Flavell suggests that "the structures of concrete operations are . . . rather like parking lots whose individual parking spaces are now occupied and now empty; the spaces themselves endure, however, and lead their owner to look beyond the cars actually present towards potential, future occupants of the vacant and to-be-vacant spaces."[83]

But concrete operations, as we have stressed before, are concrete; as Piaget puts it, "in sum, concrete thought remains essentially attached to empirical reality."[84] Like their preoperational predecessors, concrete operations always take their starting point in the real rather than the potential.[85] We must await the later section on formal operations to consider how they reverse this procedure, making the real a special sector of the possible.[86] But the important point here is that the school-age child, unlike the adolescent, cannot "delineate all possible eventualities at the outset and then try to discover which of these possibilities really do occur in the present data."[87] He can make only limited extrapolations from his ordering and organizing of the given. For, as Piaget says, "the system of concrete operations—the final equilibrium attained by preoperational thought—can handle only a limited set of potential transformations. Therefore, it attains no more than a concept of 'what is possible,' which is a simple (and not very great) extension of the empirical situation." In fact, so weak are the child's powers for dealing with the possible that Piaget only grudgingly admits that he has the ability to form hypotheses, for his hypotheses are hypotheses only in the broad sense, structures of only the reality on which the child acts, and formed only in the act. "They are hypotheses that do no more than outline plans for possible actions," says Piaget. "They do not consist of imagining what the real situation would be if this or that hypothetical condition were fulfilled, as they do in the case of the adolescent."[88]

Another limitation of this period's concreteness is the fact that the child finds it necessary, as we mentioned above in passing, to conquer the physical properties of objects and events (mass, weight, length, volume, time, etc.) one by one; only the formal operations provide sufficient abstractness to allow a "content-free, once-for-all structuring."[89]

Finally, we should note that the various structures of concrete operations exist for the most part only as isolated, unconnected units. Unlike the later, more sophisticated, formal structures, "they do not interlock to form a simple, integrated system, a system by which the child can readily pass from one substructure to another in the course of a single [complex] problem."[90]

3. Piaget and Kohlberg: Affective and Moral Development in Childhood

We have concluded our examination of the concrete operational stage of cognitive development at this point (having already given our attention to Erikson's psychosocial interpretation of the school age or latency), but before moving ahead in our consideration of personal development we must note developments in the affective and moral spheres which occur during this time. In fact, we must even push back into the previous period, for there, as we saw in looking at Erikson's interpretation of the superego's emergence, is where the first signs of morality present themselves. We shall first consider very briefly how Piaget understands various advances connected with a cluster of realities that includes feelings, will, values, and the self. Then we shall turn our attention explicitly to the subject of moral development as analyzed by Lawrence Kohlberg.

Piaget has summarized his view of the affective development of the school-age child in this way: "Affectivity from seven to twelve years is characterized by the appearance of new moral feelings and, above all, by an organization of will, which culminates in a better integration of the self and a more effective regulation of affective life."[91] A basic axiom underlying Piaget's entire analysis of affective development is that it moves in a line parallel to cognitive development (from which it is inseparable) in one general process, for "affectivity constitutes the energetics of behavior patterns, whose structures correspond to cognitive functions."[92] It follows only naturally from this, then, that the affectivity of the school-age child will bear the same general structural relationship to that of the preschooler as concrete operations bear to preoperational cognitive activities.

In characterizing the affective life of the school-age child, Piaget presupposes his analysis of its preoperational predecessor, in which he shows how its interests, feelings of self-evaluation, interpersonal emotions, and moral sentiments are all dominated by spontaneity and intuition, and "how the first moral feelings ensue from the unilateral respect of the young child for his parents or other adults and how this respect leads to the formation of a morality of obedience or heteronomy." In contrast to this, Piaget points out how at around school age, there emerges "a new feeling, which arises as a function of cooperation among children and which social life engenders, [consisting] essentially of mutual respect." This new feeling of mutual respect, by which "two individuals attribute to each other equivalent personal value and do not confine themselves to evaluating each other's specific actions,"[93] seems clearly to be an advance in the direction of decentration when set against the earlier egocentric social exchanges of the preoperational period, which Piaget characterizes as "precooperative; that is, at once social from the point of view of the subject and centered upon the child and his own activity from the point of view of the observer."[94]

The most significant and distinctive affective development of this school-age period, in Piaget's view, is the emergence of an *organized system of values* and *will*. Mutual respect and cooperation, which recognize the relative autonomy of individual conscience, lead to an organized system or scale of personal values—honesty, a sense of justice, reciprocity—comparable to the logic of concrete operations. At the same time, will is the affective equivalent of the cognitive operation within this system, regulating and maintaining an equilibrium of its autonomous moral values.[95]

Piaget concludes his consideration of this school-age period in one of his later works with the comment that a comparison of the preoperational period with the period of operations between seven or eight and eleven or twelve reveals "the unfolding of a long, integrated process that may be characterized as a transition from subjective centering in all areas to a decentering that is at once cognitive, social, and moral." And for Piaget, "this process is all the more remarkable in that it reproduces and develops on a large scale at the level of thought what has already taken place on a small scale at the sensorimotor level. . . ."[96]

With this immediate backdrop, and a recalling of our earlier thesis on the bipolarity and correlative development in the process of subject-object interaction, we can appreciate Elkind's statement that during childhood, according to Piaget, "the self system evolves from one which is entirely egocentric, or self-centered, to one which can take the other person's point of view into account when making judgments" and decisions. This relatively decentered self system, though still tied to the concreteness of the school age's dominating imagination, constitutes a clear advance in self-awareness over the narcissistic but actually selfless infant as well as the child of four or five who is not yet aware, for example, that she is herself the sister of her brother or sister. In other words, says Elkind, "in personal and interpersonal matters, the development of the self system reveals the same progressive objectification which occurs with respect to physical reality,"[97] an objectification which realizes the same major leap of self-transcendence at the subject-pole that operations and groups, will and values effect at the correlative object-pole.

Later, when we examine the developments of adolescence, we shall note how the limitations of the concrete self system of imagination are transcended by the emergence of what Piaget calls "personality," just as the formal operations of adolescence conquer the limitations of concrete operations.

As early as 1932 Piaget had published his now classic study of moral development, *The Moral Judgment of the Child.* [98] Piaget's methodology still concentrated on the verbal plane in this study, and his descriptive analysis had not yet reached the full explanatory power of his later work; nevertheless, the accuracy of his observations and analysis has made this work the most dominant influence in the field of moral development over the last forty years. William Kay's review of the field shows quite clearly that "during the years since [Piaget] first investigated the development of moral judgment in children, his conclusions have gained wider and wider acceptance." This is not to say that they have received categorical endorsement, but subsequent studies (for the most part stimulated by Piaget's) "have shown that Piaget's conclusions are still valid although somewhat oversimplified." While confirming the general outline of Piaget's theories, in other words, they have also "shown that moral judgments are more complex than Piaget realized."[99]

By now, says Kay, it is "axiomatic that a child's moral judgment changes as he grows older." And there is hardly a developmental psychologist who would disagree with Piaget's most fundamental thesis that, in the words of Kay's summary statement, the child "begins with a morality of constraint in which moral judgments are based on external authority and a rigid interpretation of rules and regulations, and passes finally to a morality of cooperation in which judgments are based on social considerations and a flexible interpretation of what had previously been inflexible rules."

Acceptance of Piaget's basic thesis at this level of generality must be distinguished, however, from the many qualifications and exceptions which subsequent researchers have made regarding specific points. For example, as we have noted, Piaget placed the shift from heteronomy to moral autonomy during the school age, that is, with the emergence of concrete operations. But, as Kay points out, "Havighurst and Taba were convinced that very few of the children they studied had actually reached the level of moral autonomy,"[100] and this despite the fact that their subjects ranged in age from ten to sixteen years.

One may immediately wonder whether this kind of discrepancy is not traceable to the fact that Piaget based his conclusions on data drawn to a large extent from a study of children in the context of the game of marbles and its rules, a context which constitutes a severely limited—indeed, closed—world. As interesting as it would be to compare and contrast the results of subsequent studies with those of Piaget, my strategy at this point will be to concentrate on the work of one current researcher and theorist, Lawrence Kohlberg, whose studies are important not only as significant reinterpretations and extensions of Piaget, but as themselves highly valuable contributions to the analysis of moral development. In pursuing this line I am not rejecting the contribution of Piaget; on the contrary, I hope to give it—like a rough diamond—the benefit of some forty years of cutting and polishing as summed up in the work of Kohlberg. Indeed, not only will Piaget shine through our immediate consideration of Kohlberg, but we shall before long be turning to some of the original insights of Piaget himself.

The center around which all else turns in Kohlberg's perspective is a schema of six stages of moral judgment divided into three major levels of development:

Level I. Preconventional:
    Stage 1. Punishment and obedience orientation.
    Stage 2. Naive instrumental-relativist orientation.
Level II. Morality of conventional role conformity:
    Stage 3. "Good-boy"/"nice girl" morality of maintaining good relations, approval by others.
    Stage 4. Authority maintaining morality.
Level III. Postconventional morality of self-accepted principles:

Stage 5. Morality of contract, of individual rights, and of demo-
cratically accepted law.
Stage 6. Morality of universal principles of conscience.[101]

The significance of this outline can be best shown by placing it within
the context of Kohlberg's understanding of Piaget's study.

As Kohlberg interprets him, Piaget "starts from a conception of
morality as respect for rules, a respect derived from personal respect for
the authorities who promulgate and teach the rules."[102] Originally
unilateral and absolutistic in the young child, this respect becomes
mutual, reciprocal, and relativistic in the child between eight and
twelve years. Supported by egocentrism and cognitive realism, unilateral respect inspires a heteronomous morality in which adult rules are
held as sacred and unchangeable. For Piaget, cognitive development
and peer group role-taking experiences gradually transform the child's
perception of rules from external authoritarian commands to internal
moral principles—essentially, logical principles of justice, concern for
reciprocity and equality between individuals.[103] Piaget believes that
such an autonomous morality of justice naturally develops in middle
childhood, eventually replacing the young child's heteronomous
morality rooted in unquestioning respect for adult authority.[104]

Now, as I have already indicated, subsequent research has supported
the basic lines of Piaget's theory, but not in every respect. For example, Piaget's stage theory suggests several cross-culturally universal age
trends in the development of moral judgment.[105] Kohlberg emphasizes
three of these universal trends which have been verified in a variety of
Western, Oriental, and aboriginal cultures—relativism and intentionality in judgment, and independence of sanctions: whereas young
children tend to judge an act as either totally right or totally wrong (as
defined univocally by adults) in terms of its actual physical consequences and punishment, the older child, in contrast, considers a
possible diversity in views, as well as the intention to do harm, the
violation of a rule, and so forth. And, says Kohlberg, "the young
child's absolutism, nonintentionalism, and orientation to punishment
do not appear to depend upon extensive parental use of punishment.
Even the permissively reared child seems to have a natural tendency to
define good and bad in terms of absolutism and punishment. . . ."
Extreme punishment practices, however, may lead to the persistence
of the young child's moral ideology of punishment into adolescence or
adulthood.

It is Kohlberg's judgment, then, that Piaget "appears to be correct
in assuming certain characteristics of the young child's moral judg-

ment in any society, characteristics which arise from the child's cognitively immature interpretation of acts labeled good and bad by adults, according to the derivation of their goodness or badness from their association with good and bad consequences of physical harm— punishment and reward." What has not been supported, however, is Piaget's interpretation that these characteristics of the young child's morality derive from the "child's sense of the sacredness of the rule and of adult authority." While it may be true, as Piaget claimed, that rigid attitudes toward game rules decrease with age in children between five and twelve, systematic research suggests that "attitudes expressing the rigidity or sacredness of moral rules or of laws increase in this period, rather than decline."[106]

Moreover, according to Kohlberg, studies show that Piaget also seems to have been off the mark "in postulating a general trend from an authoritarian to a peer group, or democratic, ethic. Postulated general age shifts from obedience to authority to peer loyalty, from justice based on conformity to justice based on equality, have not been generally found."[107]

The most important point concerning Piaget in the findings of Kohlberg's research, however, is that "more broadly," as he says,

> Piaget is correct in assuming a culturally universal age development of a sense of justice, involving progressive concern for the needs and feelings of others and elaborated conceptions of reciprocity and equality. As this sense of justice develops, however, it reinforces respect for authority and for the rules of adult society; it also reinforces more informal peer norms, since adult institutions have underpinnings of reciprocity, equality of treatment, service to human needs, etc.[108]

This basic conclusion regarding Piaget's theory on the moral judgment of the child leads us directly to the heart of Kohlberg's own position, for it is drawn from his major cross-cultural research on children's responses to hypothetical moral dilemmas, such as that of the by now famous Heinz, who was faced with the choice of watching his wife die or stealing the expensive drug that could save her life. From this research Kohlberg found that every response of a subject could be reliably matched with one of his six stages of development that we set down at the outset of our discussion here. As we have also indicated, Kohlberg divides these six stages into pairs on "three major levels, the *preconventional*, the *conventional*, and the *postconventional* or autonomous."[109]

According to Kohlberg, the preadolescent child "has not yet come to really understand and uphold conventional or societal rules and expectations." At the first stage of this preconventional level, the child with emerging concrete operations is often "well-behaved" and responsive to cultural labels of good and bad, but understands these labels in terms of 1) avoidance of breaking punishment-backed rules; 2) obedience for its own sake; and 3) avoidance of physical damage to persons and property.[110]

At Stage 2, the older child, now aware that everyone has individual interests, and that these conflict with the interests of others, understands right behavior as "acting to meet one's own interests and needs and letting others do the same," sometimes through fair exchange, a "deal." "You scratch my back, and I'll scratch yours."[111]

Kohlberg's theory thus indicates a measure of development in moral consciousness even from early to later, preadolescent childhood— development in a direction from an egocentric preoccupation with punishment and obedience towards the self-transcendence of social perspective taking and equal exchange. But just as the cognitive self-transcendence achieved through the emergence and development of concrete operations during this period is fundamentally limited by the intrinsic concreteness of the operations, so the limited moral self-transcendence effected in the development from Stage 1 to Stage 2 is excessively oriented toward the concrete interests of the self.

Adolescence, as we will now see, is the time when the roots of the movement toward self-transcendence begin to take hold—with the transformation of concrete into formal cognitive operations, with the crisis of personal identity, and with the emergence of a socially oriented morality. There seems no better place to begin our consideration of the crucial subject of adolescence than the psychosocial theory of Erik Erikson, for if there has been a single key focus to his work, it has been the identity crisis of adolescence.

C. IDENTITY AND FORMAL OPERATIONS

1. Erikson: Identity Crisis of Adolescence

Identity is at once such a complex concept and so vitally crucial to our thesis on self-transcending subjectivity that it will need much clarification as we go along. We shall begin by simply explicating the broad lines of Erikson's understanding of the adolescent crisis of identity.

In *Childhood and Society* Erikson states the general problem of adolescence this way:

> With the establishment of a good initial relationship to the world of skills and tools, and with the advent of puberty, childhood proper comes to an end. Youth begins. But in puberty and adolescence all samenesses and continuities relied on earlier are more or less questioned again, because of a rapidity of body growth which equals that of early childhood and because of the new addition of genital maturity. The growing and developing youths, faced with this physiological revolution within them and with tangible adult tasks ahead of them, are now primarily concerned with what they appear to be in the eyes of others as compared with what they feel they are, and with the question of how to connect the roles and skills cultivated earlier with the occupational prototypes of the day. In their search for a new sense of continuity and sameness, adolescents have to refight many of the battles of earlier years, even though to do so they must artificially appoint perfectly well-meaning people to play the roles of adversaries; and they are ever ready to install lasting idols and ideals as guardians of a final identity.[112]

For Erikson, then, adolescence is, "above all, a moratorium for the integration of the identity elements" which define the earlier childhood stages—and this integration must occur within the new, larger, somewhat vague but also demanding context called "society."[113] We can follow Erikson in a review of these elements.

First, as infancy established a need for trust in oneself and others, now the adolescent "looks most fervently for men and ideas to have *faith* in, which also means men and ideas in whose service it would seem worthwhile to prove oneself trustworthy."[114]

Further, just as the second stage specified self-definition in terms of what one can freely will, so the adolescent "now looks for an opportunity to decide with free assent on one of the available or unavoidable avenues of duty and service, and at the same time is mortally afraid of being forced into activities in which he would feel exposed to ridicule or self-doubt."[115]

"If an unlimited *imagination* as to what one might become is the heritage of the play age," Erikson continues, "then the adolescent's willingness to put his trust in those peers and leading, or misleading, elders who will give imaginative, if not illusory, scope to his aspirations is only too obvious."[116]

Finally, if the gift of the school age is the desire to make something not only work, but work well, it is not surprising that "the choice of an

occupation assumes a significance beyond the question of remunera-
tion and status" for the adolescent.[117]

From this it follows somewhat clearly that the critical period of
adolescence will be, as Erikson says, less "stormy" for those youths
who are gifted and trained in a way that permits them to move easily
in the pursuit of productivity within the economic and technological
trends of their times, and thus be satisfied with an implicit ideology.
When these conditions for facile absorption into adult society are not
fulfilled, however, "the adolescent mind becomes a more explicitly
ideological one, . . . searching for some inspiring unification of tradition or anticipated techniques, ideas, and ideals." But, on the other
hand, instead of encountering a genuine response from the ideological
potential of a society, "should a young person feel that the environment tries to deprive him too radically of all the forms of expression
which permit him to develop and integrate the next step, he may resist
with the wild strength encountered in animals who are suddenly
forced to defend their lives. For, indeed, in the social jungle of human
existence, there is no feeling of being alive without a sense of identity."[118]

The essential thrust of identity, and its centrality in his epigenetic
scheme, is spelled out by Erikson in this key passage from *Childhood
and Society:*

> The integration now taking place in the form of ego identity is . . . more
> than the sum of the childhood identifications. It is the accrued experience
> of the ego's ability to integrate all identifications with the vicissitudes
> of the libido, with the aptitudes developed out of endowment, and with
> the opportunities offered in social roles. The sense of ego identity, then,
> is the accrued confidence that the inner sameness and continuity prepared
> in the past are matched by the sameness and continuity of one's meaning
> for others, as evidenced in the tangible promise of a "career" [and life
> style].[119]

While recognizing the adolescent's well-known alternation between
regressive yet powerful impulsiveness and compulsive restraint,[120]
Erikson points in all of this to "an 'ideological' seeking after an inner
coherence and a durable set of values" and names the specific ego
strength or virtue which emerges with and from adolescence, *fidelity,
"the ability to sustain loyalties freely pledged in spite of the inevitable con-
tradictions of value systems."* For Erikson, this fidelity is "the cornerstone of identity and receives inspiration from confirming ideologies and affirming companions."[121] Again, from a slightly different
angle, fidelity is the "opportunity to fulfill personal potentialities

(including erotic vitality or its sublimation) in a context which permits the young person to be true to himself and true to significant others." The self-transcendence of mutuality that characteristically emerges in adolescence is especially manifest in the experience of "falling in love" which often includes, according to Erikson, "an attempt to arrive at a self-definition by seeing oneself reflected anew in an idealized as well as eroticized other."[122] In this we have another instance of a developing realization of self and its potential for further self-transcendence in the very process of reaching out to another in mutuality.

In youth, says Erikson, the truth of fidelity verifies itself in many ways:

> A high sense of duty, accuracy, and veracity in the rendering of reality; the sentiment of truthfulness, as in sincerity and conviction; the quality of genuineness, as in authenticity; the trait of loyalty, of "being true"; fairness to the rules of the game; and finally all that is implied in devotion—a freely given but binding vow, with the fateful implication of a curse befalling traitors. When Hamlet, the emotional victim of his royal parents' faithlessness, poses the question, "To be or not to be," he demonstrates in word and deed that to him "to be" is contingent on being loyal (to the self, to love, to the crown) and that the rest is death.[123]

The drive for self-transcendence, the radical dynamism to reach out beyond oneself embodied in Erikson's analysis of youth needs no further elaboration or emphasis, I think.

For Erikson, identity is not merely personal in an individualistic sense; indeed, in his view, identity functions as an essential link connecting—or, rather, reconnecting—human past with human future. Even in personal history, Erikson views identity formation as a "restructuring of all previous identifications in the light of an anticipated future."[124] But, further, Erikson sees identity as owing "its evolutionary and historical significance to the fact that, so far, social groups of men, no longer constituting a species in nature and not yet the mankind of history, have needed to feel with vanity or conviction that they were of some *special* kind, which promised to each individual the participation in a select identity."[125]

The problem here, however, as Erikson reminds us and newspaper and television reports constantly confirm, is that "tribal, national, and class identity . . . demand that man consider otherness inimical, and at least some men have overdefined others as enemies, treating them with an arbitrary ferocity absent from the animal world. At any rate, the need for superior status-identity combined with technological pride has made man exploit and annihilate other men with complete equanimity." The fundamental question at a time of technological expansion that seems to know no limits, then, the key question of survival, really, will be, as Erikson puts it, "what man can afford and decide *not* to use, *not* to invent and *not* to exploit—and yet save his identity."[126]

This question is, of course, a radically ethical one. And, as we have already observed, adolescence is essentially a moratorium, not only a moratorium between childhood and adulthood, but, and what is important here, "between the morality [moralism] learned by the child, and the ethics to be developed by the adult."[127]

Such, in outline, are the characteristics of Erikson's identity crisis. Before pursuing at greater length the question of ethics raised in the preceding paragraph, it seems strategically appropriate at this point to complete our sketch of Erikson's epigenetic schedule of crises and ego strengths—beginning with the question of intimacy and then moving directly on to the fully adult issues of generativity and integrity.

2. Erikson: Intimacy, Generativity, and Integrity

"The strength acquired at any stage," says Erikson, "is tested by the necessity to transcend it in such a way that the individual can take chances in the next stage with what was most vulnerably precious in the previous one."[128] This principle is clearly illustrated in the epigenetic relationship between the crisis of identity and that of intimacy. For, in Erikson's perspective, "consolidated identity permits the self-abandonment demanded by intimate affiliations, by passionate sexual unions, or by inspiring encounters."[129] In other words, as Erikson sums it up, "the young adult, emerging from the search for and the insistence on identity, is eager and willing to fuse his identity with that of others. He is ready for intimacy, that is, the capacity to commit himself to concrete affiliations and partnerships and to develop the ethical strength to abide by such commitments, even though they may call for significant sacrifices and compromises."[130] Again, Erikson says that "intimacy is really the ability to fuse your identity with somebody else's without fear that you're going to lose something yourself."[131]

If the obvious danger of this stage is isolation, "the avoidance of contacts which commit to intimacy,"[132] the greatest danger, perhaps, is the counterpart to intimacy that Erikson calls *distantiation:* "the readiness to repudiate, isolate, and, if necessary, destroy those forces and people whose essence seems dangerous to one's own."[133] This aberration, a "joint selfishness in the service of some territoriality" or other,[134] is essentially a corruption of love, the central virtue which Erikson specifies in this stage.

There are, of course, many different forms of love characteristic of the various stages, but here Erikson means love in the evolutionary and generational sense, "the transformation of the love received throughout the preadolescent stage of life into the care given to others during adult life." Erikson expresses the significance of this love in the following way: "It must be an important evolutionary fact that man, over and above sexuality, develops a selectivity of love: I think it is the *mutuality of mates and partners in a shared identity*, for the mutual verification through an experience of finding oneself, as one loses oneself, in another."[135] In serving the "need for a new and shared identity in the procession of generations," this "love is the guardian of that elusive and yet all-pervasive power of cultural and personal style which binds into a 'way of life' the affiliations of competition and cooperation, procreation and production."[136]

Ideally, the self-seeking of identity-hungry adolescence is gradually absorbed in adult sexuality "as the differences between the sexes become a full polarization within a joint lifestyle. For the previous vital strengths have helped to make the two sexes first become similar in consciousness, language, and ethics in order to then permit them to be maturely different." However, as Erikson points out, "a remnant of adolescent danger is to be found where intimate, competitive, and combative relations are experienced with and against the selfsame people." But the hope implicit in the generational process is that "as the areas of adult responsibility are gradually delineated, as the competitive encounter, the erotic bond, and merciless enmity are differentiated from each other, they eventually become subject to that *ethical sense*,"[137] the mark of an adult, which "emerges as a further differentiation of ideological conviction (adolescence) and a sense of moral obligation (childhood)."[138] This ethical sense is concretized most effectively, of course, in the love of mutual devotion which "overcomes the antagonisms inherent in sexual and functional polarizations, and is the vital strength of young adulthood." This all becomes clear in Erikson's attempt to sum up the matter in first person terms: "If we should continue the game of 'I am' formulations 'beyond identity,'" he says, "we should have to change the tune. For now the increment of identity is based on the formula '*We are what we love.*'"[139] In the love of intimacy, then, self-transcendence is radically "personified" insofar as the very meaning of identity is transformed to include in it the other to whom one reaches out.

In his discussion of intimacy in *Childhood and Society* Erikson reminds us of Freud's reported answer when he was once asked what a normal person should be able to do well. His well-known answer was, of course, "*Lieben und Arbeiten.*"[140] Now, if the first half of his answer, when properly understood, characterizes Erikson's sixth stage of young adulthood, the second half highlights the dominant trend of the seventh stage that Erikson names, *maturity.* For here the crisis is one of *generativity* versus stagnation, where generativity is meant in the broadest sense, including not only productivity in the economic sense, but the bringing forth of "everything that is generated from generation to generation: children, products, ideas, *and* works of art."[141] But generativity is "primarily the concern with establishing and guiding the next generation." For, as Erikson puts it, "evolution has made man the teaching and instituting as well as the learning animal."[142] Dependency and maturity are, in his view, reciprocal.

The self-transcendence that defines the human person in his or her radical exigence is revealed unmistakably in the psychosocial understanding that "adult man is so constituted as to *need to be needed* lest he suffer the mental deformation of self-absorption, in which he becomes his own infant and pet."[143] At the same time, "maturity is guided by the nature of that which must be cared for." Thus, "from the crisis of generativity emerges the strength of care." For Erikson, this "care is the broadening concern for what has been generated by love, necessity, or accident—a concern which must consistently overcome the ambivalence adhering to irreversible obligation and the narrowness of self-concern."[144]

"In the aging person who has taken care of things and people and has adapted to the triumphs and disappointments of being, by necessity, the originator of others and the generator of things and ideas— only in him the fruit of the seven stages gradually ripens."[145] Appropriately enough, Erikson names the positive balance of psychic powers of this final stage *integrity.* By this he means "the ego's accrued proclivity for order and meaning. It is a postnarcissistic love of the human ego—not of the self—as an experience which conveys some world order and spiritual sense, no matter how dearly paid for."[146] At the same time, "it is the acceptance of one's one and only life cycle and of the people who have become significant to it as something that had to be and that, by necessity, permitted of no substitutions. It thus means a new and different love of one's parents, free of the wish that they should have been different, and an acceptance of the fact that one's life is one's own responsibility."[147]

The strength or specific virtue of this stage takes the form of "wisdom in its many connotations—ripened 'wits,' accumulated knowledge, inclusive understanding, and mature judgment. Wisdom maintains and conveys the integrity of experience, in spite of the decline of bodily and mental functions."[148] In the explicit, conceptual sense, Erikson does not claim that "each man can evolve wisdom for himself. For most, a living tradition provides the essence of it."[149] And for this reason Erikson is not entirely satisfied with "wisdom" as a label designating the strength of this last stage. For, while there is an obvious conceptual element in wisdom, it is often overlooked that to be meaningfully effective in life wisdom's roots must be able to take firm hold in a ground of fundamental psychic wholeness. This is why, perhaps, Erikson stresses the integrity of *experience,* and why he says that integrity "implies an emotional integration faithful to the image bearers of the past and ready to take (and eventually to renounce) leadership in the present."[150] We should agree, perhaps, that fundamental integrity and wholeness of experience is to be found in more people than the gifted few who are able to articulate such emotional wholeness of their own into explicit, conceptual "wisdom," but also that it is to be found in a very much smaller group than the mass of people who only repeat the verbal shell of such conceptual wisdom, either half-heartedly or with a conviction of voice that belies an aching doubt.

Meaningful old age, says Erikson, can provide that "integrated heritage which gives indispensable perspective to those growing up, 'adolescing,' and aging. But the end of the cycle," he points out, "also evokes 'ultimate concerns.'"* And while he readily grants that the paradoxes of such ultimate concerns must be left to philosophers and theologians, he wants to emphasize that from the psychosocial perspective, "whatever chance man has to transcend the limitations of his self seems to depend on his full (if not tragic) engagement in the one and only life cycle permitted him in the sequence of generations." He reminds us that even the "great philosophical and religious systems dealing with ultimate individuation seem to have remained (even in their monastic establishments) responsibly related to the cultures and civilizations of their times. Seeking transcendence by renunciation, they remain ethically concerned with the maintenance of the world."[151]

By the same token, then, for the individual "*wisdom... is detached concern with life itself, in the face of death itself.*" For, in Erikson's view, "if there is any responsibility in the cycle of life it must be that one generation owes to the next that strength by which it can come to face ultimate concerns in its own way—unmarred by debilitating poverty or by the neurotic concerns caused by emotional exploitation."[152]

Concluding his reflections on the "Eight Ages of Man" in *Childhood and Society*, Erikson tells us that he found Webster's Dictionary helpful in specifying the generational link in the life cycle. For there, though he suspects that the context is business rather than babies, trust (the first ego-value) is defined as "the assured reliance on another's integrity" (the last of the cycle's values). And it seems possible, he says, "to further paraphrase the relation between adult integrity and infantile trust by saying that healthy children will not fear life if their elders have integrity enough not to fear death."[153]

Our brief consideration of the crisis of identity and the stages following it has been sufficient, I think, to indicate the implicit but fundamental core of self-transcendence in Erikson's thought, and thus to provide a concrete psychosocial context in which to discuss its implications for an ethics of self-transcendence. Our immediate step in this direction will be a consideration of the ethical implications which Erikson himself sees in this psychosocial perspective on self-transcending subjectivity.

3. Erikson: The Ethical Orientation

In his 1970 "Reflections on the Dissent of Contemporary Youth," Erikson presents some of his most explicit and systematic thought on the development of the human person's "moral and ethical orientation." Erikson views this development in terms of a basic threefold division: "I will speak of *moral learning* as an aspect of childhood; of *ideological experimentation* as a part of adolescence; and of *ethical consolidation* as an adult task." But these dividing lines are not to be taken as stone walls, for, he points out, "as we know from the study of psychosexuality, the earlier stages are not replaced, but—according to the epigenetic principle—absorbed into a hierarchic system of increasing differentiation."[154]

In the sphere of moral development, this principle means, as Erikson writes, that "if the child learns to be moral, by which I mean primarily to *internalize the prohibitions* of those significant to him, his moral conflicts continue in adolescence but come under the primacy of ideological thinking." Here ideology means a "*system of commanding ideas* held together more (but not exclusively) by totalistic logic and utopian conviction than by cognitive understanding or pragmatic experience."[155] "By definition," says Erikson, ideologies "cannot consist of mature values."[156] The fundamental human hope (and exigence) is that this ideological orientation as well as its moral predecessor will in its turn in the life cycle be absorbed (though never fully replaced) by what Erikson calls that "ethical orientation which really marks the difference between adulthood and adolescence—'ethical' meaning a *universal sense of values assented to* with insight and foresight, in anticipation of immediate responsibilities, not the least of which is a transmission of these values to the next generation."[157]

I refer to the emergence of the ethical orientation as a hope because the scheme of moral development comes with no guarantee. There is, on the contrary, always the real liability of arrest or retrogression. In the following passage Erikson outlines the various forms in which this liability can actualize itself from the perspective of adolescence, but the structure of the mechanism applies equally (though analogously) to the adult (i.e., the older person who is an adult in the chronological if not ethically normative sense):

> In youth, this [liability] can be seen in an arrest on the ideological level or a backsliding to infantile conflicts over moral interdicts; wherefore aggravated and especially agitated youth alternately reenacts a *premoral* position which denies any need for morality; an *amoral* position which flaunts accepted norms; an *antimoral* position which militantly negates all authority; and finally, an *antiauthoritarian* and yet *moralistic* position which condemns the adult world with righteous fervor—all in the context of an insistence that the stubborn vitality of youth must not be surrendered to the existing system.[158]

One of the most significant points in Erikson's conception of moral development, of course, is the distinction between what he calls the "moral" orientation and the "ethical" orientation. The semantics here are important, but not crucial. Some clarification seems necessary, however, inasmuch as Erikson's linguistic distinction is not exactly parallel to the one in general use throughout this study. I have preferred to use "moral" in a fully positive sense, much like the dictionary's "relating to, dealing with, or capable of making the distinction between, right and wrong in conduct," while generally restricting "ethical" or "ethics" to "the study of standards of conduct and moral judgment,"[159] that is, moral philosophy or moral theology. In this sense, persons or their behavior may be moral, but studies and their methodologies are ethical. This, as I say, is merely a preference, based on a desire to distinguish systematic reflection from its performative subject matter. It does not pretend to be a hard and fast rule; thus I have no difficulty in also describing someone's conduct as "ethical." However, I do resist Erikson's restriction of the term "moral" to a meaning I find better expressed by "moralistic," a usage Erikson himself sometimes follows. While I have not adopted Erikson's language for general use, I have found the meaning of his distinction a profoundly significant one (and use his terminology in discussing it). Let us listen again as he rephrases this basic developmental differentiation:

> I would propose that we consider *moral rules* of conduct to be based on a fear of *threats* to be forestalled. These may be outer threats of abandonment, punishment, and public exposure, or a threatening inner sense of guilt, of shame, or of isolation. In either case, the rationale for obeying a rule may not be too clear; it is the threat that counts. In contrast, I would consider *ethical rules* to be based on *ideals* to be striven for with a high degree of rational assent and with a ready consent to a formulated good, a definition of perfection, and some promise of self-realization.[160]

The fundamental thesis here is that what Erikson calls "the moral and the ethical sense are different in their psychological dynamics, because the moral sense develops on an earlier, more immature level." The immaturity of the moral orientation, however, does not mean that it could (or should) in some way be skipped over, for, as Erikson points out according to the principle of epigenesis, "all that exists layer upon layer in the adult's mind has been developed step by step in the growing child's, and all the major steps in the comprehension of what is considered good behavior in one's cultural universe are—for better or for worse—related to different stages in intellectual maturation," all of which are necessary to one another.[161]

In emphasizing Erikson's distinction between the moral orientation of the child and the ethical orientation of the adult, I do not mean to ignore the mediating perspective of adolescence in which, as Erikson says, the universal good is perceived in ideological terms. For, as "the adolescent learns to grasp the flux of time, to anticipate the future in a coherent way, to perceive ideas and to assent to ideals, to take—in short—an *ideological* position for which the younger child is cognitively" unprepared, "an ethical view is approximated, but it remains susceptible to an alternation of impulsive judgment and odd rationalization." As Erikson stresses throughout his exposition of the stages of the life cycle, "it is the joint development of cognitive and emotional powers paired with appropriate social learning which enables the individual to realize the potentialities of a stage."[162] Here we see Erikson specifying cognitive development as a critical differentiating factor not only between the morality of childhood and the ideology of adolescence, but also between the latter orientation and its adult, ethical successor. We shall pay careful attention to these differences when we return to our consideration of Piaget's study of cognitive development (most of Erikson's reflections on this subject, in fact, are drawn explicitly from Piaget), but I think our purposes will be served best here if—while keeping adolescent ideology in mind—we concentrate especially on the distinction between the orientation of the child and that of the adult.

Indeed, it might be even more helpful if, while remaining aware that there are important distinctions to be made between adolescent ideology and adult ethics, we think of the major differentiation here as one between a childhood orientation and a postchildhood orientation. For at the basis of Erikson's distinction between a morality of childhood and an ethics of adulthood is the fundamental differentiation between an orientation dominated by the superego and one dominated by the strength of ego identity.

We have already seen that Erikson understands an ethical capacity to be the criterion of identity, and in this sense, while identity as a *crisis* may be peculiar to adolescence, identity as a definite (though ongoing) *consolidation* is the defining property of the young adult. Moreover, it also seems clear from the definitions which we have already seen, that Erikson's notion of ethical orientation, while supported by the identity of a strong ego, is essentially an orientation of the conscious "I," for it is characterized, in Erikson's words, at one time as a sense of "*ideals* to be striven for with a high degree of rational assent and with a ready consent to a formulated good, a definition of perfection, and some promise of self-realization,"[163] and again, as "a *universal sense of values assented to* with insight and foresight, in anticipation of immediate responsibilities. . . ."[164] This emphasis on a *striving for ideals and values with insight and rational assent* seems decisively to constitute the ethical orientation as essentially and predominantly conscious, in contrast to the earlier and less mature moral orientation which, though conscious, of course, seems to be influenced most heavily by activities of the unconscious superego.[165]

In light of the foregoing discussion, then, the thesis that I am advancing is that Erikson's psychosocial approach to identity provides ethical theorists with a perspective that focuses at once on the "psycho" and the "social," the conscious as well as the unconscious elements in human living. By distinguishing a mature "ethical" orientation from the more primitive, superego-dominated "moral" orientation of childhood, this perspective opens up the possibility of understanding conscience not as the mere internalization of social prohibitions, but as an active, critical striving for ideals with "a *universal sense of values assented to* with insight and foresight, in anticipation of

immediate responsibilities."[166] Further, by identifying conscience
with a mature ethical orientation, Erikson helps us to understand that
a fully human conscience is not part of a person's birthright, but an
achievement of normative human development. There is no need,
then, to think that everybody has a "conscience" in the fully human
sense of the word, just because everybody seems to have some moral
sense.

But in distinguishing a mature conscience from its unconscious
predecessor, which it supersedes but never fully replaces, Erikson's
perspective at the same time indicates the vitally important role
played by the conscience's true partner in the person's unconscious
life, the ego—and especially the strength of its identity. This perspective, then, does not leave the ethical theorist with a choice between
on the one hand a rationalistic conscience, paper-thin and woefully
ignorant of the dynamism of the unconscious, and, on the other, a
totally unconscious superego whose truncated vision is dominated by
the fear of threats, whether they be "outer threats of abandonment,
punishment, and public exposure, or a threatening inner sense of
guilt, of shame, or of isolation."[167] The psychosocial approach to
identity, on the contrary, is neither entirely conscious nor unconscious, and its developmental angle of vision can specify both the
negative and the positive in the human person, possibilities for self-
destruction as well as self-transcendence. It offers, then, an integration which brings together in a single focus that is both radically social
and historical the luminous rationality of the conscious "I" and the
equally important developmental strengths of the identity of the unconscious ego.

My thesis concerns self-transcending subjectivity. My purpose in
this section—and the preceding ones on Erikson—has been to sketch
the broad lines of his model of the human person in such a way that it
will become clear how central (though implicit for the most part) the
normative function of self-transcendence is to it.[168] There is, of course,
a certain kind of self-transcendence present in the very principle of
epigenesis according to which psychosocial development unfolds. But
this is not our main concern, for not every model of development
is self-transcending in the more important way that Erikson's is. The
critical point to be grasped here is that within Erikson's epigenetic
model every crisis that marks a further developmental stage has a
built-in criterion of self-transcendence. In other words, one develops
in a fully human way only insofar as at each critical juncture one
achieves a measure of self-transcendence. For Erikson's model does
not concern just any kind of development. It is a model for the *growth*

of the *healthy* personality.[169] Thus each crisis is defined normatively in terms of positive and negative factors, and a *healthy* resolution demands a ratio favoring the positive, e.g., basic trust over mistrust. In such favorable resolutions there emerge fundamental virtues or ego strength, e.g., hope. The acquisition and consolidation of such strengths establish a psychosocial foundation that is a *sine qua non* for a healthy, fully human life.

It is no accident, I think (and this is my main contention), that these virtues or ego strengths, as defined by Erikson, are, first and foremost, springboards pointed in the direction of self-transcendence. Whether he is speaking about—to mention a few—the hope of infancy, the fidelity of adolescence, or the love, care, and wisdom of adulthood, it is clear that Erikson is telling us that one becomes one's truly and fully human self only insofar as, and to the extent that, one reaches out beyond oneself to others; that, in short, *self-realization is self-transcendence.*

This basic thrust of Erikson's adult ethical orientation is summed up well in his psychosocial reinterpretation of the Golden Rule in terms of what he calls active mutuality. This mutuality, which first emerges in the successful resolution of the crisis of basic trust in infancy and which comes into its own most fully and explicitly during young adulthood, is fundamentally a relationship in which partners strengthen each other—and themselves—in a way appropriate to their respective age, stage, and condition. Erikson's version of the Golden Rule, then, says that "it is best to do to another what will strengthen you even as it will strengthen him—that is, what will develop his best potentials even as it develops your own."[170] Erikson's basic point, then, is that the true ethical sense which normatively emerges in and characterizes young adulthood involves the radical human possibility of self-transcendence, and that such self-transcendence is self-realization in its deepest and truest sense.

Having examined the basic elements of Erikson's psychosocial life cycle and ethical orientation, this is an appropriate point to shift our attention back to Piaget for a consideration of the special cognitive developments that are proper to and characterize adolescence.

4. Piaget: Formal Operations

We have seen in our consideration of the identity crisis and ideological orientation of adolescence just how central a role in these phenomena Erikson assigns to the special cognitive development that characterizes the adolescent stage. We noted with Erikson that—to repeat—"the adolescent learns to grasp the flux of time, to anticipate the future in a coherent way, to perceive ideas and to assent to ideals, to take—in short—[what Erikson designates] an *ideological* position for which the younger child is cognitively not prepared." We noted also how congenial Erikson finds Piaget's explanation of these cognitive abilities in terms of the formal operations of hypothetico-deductive modes of thought.

In this section, then, we will continue our consideration of Piaget's analysis of cognitive development, for not only does its central theme of the striving for equilibrium through the dialectic of egocentrism and decentration offer a particularly clear and persuasive model of self-transcendence in itself, but, as I have just suggested, this cognitional analysis forms a highly valuable explanatory complement to the model of self-transcendence we have recognized in Erikson's epigenetic theory of psychosocial development. I must emphasize here just how important this complementarity is, for it would be a serious misunderstanding (not always avoided in the past) to regard the affective or cognitive aspects of personal development—distinguished here methodologically in the works of Erikson and Piaget—as separate, independent processes. Erikson reminds us of the necessity of an integrated view of the dynamic and cognitional, and confirms Piaget's perspective of these elements as two sides of the one human reality, when he says that "the employment of the particular cognitive gains of any stage of life is . . . not just a matter of exercising intelligence, for these gains are part of a new pattern of verification which pervades a person's whole being."

Thus, in adolescence, for example, Erikson points out how the formal operations described by Piaget form the basis of a "*historical perspective,* which makes room not only for imaginative speculation about all that could have happened in the past,"[171] but also "a sense of the irreversibility of significant events"[172] and a "deepening concern with the narrowing down of vast possibilities to a few alternatives. . . ."[173] Such a cognitive orientation, then, which permits a systematic exploration of the full range of historical possibilities, forms, in Erikson's mind, "not a contrast but a complement to the need of the young person to develop a sense of identity, for, among all possible and imaginable relations, he must make a series of ever-narrowing selections of personal, occupational, sexual, and ideological commitments."[174] With this brief introduction on the relation between the analyses of Erikson and Piaget, we can move directly to our consideration of Piaget's explanation of adolescent cognitive development, paying special attention to its implicit norm of self-transcendence.

"By comparison with a child," says Piaget, "an adolescent is an individual who constructs systems and 'theories.' The child does not build systems." Whatever systematic qualities the child has are unconscious or at least, says Piaget, preconscious, in the sense that they are neither formulated nor reflected upon. "In other words, he thinks concretely, he deals with each problem in isolation and does not integrate his solution by means of any general theories from which he could abstract a common principle. By contrast, what is striking in the adolescent is his interest in theoretical problems not related to everyday realities."[175] This is the age, says Piaget, of an orientation toward the future and of great ideals. But while the affective and social impulse of adolescence has often been described, Piaget points out that "it has not always been understood that this impulse is dependent upon a transformation of thought that permits the handling of hypotheses and reasoning with regard to propositions removed from concrete and present observations."

In slightly different terms, then, Piaget is saying that if the adolescent is characterized affectively and socially by a "liberation from the concrete in favor of interest oriented toward the nonpresent and the future," it is because as a cognitive subject he has succeeded "in freeing himself from the concrete and locating reality within a group of possible transformations."[176] The key, operative word here is "possible." For, as John Flavell rightly emphasizes in his lengthy and detailed study, "the most important general property of formal-operational thought, the one from which Piaget derives all others, concerns the *real* versus the *possible*."[177] Unlike the child at the stage of concrete operations, the adolescent attacks a problem by trying to conceive all the possible sets of relations suggested by a reading of the data and then, by experimentation and logical analysis, attempts to determine which sets of relations can in fact be verified in the data. "Reality is thus conceived as a special subset within the totality of things which the data would admit as hypotheses; it is seen as the 'is' portion of a 'might be' totality, the portion it is the subject's job to discover."[178]

As we saw in our earlier sections on cognitive development, the transition from a preoperational stage to concrete operations constitutes an "initial and major step towards liberation from a slavish and distorting accommodation to immediate reality." Concerned to emphasize the profound epistemological implications in cognitive development, Flavell points out that this "liberation takes another giant stride in adolescence with [the] reversal in roles between the real and the possible," a reversal, he says, which "amounts to a fundamental reorientation towards cognitive problems."[179] In one of his later works, Piaget explains the distinctive character of formal thought this way:

> The great novelty of [the stage of formal operations] is that by means of a differentiation of form and content the subject becomes capable of reasoning correctly about propositions he does not believe, or at least not yet; that is, propositions that he considers pure hypotheses. He becomes capable of drawing the necessary conclusions from truths which are merely possible, which constitutes the beginnings of hypothetico-deductive or formal thought.[180]

From what we have already seen about the nature of adolescent thought, it must be apparent that there are many similarities between its structures and those of formal symbolic or mathematical logic. Indeed, Piaget's analytical method depends to a great extent on a systematic revelation and exploitation of their similarities. Flavell has isolated three key characteristics of formal thought which highlight these similarities; we can attain some clear understanding of the structure of adolescent thought, he thinks, if we appreciate—via Piaget's analysis—that it is *hypothetico-deductive, propositional,* and *combinatorial.*[181] I will briefly sketch out the broad lines of each of these basic characteristics.

"Formal thought is 'hypothetical-deductive,'" says Piaget, "in the sense that it permits one to draw conclusions from pure hypotheses and not merely from actual observations. These conclusions can even have a validity independent of their factual truth."[182]

But if hypothetico-deductive thought can prescind from the real in dealing with the merely hypothetical, it can also discover the real among the possible by entertaining the possible "as a set of hypotheses to be successively confirmed or infirmed. Hypotheses which the facts infirm can then be discarded; those which data confirm go to join the reality sector."[183]

Above all else, though, formal thinking is propositional. Adolescent reasoning manipulates not only the concrete objects of childhood thought, but also—and especially—propositions about those objects. In other words, the adolescent "takes the *results* of . . . concrete operations, casts them in the form of propositions, and then proceeds to operate further upon them, i.e., make various kinds of logical connections between them (implication, conjunction, identity, disjunction, etc.).'' Formal operations, then, are performed on the results of prior (concrete) operations or upon the operations themselves (algebra, for example) and thus it is that Piaget refers to them as *second-degree operations* or *operations to the second power.*[184]

By adding the method of combinatorial analysis to the hypothetico-deductive and propositional aspects of formal thought we complete its basic structural analogy to symbolic logic. For while the "child of twelve to fifteen of course does not establish the relevant laws of logic, . . . it is remarkable that at the level at which he becomes capable of combining elements by an exhaustive and systematic method he is also capable of combining ideas or hypotheses in affirmative and negative statements. . . ."[185] Thus, when confronted with a problem, the adolescent seeks to exhaustively inventory all the possible relations in the problem by systematically isolating every individual variable plus all the possible combinations of these variables.[186]

In summary, then, it is accurate to say that for Piaget formal thought is "not so much this or that specific behavior as it is a generalized *orientation,* sometimes explicit and sometimes implicit, towards problem solving: an orientation towards organizing data (combinatorial analysis), towards isolation and control of variables, towards the hypothetical, and towards logical justification and proof."[187]

To put the matter in simple descriptive terms, we can say that the adolescent improves on and combines the best qualities of the previous cognitive periods: he or she exhibits the fundamental wonder of the preoperational child, but it is now a carefully planned and controlled wonder; viewed from the other side, the adolescent maintains the concrete operational child's concern for order and pattern, but frees it from a slavish obsession with the empirically real by opening up the hypothetical world of possibility.[188]

But the real power that Piaget has brought to the area of adolescent cognitional theory is rooted in the explanatory range and precision of the logico-mathematical structures that direct his analysis. For just as he does with concrete operations, Piaget uses logico-mathematical structures as models for the formal operations of adolescence, only here the logical structure is the integrated lattice-group rather than incomplete concrete groupings. Piaget's point is that as the child approaches her teen years she develops the capacity to move into the world of possibilities and reason in a hypothetico-deductive fashion, the implicit structure of which is reflected explicitly in formal mathematical logic. Piaget, in other words, has chosen formal logic as an appropriate model to exhibit in clear and explicit fashion the cognitive structure according to which the older child and adolescent (in contrast to younger and middle children) implicitly operate. Piaget is not claiming that subjects on the formal level of operation know formal logic in any explicit way; insofar as they can perform logically, we may say that in Michael Polanyi's terms these subjects have a *tacit* operative knowledge of logic, but they have no spontaneous conceptual or explicit knowledge of logic or its rules.

We might think that the formidable power of formal operations would eliminate cognitive egocentrism once and for all. But even the great achievement of formal operational thought does not automatically mean the disappearance of egocentrism. In fact, there is a specific egocentrism characteristic of adolescence which occurs "as a consequence of the extension of reflective thought into the realm of the possible and hypothetical."[189] And, as at previous stages, this "new mental ability starts off by incorporating the world in a process of egocentric assimilation." Only later, says Piaget, does formal thought "attain equilibrium through a compensating accommodation to reality." Most generally, according to Piaget, "adolescent egocentricity is manifested by belief in the omnipotence of reflection, as though the world should submit itself to idealistic schemes rather than to systems of reality." Seeming to equate metaphysics in some way with idealistic schemes, Piaget tells us that adolescence is "the metaphysical age *par excellence;* the self is strong enough to reconstruct the universe and big enough to incorporate it."[190] The egocentrism of adolescence, then, is "a kind of naive idealism, bent on intemperate proposals for reforming and reshaping reality and—here the 'omnipotence of thought' characteristic of all egocentrism—with an immoderate belief in the efficacy of its thought coupled with a cavalier disregard for the practical obstacles which may face its proposals."[191] This egocentric situation of adolescent thought is summed up by Piaget in this fashion:

> The indefinite extension of powers of thought made possible by the new instruments of propositional logic at first is conducive to a failure to distinguish between the ego's new and unpredicted capacities and the social or cosmic universe to which they are applied. . . . This is obviously a form of cognitive egocentrism. Although it differs sharply from the child's egocentrism . . . it results, nevertheless, from the same mechanism and appears as a function of the new conditions created by the structuring of formal thought.[192]

The interesting paradox about this egocentrism, of course, is that it results from the acquisition of new cognitive powers more flexible and powerful than any previously possessed. But if an imbalance in the functioning of these new capacities brings about an egocentric orientation, it is also true that these new powers not only establish thought on a new and qualitatively distinct level, but, in so doing, also ground the whole of adolescent life as a realm of experience worlds apart from that of the child. Unlike the child, who lives mostly in the here and now present, the adolescent lives not only in the present, but also in a nonpresent, hypothetical world full of plans for his or her future as well as society's. Transposing this cognitive difference into Erikson's context of the identity crisis, we can appreciate the adaptive significance it has for the adolescent who is beginning to look to the adult world with all its possibilities for personally important choices.

Clearly, then, Piaget, like Erikson, sees an intimate connection between the new cognitive orientation and concerns of adolescence on the one hand, and the structural power of the recently acquired formal operations on the other.

Piaget also sees in the new concerns and practical orientation toward future choices of the adolescent the very lever which will gradually but almost surely bring his new cognitive powers into balance through a "decentering process which ... makes it possible for the adolescent to get beyond the early relative lack of differentiation and to cure himself of his [egocentric crisis of idealism]—in other words, the return to reality which is the path from adolescence to the true beginnings of adulthood."[193]

This movement beyond the egocentrism of adolescence has many facets, says Piaget,

> But the focal point of the decentering process is the entrance into the occupational world or the beginning of serious professional training. The adolescent becomes an adult when he undertakes a real job. It is then that he is transformed from an idealistic reformer into an achiever. In other words, the job leads thinking away from the dangers of formalism back into reality. Yet observation shows how laborious and slow this reconciliation of thought and experience can be. One has only to look at the behavior of beginning students in an experimental discipline to see how long the adolescent's belief in the power of thinking endures and how little inclined is the mind to subjugate its ideas to the analysis of facts. (This does not mean that facts are accessible without theory, but rather that a theoretical construction has value only in relation to empirical verification.)[194]

This process of decentering that occurs as the adolescent moves into young adulthood and the occupational world (and Piaget is not entirely clear on whether it makes adult work possible or, as above, is made possible by the hard realities of the adult world of jobs) is actually a continuation of a development in adolescent cognition that has already made its mark by the age of fifteen. For many of Piaget's experiments with subjects at the level of formal operations show that within the formal stage itself there is a development from the ability to use merely deductive methods (among eleven to fourteen-year-olds) to the "capacity to use both deduction and experimental induction at the same time"[195] (which is found in fifteen-year-olds, allowing them not only to solve problems, but to set up rigorous and exhaustive methods of proof or verification). The overall direction of decentering on this level, then, is from the ideal to the real, from the possible to the factual (where the real and the factual are no longer the merely empirically real and factual of childhood but the factual reality reasonably affirmed within the larger context of the possible). The equilibrium of this stage is attained, says Piaget, "when the adolescent [or young adult] understands that the proper function of reflection is not to contradict but to predict and interpret experience. This formal equilibrium surpasses by far the equilibrium of concrete thought because it not only encompasses the real world but also the undefined constructions of rational deduction and inner life."[196] In short, a careful reading of Piaget demonstrates that as powerful as the structures of formal thought are, and as fascinating as their hypotheses are, their own cognitive nature requires that they transcend themselves in an objective movement toward and subordination to the real.

The great strength of Piaget's thought lies, of course, in the area of cognitive development that we have just examined. But, as we have already seen at the concrete level, his analysis extends in many interesting ways into the areas of affectivity, values, and the development of the entire person. Before concluding our consideration of Piaget, then, I will try to show how the same movement toward a critical self-transcendence is manifested by his investigations in these areas.

In accord with his principle that the affective and cognitive are intimately connected and must be treated as such, Piaget reminds us that the fundamental distinction between concrete and formal operations—as realized particularly in the radical liberation of perspective that the latter bring about—is "as important for affective as for cognitive development, for the world of values also can remain bound by concrete and perceptible reality, or it can encompass many interpersonal and social possibilities." An important part of Piaget's thesis here, of course, is that "each new mental structure, by integrating the preceding ones, succeeds both in partly liberating the individual from his past and in inaugurating new activities which at the formal oper-atory level are mainly oriented toward the future." In Piaget's view, then, the "moral autonomy" which he sees emerging "on the interpersonal level between the ages of seven and twelve acquires, with formal thought, an added dimension in the application of ideal or supra-individual values." He says, for example, that in studying the development of the concept "native land," he "observed that this concept did not acquire adequate affective value until after the age of twelve or over. The same," he says, "is true of the concept of social justice and of rational, aesthetic, or social ideals."[197]

"As a result of the acquisition of such values," says Piaget, "decisions, whether in opposition to or in agreement with the adult, have an altogether different significance than they do in the small social groups of younger children. . . . The possibilities opened up by these new values are obvious in the adolescent, who differs from the child in that he is not only capable of forming theories but is also concerned with choosing a career that will permit him to satisfy his need for social reform and for new ideas."[198] At the concrete level, on the other hand, "there is no operation available . . . which would make it possible for the child to elaborate an ideal which goes beyond the empirically given."[199]

From a slightly different angle Piaget suggests that "adolescent affectivity asserts itself through the development of the personality and its injection into adult society," and that this occurs, again, in a way "exactly parallel to the elaboration of the formal operations. . . ." Here the key term is "personality," and it is to be understood as distinct from and in contrast to the "self."[200]

"The self," says Piaget, "while it may not appear immediately, is at any rate relatively primitive. It is the center of one's activity and is characterized by its conscious or unconscious egocentricity." On the other hand, personality, according to Piaget's meaning, "results from the submission, or rather the autosubmission, of the self to some kind of discipline." For example, says Piaget, "a man is not said to have a strong personality when everything is egotistically determined and he remains incapable of dominating the self. He is said to have a strong personality when he incarnates an ideal or defends a cause with all his activity and will." For Piaget personality is a social reality, and implies cooperation as well as personal autonomy.[201]

David Elkind has pointed out that "just as formal operations build upon and incorporate the concrete operational structures, so does personality build upon and incorporate the self system," and it is in this sense that Piaget asserts that "personality formation begins in middle to late childhood (eight to twelve years) with the autonomous organization of rules and values, and the affirmation of will with respect to the regulation and hierarchical organization of moral tendencies." But personality itself, or a personal system, "does not emerge until adolescence and the appearance of formal operations which enable the young person to form life plans that project his activity into the future and which go beyond personal concerns and have consequences for society as a whole."[202] For "a life plan is above all a scale of values which puts some ideals above others and subordinates the middle-range values to goals thought of as permanent. But this scale of values is the affective organization corresponding to the cognitive organization of his work which the new member in the social body says he will undertake. A life plan is also an affirmation of autonomy, and the moral autonomy finally achieved by the adolescent who judges himself the equal of adults is another essential affective feature of the young personality preparing himself to plunge into life."[203]

One important aspect of the relationship between personality and self we should note is that "personality implies a kind of decentering of the self which becomes part of a cooperative plan which subordinates itself to autonomous and freely constructed discipline." It follows, says Piaget, that "disequilibrium will recenter the self on itself, so that oscillations between the personality and the self are possible at all levels." Piaget cites the megalomaniac egocentrism of adolescence as an obvious example,[204] but in the sphere of performance adolescents seem to have no monopoly on self-centered behavior.

We have by no stretch of the imagination considered Piaget's theory in anything like the depth and detail that its complexity and richness demands, but we have touched upon most of the highpoints in the course of our discussion. We can do no better at this point, perhaps, than to turn to Piaget himself for a brief summary:

> In conclusion [he says], let us point out the basic unity of the processes [of mental development] which, from the construction of the practical universe by infantile sensorimotor intelligence, lead to the reconstruction of the world by the hypothetico-deductive thinking of the adolescent, via the knowledge of the concrete world derived from the system of operations of middle childhood. We have seen how these successive constructions always involve a decentering of the initial egocentric point of view in order to place it in an ever-broader coordination of relations and concepts, so that each new terminal grouping further integrates the subject's activity by adapting it to an ever-widening reality. Parallel to this intellectual elaboration, we have seen affectivity gradually disengaging itself from the self in order to submit, thanks to the reciprocity and coordination of values, to the laws of cooperation. Of course, affectivity is always the incentive for

the actions that ensue at each new stage of this progressive ascent, since affectivity assigns value to activities and distributes energy to them. But affectivity is nothing without intelligence. Intelligence furnishes affectivity with its means and clarifies its ends. It is erroneous and mythical to attribute the causes of development to great ancestral tendencies as though activities and biological growth were by nature foreign to reason. In reality, the most profound tendency of all human activity is progression toward equilibrium. Reason, which expresses the highest forms of equilibrium, reunites intelligence and affectivity.[205]

Having come this far with our consideration of Erikson and Piaget, I think we are in a good position to appreciate the force of Elkind's judgment that "for both Piaget and Erikson, the person does not become a true individual or personality until he has integrated his thoughts and feelings about himself into a total life perspective which expands beyond personal interest to the whole of mankind."[206] Or, in the language of my basic thesis, for both psychologists not only is authentic subjectivity genuine objectivity, but personal self-realization is no more *and no less* than personal self-transcendence.

Before moving on to the completion of our consideration of Kohlberg's analysis of moral judgment, we might consider the possibility of correlating Erikson's concept of *identity* with Piaget's *personality*. Here, in a brief anticipation of Lonergan's notion of insight, I would like to expand on this correlation by pointing out the complementarity that exists between Piaget's explication of formal operations and Erikson's understanding of identity. According to Piaget, self-transcending *personality* can emerge only from a foundation supported by the strength of formal operations. We have already seen that Erikson makes the same assertion about identity.[207] And, just as Piaget understands formal operations (personality) as incorporating but moving beyond the structures of concrete operations (self), so, for Erikson, the integration that takes place in the form of ego identity is "more than the sum of childhood identifications."[208] Erikson tells us that "the limited usefulness of the mechanism of identification becomes obvious at once if we consider the fact that none of our identifications of childhood . . . could, if merely added up, result in a functioning personality." Identity formation, in fact, "begins where the usefulness of identification ends." Identifications are important, however, for while identity formation involves some "selective repudiation," it arises fundamentally from a "mutual assimilation of childhood identifications and their absorption in a new configuration." Thus Erikson says that "from a genetic point of view . . . the process of identity formation emerges as an evolving configuration—a configuration

which is gradually established by successive ego syntheses and resynthe-
ses throughout childhood." Now it is clear that for Erikson identifications are partial, immediate, concrete, and, as he says, heavily influenced by "the nature of infantile fantasy which only gradually gives
way to more realistic judgment."[209] In short, it seems that for Erikson
identifications are dominated by the imagination. Now, as we shall see
at greater length in chapter three, one of the cornerstones in Bernard
Lonergan's cognitional theory is the fundamental distinction between
imagination and *insight* (or understanding). Insight is the illuminating
act of understanding. Insight, according to this analysis, is always *into*
the image. In more concrete patterns of thought insight permeates this
image in order to illuminate its meaning. But in other patterns of
thought, insight uses images as springboards and tends to express itself
on its own level of *conceptual* understanding rather than in the immediacy and concreteness of images. Thus, from the genetic perspective, we have Piaget's distinction between concrete and formal operations.

Now, in this context, I suggest that identity in Erikson's sense of the
term can emerge only after the acquisition of formal operations because, unlike identifications which remain bound to given images of
childhood, identity is essentially the expression of an individual's
self-understanding that constitutes him or her as a person. This fundamental insight into the self has its origin in the specific, concrete,
feeling-laden images of childhood identifications—and would, in fact,
amount to only an empty conceptualization without their richness.
But the final achievement is a grasp of unity, identity, and wholeness
in the data of past identifications that structures them in a new personal reality which, while nourished by all past images and feelings, is
tied finally to none of them. It is this identity, this new personal
reality that prompts a voice—in the words that Erikson quotes from
James—to speak and say: "*This* is the real me!"[210] Sharing the transcendence and universal quality of the insight which gave it birth, the
personal identity of Erikson and Piaget which emerges and establishes
itself in young adulthood is self-transcending subjectivity—or, at least,
a subjectivity with both the exigence and real possibility for self-
transcendence. For, as Piaget says, egocentrism is always a possibility,
and the achievement of personal identity is never permanent, but
must always be re-won.

It may be premature to bring this section to a close by placing an
"equals" sign between "identity" and "insight," but I think it is appropriate to suggest that as both discovery and creation the insight of
personal identity is clearly the most significant instance of a knowing

that is constitutive as well as cognitive. As we pursue the argument for self-transcending subjectivity, then, it should come as no surprise that the *conscience* which emerges from the fire of self-constituting understanding (in contrast to less mature moral agencies) will take its stand not on conformity to some "already-out-there-now" code or set of moral rules, but on the novelty of a creative understanding that will settle for nothing less than the most fully human response to each situation. We shall begin our analysis of this creative conscience in the following section on Kohlberg's study of adolescent and adult moral judgment.

D. KOHLBERG: MORAL DEVELOPMENT IN THE ADOLESCENT AND ADULT

Adolescence, according to Kohlberg's analysis, is the period when for the first time "maintaining the expectation and rules of the individual's family, group, or nation is perceived as valuable in its own right." There is now concern "not only with conforming to the individual's social order, but also in maintaining, supporting, and justifying this order."[211]

During the first phase of this conventional level (Stage 3), Kohlberg notes, "good behavior is that which pleases or helps others and is approved by them. There is much conformity to stereotypical images of what is majority or 'natural' behavior. Behavior is often judged by intention—'he means well' becomes important for the first time and is overused. One seeks approval by being 'nice.' "[212]

Later (Stage 4), "right behavior consists of doing one's duty, showing respect for authority, and maintaining the given social order for its own sake. One earns respect by performing dutifully."[213] The older adolescent now takes the social perspective of the system that defines roles and rules, and views individual relations in terms of their place in the social system.[214]

The social orientation of conventional morality, especially the social system perspective of Stage 4, it should be clear, depends cognitively on the abstracting power of at least elementary formal thought.

As we might expect from a theoretician who takes his basic orientation from Piaget, Kohlberg places great emphasis on formal operations in his analysis of mature moral judgment. But as I pointed out at the end of the last section and will continue to reinforce, Kohlberg clearly recognizes that "what is of special importance for understanding adolescence . . . is not the logic of formal operations, but its epistemology, its conception of truth and reality." He recognizes, in fact, that the advent of formal operations brings about an epistemological revolution which is in some ways the first major step toward the radical intellectual conversion to *critical* realism that we will be examining in chapter three. For Kohlberg correctly emphasizes that the child of concrete operations, unlike his or her younger brother or sister, differentiates the subjective and objective in terms of the internal and external and equates reality with the external and the physical, identifying the subjective and mental with fantasies, while the adolescent or young adult with formal operations assumes a profoundly different orientation toward the external and physical, seeing them as "only one set of many possibilities of a subjective experience." No longer is the external necessarily the real or the objective, and the internal the unreal. Now, says Kohlberg, "the internal may be real and the external unreal. At its extreme," he says, "adolescent thought entertains solipsism or at least the Cartesian cogito, the notion that the only real thing is the self."[215]

According to Kohlberg, however, there is more to the matter, for "if the discovery of subjective experience and the transcendental self is one side of the new differentiation of subjective and objective made by the adolescent, the clouding and questioning of the validity of society's truths and its rightness is the other."[216]

The foundation of Piaget's analysis of adolescence, then, is the revolutionary shift in cognition from concrete to formal operations "by which old conceptions of the world are restructured in terms of a new philosophy." Kohlberg reminds us that "Piaget defined the preschool child as a philosopher, revolutionizing child psychology by demonstrating that the child at each stage of development actively organizes his experience and makes sense of the physical and social world with which he interacts in terms of the classical categories and questions of philosophers concerning space, time, causality, reality, and so on."[217] But it is really only in adolescence with the emergence of formal thought that the child becomes a philosopher in any explicit sense. Thanks to Kohlberg and his many colleagues in the field of moral development, the adolescent emergence of philosophical questioning has been studied in particularly great detail in the moral realm, where it grounds the possibility of the transition from a conventional to a postconventional stance. Kohlberg sums up the situation this way:

> The shift in adolescence from concrete to formal operations, the ability now to see the given as only a subset of the possible and to spin out the alternatives, constitutes the necessary precondition for the transition from conventional to principled moral reasoning. It is in adolescence, then,

that the child has the cognitive capability for moving from a conventional to a postconventional, reflective, or philosophic view of values and society.

The rejection of conventional moral reasoning begins with the perception of relativism, the awareness that any given society's definition of right and wrong, however legitimate, is only one among many, both in fact and theory.[218]

An example of such a relativistic view is found in the following student statement:

Dan: Immoral is strictly a relative term which can be applied to almost any thought on a particular subject... if you have a man and a woman in bed, that is immoral as opposed to if you were a Roman a few thousand years ago and you were used to orgies all the time, that would not be immoral. Things vary so when you call something immoral, it's relative to that society at that time and it varies frequently.[219]

This statement is representative of a group of students who from the viewpoint of moral stage theory are in a transitional period, which Kohlberg calls Stage 4½. For while they understand and can use conventional moral thinking, they view it as "arbitrary and relative."[220] At the same time, they do not yet have, says Kohlberg, "any clear understanding of, or commitment to, moral principles which are universal, which have a claim to some nonrelativistic validity. Insofar as they see any 'principles' as nonrelativistic, it is the principle of 'do your own thing, and let others do theirs.'"[221]

In addition to the revolutionary cognitive power of formal operations, Kohlberg specifies another significant factor in the movement from a conventional to relativistic orientation: the personal "experience of leaving home and entering a college community with conflicting values...."[222] In the context of psychosocial moratorium and identity questioning, this experience can trigger a breakthrough of the absolute "givenness" which the social system enjoys in Stage 4.

On the cognitive side, Kohlberg suggests that "the very questioning of the arbitrariness of conventional morality presupposes a dim intuition of nonarbitrary moral principles. A purely conventional person can accept the relativity of the rules of his group because he seeks nothing more. Intense awareness of relativity, however, implies a search for, or dim awareness of, universal principles in terms of which conventional morality seems arbitrary. Royce," he says, "pointed this out long ago, and termed 'the moral insight' the recognition that the sense of relativity itself presupposes an implicit valid universal principle."[223]

There does seem to be a genuine insight into the relativity of reality, then, that is necessary for the emergence of principled morality. And though "moral relativism" may be a transitional period in Kohlberg's developmental schema, to be succeeded, normatively, by the morality of a principled conscience, such a principled conscience, I suggest, exists and functions within the context of an enduring and valid perception of relativity. This is not an extreme relativism, however, for the point that one discovers in an authentic grasp of relativity is *not* that *everything* is relative and arbitrary, but that reality (especially *human* reality) is complex and ambiguous, and that absolute, abstract, and predetermined answers to problematic situations cannot do justice to their reality. Further, one discovers that fundamental values like love, fidelity, and honesty (while absolute in the sense that they *always* inform a truly *human* response—and that their opposites *never* do) are *relative* inasmuch as their meaning in specific, concrete circumstances is never pre-given, but must be determined in the particular situation by creative, sensitive understanding and critical judgment. Such an insight into the character of human reality and knowing is at the heart of the appropriation of one's critical intelligence that constitutes the intellectual conversion we shall examine in chapter three.

This discussion of Kohlberg's analysis of relativism, as well, of course, as the various stages of moral judgment, has been carried on within the normative context of a mature morality of principled conscience. If a personal transition from relativism to such a principled moral orientation is to be achieved, however, more than advanced cognitive development is necessary.

On the question of the relationship between moral and cognitive development, Kohlberg deliberately aligns himself with Piaget in stating that "both types of thought and types of valuing (or of feeling) are schemata which develop a set of general structural characteristics representing successive forms of psychological equilibrium. The equilibrium of affective and interpersonal schemata, justice or fairness, involves many of the same basic structural features as the equilibrium of cognitive schemata logicality." From this perspective, then, "justice (portrayed as balancing the scales) is a form of equilibrium between conflicting interpersonal claims," so that, as Kohlberg quotes from Piaget's *Moral Judgment of the Child,* "in contrast to a given rule imposed upon the child from outside, the rule of justice is an immanent condition of social relationships or a law governing their equilibrium."[224]

The central point being asserted by Kohlberg, therefore, "is not that moral judgment stages are cognitive—they are not the mere application of logic to moral problems—but that the existence of moral stages implies that [moral] development has a basic cognitive-structural component."[225] In other words, the Piagetian rationale just put forth by Kohlberg maintains that "cognitive maturity is a necessary, but not a sufficient condition for moral judgment maturity. While formal operations may be necessary for principled morality, one may be a theoretical physicist and yet not be able to make moral judgments at the principled level."[226]

This is a critical point because Kohlberg claims that his studies show that most persons (even those with formal operations) never advance to the principled stage of moral development, and that those who do reach it do so no earlier than young adulthood. Besides cognitive maturity, then, what else does Kohlberg see as necessary for development to principled morality? In addition to the experience of identity crisis, in which responsibility is only for the self and freedom is to make one's choices for oneself, Kohlberg suggests that for development to principled moral reasoning there must also be adult moral "experience of *sustained responsibility for the welfare of others* and the experience of irreversible choice...."[227]

Kohlberg tells us that the postconventional level is "characterized by a major thrust toward autonomous moral principles which have validity and application apart from [the] authority of the groups or persons who hold them and apart from the individual's identification with those persons or groups." Like the other levels, the postconventional comprises two stages of development, the fifth and sixth of the overall scheme. In the following summary passage Kohlberg characterizes Stage 5 as

a social-contract orientation, generally with legalistic and utilitarian overtones. Right action tends to be defined in terms of general rights and in terms of standards which have been critically examined and agreed upon by the whole society. There is a clear awareness of the relativism of personal values and opinions and a corresponding emphasis upon procedural rules for reaching consensus. Aside from what is constitutionally agreed upon, right or wrong is a matter of personal values and opinion. The result is an emphasis upon the legal point of view, but with an emphasis upon the possibility of changing law in terms of rational considerations of social utility, rather than freezing it in the terms of Stage 4, law and order. Outside the legal realm, free agreement and contract are the binding elements of obligation. This is the official morality of American government, and finds its ground in the thought of the writers of the Constitution.[228]

A definite advance upon this moral perspective, but one that does not yet qualify as a totally new stage, is designated by Kohlberg as

Stage 5B, and consists of an "orientation to internal decisions of conscience but without clear rational or universal principles."[229]

Stage 6, on the other hand, is an orientation of conscience toward ethical principles which appeal to "logical comprehensiveness, universality, and consistency. These principles are abstract and ethical (the Golden Rule, the categorical imperative); they are not concrete moral rules like the Ten Commandments. Instead, they are universal principles of justice, of the reciprocity and equality of human rights, and of respect for the dignity of human beings as individual persons."[230]

Kohlberg has defined these highest stages of moral orientation, as well as their earlier predecessors, in terms of the specific stance they take on some thirty-two different aspects of morality. For example, on "Conscience, Motive Given for Rule Obedience or Moral Action,"[231] the stages are:

Stage 1. Obey rules to avoid punishment.
Stage 2. Conform to obtain rewards, have favors returned, and so on.
Stage 3. Conform to avoid disapproval, dislike by others.
Stage 4. Conform to avoid censure by legitimate authorities and resultant guilt.
Stage 5. Conform to maintain the respect of the impartial spectator judging in terms of community welfare.
Stage 6. Conform to avoid self-condemnation.[232]

This example clearly involves "successive degrees of internalization of moral sanctions." Other issues studied by Kohlberg represent "successive cognitional reorganization of the meaning of culturally universal values." For example, even though "cultures differ in their definition of the universality of [the value of life] or of the conditions under which it may be sacrificed for some other value," human life is a basic value in every society. Kohlberg found that it falls into stages this way:

Stage 1. The value of a human life is confused with the value of physical objects and is based on the social status [or] physical attributes of its possessor.
Stage 2. The value of a human life is seen as instrumental to the satisfaction of the needs of its possessor or of other persons.
Stage 3. The value of a human life is based on the empathy and affection of family members and others toward its possessor.
Stage 4. Life is conceived as sacred in terms of its place in a categorical moral or religious order of rights and duties.
Stage 5. Life is valued both in its relation to community welfare and as a universal human right.

Stage 6. Life is valued as sacred and as representing a universal human value of respect for the individual.[233]

For Kohlberg these orientations are stages in the strong sense inasmuch as they "represent an invariant developmental sequence. True stages," he says, "come one at a time and always in the same order." Further, "all movement is forward in sequence and does not skip steps. Children may move through these stages at varying speeds, of course, and may be found half in and half out of a particular stage. An individual may stop at any given stage and at any age, but if he continues to move," says Kohlberg, "he must move in accord with these steps. Moral reasoning of the conventional or Stage 3–4 kind never occurs before the preconventional Stage 1 and Stage 2 thought has taken place. No adult in Stage 4 has gone through Stage 6, but all Stage 6 adults have gone at least through 4."[234]

It is important to note here that "at each stage, the same basic moral concept or aspect is defined, but at each higher stage this definition is more differentiated, more integrated, and more general or universal." For example, says Kohlberg, "when one's concept of human life moves from Stage 1 to Stage 2 the value of life becomes more differentiated from the value of property, more integrated (the value of life enters an organizational hierarchy where it is 'higher' than property so that one steals in order to save life) and more universalized (the life of any sentient being is valuable regardless of status or property)." And each stage is accompanied by the same kind of advance. "Each step of development, then, "is a better cognitive organization than the one before it, one which takes account of everything present in the previous stage, but making new distinctions and organizing them into a more comprehensive or more equilibrated structure."[235]

The postconventional structure is an "orientation not only to actually ordained social rules but to principles of choice involving appeal to logical universality and consistency."[236] From the genetic perspective, "the general direction of maturity of moral judgment is a direction of greater morality," says Kohlberg.[237] For his meaning of "greater morality," here, Kohlberg relies on the thought of such standard moral philosophers as Kant, Sidgwick, and Hare. Thus, he says,

Each of the Kohlberg stages of moral judgment represents a step toward a more genuinely or distinctly moral judgment. We do not mean by this that a more mature judgment is more moral in the sense of showing closer conformity to the conventional standards of a given community. We mean that a more mature judgment more closely corresponds to genuine moral judgments as these have been defined by philosophers. While philosophers have been unable to agree upon any ultimate principle of the good that would define "correct" moral judgments, most philosophers agree upon the characteristics that make a judgment a genuine moral judgment. Moral judgments are judgments about the good and the right of action. Not all judgments of "good" or "right" are moral judgments, however; many are judgments of esthetic, technological, or prudential goodness or rightness. Unlike judgments of prudence or esthetics, moral judgments tend to be universal, inclusive, consistent, and to be grounded on objective, impersonal, or ideal grounds.[238]

Kohlberg offers "the right way to make a Martini is five to one" as a statement about the good and right that is not a moral judgment inasmuch as it lacks the above specifically moral characteristics. In this view, "if we say, 'Martinis should be made five to one,' we are making an esthetic judgment, and we are not prepared to say that we want everyone to make them that way, that they are good in terms of some impersonal ideal standard shared by others, and that we and others should make five-to-one Martinis whether they wish to or not."[239] Having made this distinction between moral and nonmoral value judgments, Kohlberg goes on to apply it to his developmental scheme when he argues that:

> In a similar fashion, when a ten-year-old answers the "moral should" question "Should Joe tell on his older brother?"—in stage 1 terms of the probabilities of getting beaten up by his father and by his brother—he does not answer with a moral judgment that is universal (applies to all brothers in that situation and ought to be agreed upon by all people thinking about the situation) or one that has any impersonal or ideal grounds. In contrast, stage 6 statements not only use specifically moral words like "morally right" or "duty" but use them in a moral way: e.g., phrases such as "regardless of who it was" and "by the law of nature or of God" imply universality; "Morally, I would do it in spite of fear of punishment" implies impersonality and ideality of obligation, and so on. Thus, the responses of subjects at lower levels to moral-judgment matters fail to be moral responses the same way that the value judgments of subjects at higher levels about esthetic or morally neutral matters fail to be moral responses.[240]

By setting up as a criterion such a formal definition of moral maturity, Kohlberg has found it possible to "define a moral judgment as 'moral' without considering its content (the action judged) and without considering whether it agrees or not with our own judgments or standards."[241] This genuinely moral judgment is what Kohlberg means by "judgment of principle," and he quotes Hare's view that "to become morally adult is to learn to make decisions of principle; it is to learn to use 'ought' sentences verified by reference to a standard or set of principles which we have by our own decision accepted and made our own."[242] The sign of moral maturity, then, says Kohlberg, is the "ability to make moral judgments and formulate moral principles" of one's own, rather than the ability to conform to moral judgments of others.[243]

In claiming that the mature moral judgment of Level III is characterized by an orientation to principles of conscience, Kohlberg is confirming the basic thesis of Piaget that moral development is marked by a progressive sense of justice, for *the* moral principle that governs the lives of morally mature men, according to Kohlberg, is justice.[244] It is evident, he claims, that

> moral development in terms of these stages is a progressive movement toward basing moral judgments on concepts of justice. To base a moral duty on a concept of justice is to base that duty on the right of an individual; to judge an act wrong is to judge it as violating such a right. The concept of a right implies a legitimate expectancy, a claim which I may expect others to agree I have. While rights may be grounded on sheer custom or law, there are two general grounds for a right—equality and reciprocity (including exchanges, contract, and the reward of merit). At stages 5 and 6 all the demands of statute or of moral (natural) law are grounded on concepts of justice, i.e., on agreement, contract, and the impartiality of the law and its function in maintaining the rights of individuals.[245]

As an illustration of the Stage 6 orientation to universal moral principles, and thus, especially, justice, Kohlberg cites the following passage from Martin Luther King's "Letter from a Birmingham Jail":

> There is a type of constructive nonviolent tension which is necessary for growth. Just as Socrates felt it was necessary to create a tension in the mind so that individuals could rise from the bondage of half-truths, so must we see the need for nonviolent gadflies to create the kind of tension in society that will help men rise from the dark depths of prejudice and racism.

> One may well ask, "How can you advocate breaking some laws and obeying others?" The answer lies in the fact that there are two types of laws, just and unjust. One has not only a legal but a moral responsibility to disobey unjust laws. An unjust law is human law that is not rooted in eternal and natural law. Any law that uplifts human personality is just, any law that degrades human personality is unjust. An unjust law is a code that a numerical or power majority group compels a minority group to obey but does not make binding on itself. This is difference made legal. I do not advocate evading or defying the law as would the rabid segregationist. That

would lead to anarchy. One who breaks an unjust law must do so openly, lovingly, and with a willingness to accept the penalty. An individual who breaks a law that conscience tells him is unjust, and willingly accepts the penalty of imprisonment in order to arouse the conscience of the community over its injustice, is in reality expressing the highest respect for law.[246]

Perhaps we can conclude our exposition of the stages of moral judgment with Kohlberg's brief interpretation of the King passage:

> King makes it clear that moral disobedience of the law must spring from the same root as moral obedience to law, out of respect for justice. We respect the law because it is based on rights, both in the sense that the law is designed to protect the rights of all and because the law is made by the principle of equal political rights. If civil disobedience is to be Stage 6, it must recognize the contractual respect for law of Stage 5, even to accepting imprisonment. That is why Stage 5 is a way of thinking about the laws which are imposed upon all, while a morality of justice which claims to judge the law can never be anything but a free, personal ideal. It must accept the idea of being put in jail by its enemies, not of putting its enemies in jail.[247]

While it is true that Kohlberg's stress on the formal aspects of moral judgments allows him to "define a moral judgment as 'moral' without considering its content" and thus "whether it agrees or not with our own judgments or standards,"[248] there are definite limitations to such an approach. For example, although Kohlberg's cross-cultural studies indicate a "significant increase or stabilization of conventional morality of a Stage 4 variety, at the expenses of preconventional stages of thought"[249] in adulthood, he discovered in their results "no way of thinking about our moral situations [that was] found in adulthood and not found in adolescence." He concluded originally, then, that "there are no adult stages in the structural sense," and that adulthood has no "moral wisdom denied to the youth," despite the fact that "there is an adult movement toward integration in the use of moral structures, in the integration of moral thought in its application to life."[250]

It was Kohlberg's insistence on the distinction between structure and content, in fact, which at first made him argue that Erikson's developmental task conceptions fall short of a truly developmental explanation. "Sexual intimacy and marriage, vocational identity and achievement, parenthood, acceptance of life's completion and conclusion are matters of content, not form," Kohlberg claimed.[251] By thus removing Erikson's insights from the structural arena of truly explanatory theory, Kohlberg was unable to take serious theoretical account of such distinctively adult virtues as love and care. The result of his original neglect of these basic human realities (proper to the adult in their full and effective form) meant that Kohlberg did less than justice to his own cognitive-developmental view "that 'cognition' and 'affect' are different aspects, or perspectives, on the same mental events, that all mental events have both cognitive and affective aspects. . . ."[252] In chapter three we shall see that moral judgments are not just "about sentiments and intuitions of persons," as Kohlberg has said they are, but that moral judgments are judgments of values, values that are apprehended in feelings. Thus, if, as Erikson argues, virtues such as love and care are proper to adults in a way that they are not to children and adolescents, Kohlberg's position that "the quality (as opposed to the quantity) of affects involved in moral judgment is determined by its cognitive-structural development"[253] was not fully adequate to the reality.

The difficulty of Kohlberg's original emphasis on the strictly formal, cognitive structure of moral judgment and its concept of justice can be formulated most clearly in a question that Kenneth Keniston put in terms of a distinction between "ethicality and zealotry."[254] Granting that a person of mature moral judgment and sense of justice will pursue just goals, we still will want to know how, concretely, he or she will pursue such goals. What means will be employed? Will he or she proceed in a style that is fully human?

In Keniston's view, when we consider "the development of a morality based on a commitment to ethical principles that are maintained even when they conflict with conventional moral wisdom . . . we are immediately confronted with a paradox." "On the one hand," says Keniston, "Kohlberg identifies such ethical reasoning with admirable men like Socrates, Gandhi, and Martin Luther King—men for whom devotion to the highest personal principles was paramount over all other considerations, and who as a result were moral leaders of their time." Yet, on the other hand, Keniston reminds us that it has been argued that such abstract personal moral principles "are intimately—perhaps inevitably—related to the development of moral self-righteousness, zealotry, dogmatism, fanaticism, and insensitivity." In pursuit of personal principles, he says, some people "will ride roughshod over others who do not share these principles, will disregard human feelings or even destroy human life."[255] While it may be claimed that many moral zealots have never reached the highest stages of moral reasoning, says Keniston, there is no reason to think that this is true of all; and while a sense of justice may forbid some of the behavior that Keniston describes, we should be aware that even

Kohlberg does not claim that all persons who reach Stage 6 have gone through Stage 5.[256]

Keniston's own solution to the paradox—in terms of Anna Freud's concept of an ideal "harmony" between "developmental lines"— suggests that "whether the highest stages of moral reasoning lead to destructive zealotry or real ethicality depends upon the extent to which moral development is matched by development in other sectors. The critical related sectors of development . . . are those which involve compassion, love, or empathic identification with others." Advanced moral development in itself is not dangerous, says Keniston (though we may wonder whether such moral development "in itself" can be moral in any serious sense of the word). "What is dangerous is *any* level of moral development . . . in the absence of a developed capacity for compassion, empathy, and love for one's fellow man . . . the combination of abstract principles with a humorless and *loveless asceticism* is especially likely to be dangerous." "In such individuals," says Keniston, "the danger of breaking human eggs to make a moral omelet, of injuring people in order to advance one's own moral principles, is all too real. Thus, neatly to identify even the highest levels of moral reasoning with human virtue, much less with mental health, maturity, and so on, would be a serious mistake."[257]

Keniston's solution, then, brings us to the notion of the complete integration of personality, fully personal equilibrium, or what Anna Freud has called "harmony." And these concepts strongly suggest, I think, that, as illuminating as it is, a contentless, structural analysis is a necessary but not sufficient approach to a fully adequate understanding of the development of moral reasoning. For there *is* in adulthood a "moral wisdom denied to the youth," and this moral wisdom, if not specified in formal structures as first analyzed by Kohlberg, is surely manifested by the adult virtues Erikson calls love and care. Kohlberg's theoretical revisions of later years—especially his attempt at a rapprochement with Erikson's theory on the postconventional level,[258] which we have seen above—indicate that he has come to appreciate the force of this point: moral reasoning is an inseparably cognitive-affective reality.

There is, of course, more to moral action than moral judgment. And if cognitive maturity is a necessary but not sufficient condition for mature moral judgment, the same is true *a fortiori* for moral behavior. In the next chapter we shall consider the key distinction between judgment and decision in the context of Lonergan's analysis, but I will suggest at this point that the only adequate answer to the problem of moral behavior (i.e., reasonable or fully human behavior in the normative sense) lies in the cognitive-affective integration of the personality. I have already described Erikson's ethical orientation at length, but it cannot be overemphasized that mature moral (ethical) behavior is nothing else than fully human behavior, and that fully human behavior only issues (in any predictable and secure way) from a concrete personal identity that has harmoniously integrated both cognitive and affective maturity of the most advanced forms in a stable, but active equilibrium.

E. SUMMARY

My purpose in this chapter has been to show that an implicit criterion of self-transcendence is operative in the developmental psychologies of Piaget, Erikson, and Kohlberg. We have seen, in fact, that transcendence plays a twofold role in developmental thought. Not only is each new stage regarded as qualitatively transcending its predecessor (as in an elevator image), but, more importantly, we have seen that this developmental transcendence is understood as *normative,* and that it is defined precisely in terms of the *subject's transcendence of self* in the operation, task, or orientation of the given stage.

Thus we have seen how Piaget's interpretation of cognitive development functions in terms of a normative *objectivity* which—ideally—is realized in an ever fuller and more sophisticated way as development progresses from sensorimotor and symbolic activities to concrete and finally formal operations through a dialectical process of decentering which achieves a significant if not complete and permanent eradication of egocentrism. Indeed, when we recall Piaget's thesis that "the objectivity of experience is an achievement of accommodation and assimilation combined, that is to say, of the intellectual activity of the subject, and not a primary datum imposed on him from without,"[259] we realize that Piaget presents us not only with a most significant instance of the basic and central position of self-transcendence in human reality, but also with a highly sophisticated model of *self-transcending subjectivity* in the fundamental sphere of cognition. This is clear when—realizing that consciousness is constitutive as well as cognitive—we remember that for Piaget there is, in Flavell's words, "simultaneously a centrifugal process of gradual objectification of external reality and a centripetal process of burgeoning self-awareness. . . ."[260]

Further, our thesis that authentic subjectivity is genuine

objectivity—in the sense that subjectivity achieves objectivity insofar as it transcends itself—was clarified and supported by our consideration of Piaget's theory, especially in his analysis of egocentrism, where he asserts, for example, that "egocentrism signifies the absence of both self-perception and objectivity," and that "through an apparently paradoxical mechanism... it is precisely when the subject is most self-centered that he knows himself the least, and it is to the extent that he discovers himself that he places himself in the universe and constructs it by virtue of that fact."[261]

If self-transcending subjectivity is central to cognitive development, it is equally important to the stages of psychosocial development conceived by Erikson in terms of tasks, crises, and virtues. For we noted that Erikson has put subjectivity right at the heart of his theory in the concept of identity—a personal identity that by definition emerges in a specific social-cultural context, and that he has interpreted the development of this identity in terms of a series of critical psychosocial tasks—tasks whose completions mark, crises whose successful resolutions are defined by, the acquisition of specific, necessary psychosocial strengths. These strengths are the true moral virtues—virtues, not in the sense of socially approved character traits that are to be striven for, but in the sense of dynamic strengths that in the healthy, fully mature personality underpin every authentic discovery, decision, and deed; virtues, in other words, that are defined by the very power they give the subject for self-transcendence, from the initial but irreplaceable hope of the trusting infant to the love and care of its parents, to the ultimate wisdom of the grandparent whose understanding and concern reach out to the generations to come. Indeed, we even saw that Erikson has extrapolated this psychosocial orientation of self-transcending subjectivity into an ethical viewpoint—a viewpoint formulated in a version of the Golden Rule revised in terms of the active mutuality that St. Francis sought when he prayed, "Lord, make me an instrument of your peace...."

We found the same self-transcending subjectivity again in the field of moral judgment, whose form, we learned through Kohlberg's study, develops normatively from a naive egocentric instrumentalism through a conventional morality of approval that perceives value as existing in "already-out-there-now" rules, to a universal orientation of principled conscience.

We have noted in this chapter that relatively few adults ever reach the fullness of cognitive powers as specified by Piaget's level of formal operations. Significantly fewer, still, ever attain the highest levels of moral judgment and personal commitment. Those who do can be said to have experienced a genuine intellectual and moral *conversion*. Such conversion is a proper object of strictly philosophical as well as psychological analysis. Kohlberg recognizes the need of philosophy when, after a discussion of "the moral strand of ego development, which is clearly philosophical," he says that while one side of ego development is the structure of the self-concept, . . . the other side is the individual's concept of the true, the good, the beautiful, and the real." And "if education is to promote self-development, ego development must be seen as one side of an education whose other side consists of the arts and sciences as philosophically conceived"; if it is "to offer some purposes and meanings which can stand up to relativistic questioning, it must learn philosophy."[262] Indeed, like Erikson, Kohlberg recognizes that ultimately the ethical orientation must be understood in generational terms, and after admitting the inadequacy of his initial attempt to integrate childhood and adult moral development into a single theoretical series, he advises us that if adults are to speak effectively to the next generation "they must try to express whatever sense of commitment they have found genuinely meaningful," and "if developmental psychology is to aid in such communication between the generations, it must learn the language of philosophy."[263]

In the next chapter I will show how the question of moral development—especially *conversion*—as explicated by Piaget, Erikson, and Kohlberg can be further illuminated from the philosophical perspective of Bernard Lonergan's transcendental method. There I will indicate how the concept of self-transcending subjectivity which we have been examining here in the context of developmental psychology (where we have been interested in learning from the major theories rather than in verifying them) can be understood as a model for a more adequate interpretation of fully human conscience, as well as verified in personal experience. Lonergan's philosophical method, rooted as it is in the transcendental analysis of the personal experience of *insight*, seems to offer an especially promising area for exploration, for this second chapter has clearly indicated, I think, how central the activity of insight—at once both concrete and universal—is to the moral dimension of consciousness, where the abstract idea misses the concreteness of the human good, and the mere image its universal context.

Notes

1. The past ten years have seen an increasing body of critical writing on specific aspects of the work of Erikson, Piaget, and especially Kohlberg. While many of these criticisms are significant, they will not receive *explicit* attention here as they do not

touch directly on the fundmental issue of self-transcendence. Interested readers may consult, on Erikson: P. Roazen, *Erik H. Erikson: The Power and the Limits of His Vision* (New York: Free Press, 1976) and C. Gilligan, "Woman's Place in Man's Life Cycle," *Harvard Educational Review* 49/4 (November 1979): 431–446; on Piaget: L. S. Siegel and C. J. Brainerd (eds.), *Alternatives to Piaget: Critical Essays on the Theory* (New York: Academic Press, 1978) and G. Brown and C. Desforges, *Piaget's Theory: A Psychological Critique* (London: Routledge and Kegan Paul, 1979); on Kohlberg: W. Kurtines and E. C. Greif, "The Development of Moral Thought: Review and Evaluation of Kohlberg's Approach," *Psychological Bulletin* 81/8 (August 1974): 453–470, E. L. Simpson, "Moral Development Research: A Case Study of Scientific Cultural Bias," *Human Development* 17 (1974): 81–106, P. J. Philibert, "Lawrence Kohlberg's Use of Virtue in His Theory of Moral Development," *International Philosophical Quarterly* 15 (December 1975): 455–497, W. E. Conn, "Postconventional Morality: An Exposition and Critique of Lawrence Kohlberg's Analysis of Moral Development in the Adolescent and Adult," *Lumen Vitae* 30 (1975): 213–230, J. C. Gibbs, "Kohlberg's Stages of Moral Development: A Constructive Critique," *Harvard Educational Review* 47/1 (February 1977): 43–61; C. Gilligan, "In a Different Voice: Women's Conceptions of Self and of Morality," *Harvard Educational Review* 47/4 (November 1977): 481–517, D. Locke, "The Illusion of Stage Six," *Journal of Moral Education* 9/2 (January 1980): 103–109, and the wide-ranging essays in B. Munsey (ed.), *Moral Development, Moral Education, and Kohlberg* (Birmingham, AL: Religious Education Press, 1980).

2. Erik Erikson, *Childhood and Society* (2nd ed.; New York: Norton, 1963), p. 249.

3. Erik Erikson, *Identity: Youth and Crisis* (New York: Norton, 1968), p. 96.

4. Erik Erikson, "Life Cycle," *International Encyclopedia of the Social Sciences,* 17 vols. (New York: Macmillan and Free Press, 1968), 9:286–292, at 288.

5. Erik Erikson, *Insight and Responsibility* (New York: Norton, 1964), p. 116.

6. Erikson, *Identity*, p. 99.

7. Erikson, "Life Cycle," p. 288.

8. Erikson, *Childhood and Society*, p. 250.

9. Erikson, *Identity*, p. 118.

10. Erikson, *Insight and Responsibility*, p. 115.

11. Ibid., p. 116.

12. Erikson, *Identity*, pp. 105, 107.

13. Erikson, *Insight and Responsibility*, pp. 116–117.

14. Jean Piaget, *The Origins of Intelligence in Children*, trans. Margaret Cook (New York: Norton, 1963; original French, 1936).

15. Jean Piaget, *The Construction of Reality in the Child*, trans. Margaret Cook (New York: Ballentine, 1971; original French, 1937).

16. Ibid., p. 397.

17. Ibid., p. 395.

18. Peter H. Wolff, *The Developmental Psychologies of Jean Piaget and Psychoanalysis*, Psychological Issues, 5 (New York: International Universities Press, 1960), p. 37.

19. Ibid.

20. Jean Piaget, *Six Psychological Studies*, trans. Anita Tenzer, ed. David Elkind (New York: Vintage, 1968; original French, 1964), p. 11.

21. Jean Piaget and Bärbel Inhelder, *The Psychology of the Child*, trans. Helen Weaver (New York: Basic Books, 1969; original French, 1966), p. 12.

22. Piaget, *Six Psychological Studies*, pp. 12–13.

23. John Flavell, *The Developmental Psychology of Jean Piaget* (New York: Van Nostrand Reinhold, 1963), p. 61.

24. Piaget, *Construction of Reality*, pp. 401–402.

25. Ibid., p. 402.

26. Piaget, *Origins of Intelligence*, pp. 367–368.

27. Flavell, *Developmental Psychology*, p. 71.

28. Piaget, *Construction of Reality*, p. xi.

29. Ibid., pp. 413–414.

30. See J. M. Tanner and Bärbel Inhelder, (eds.) *Discussions on Child Development*, Vol. 4 (New York: International Universities Press, 1960), esp. pp. 15–16; Wolff, *Developmental Psychologies of Jean Piaget and Psychoanalysis*; Henry W. Maier, *Three Theories of Child Development* (New York: Harper and Row, 1965); Jonas Langer, *Theories of Development* (New York: Holt, Rinehart and Winston, 1969).

31. Piaget, *Six Psychological Studies*, p. 16.

32. Ibid., pp. 16–17.

33. Erikson, *Identity*, p. 107.

34. Ibid., pp. 108, 109.

35. Erikson, "Life Cycle," p. 288.

36. Erikson, *Identity*, pp. 108, 109.

37. Erik Erikson, *Identity and the Life Cycle*, Psychological Issues, 1 (New York: International Universities Press, 1959), p. 68.

38. Erikson, *Identity*, p. 109.

39. Erikson, *Insight and Responsibility*, p. 119.

40. Erikson, *Identity*, p. 114.

41. Piaget, *Construction of Reality*, pp. 405–407.

42. David Elkind, *Children and Adolescents: Interpretive Essays on Jean Piaget* (New York: Oxford University Press, 1970), p. 52.

43. Ibid.

44. Piaget, *Six Psychological Studies*, pp. 24, 29.

45. Ibid., p. 30.

46. Jean Piaget, "Developmental Psychology: A Theory," *International Encyclopedia of the Social Sciences*, 17 vols. (New York: Macmillan and Free Press, 1968), 4:140–147, at 142–143.

47. Erikson, *Identity and the Life Cycle*, p. 74.

48. Erikson, *Identity*, p. 115.

49. Erikson, *Childhood and Society*, pp. 225, 255–256.

50. Erikson, *Identity and the Life Cycle*, p. 80.

51. Erikson, *Childhood and Society*, p. 256.

52. Erikson, *Identity*, p. 119.

53. Erikson, *Childhood and Society*, p. 257.

54. Erikson, *Identity and the Life Cycle*, p. 80.

55. Erikson, *Identity*, p. 121.

56. Erikson, *Insight and Responsibility*, p. 121.

57. Erikson, *Identity*, p. 121.

58. Erikson, "Life Cycle," p. 289.

59. Erikson, *Insight and Responsibility*, p. 122.

60. Erikson, *Identity*, p. 122.

61. Ibid.

62. Erikson, *Insight and Responsibility*, p. 123.

63. Erikson, "Life Cycle," p. 289.

64. Erikson, *Identity*, pp. 123–124.

65. Erikson, *Insight and Responsibility*, p. 123.

66. Erikson, "Life Cycle," p. 289.

67. Erikson, *Childhood and Society*, pp. 260–261.

68. Erikson, *Identity*, p. 127; Erikson, *Childhood and Society*, p. 261.

69. Erikson, *Insight and Responsibility*, p. 124.

70. Erikson, *Identity*, pp. 127–128.

71. Flavell, *Developmental Psychology*, p. 166.

72. Ibid.

73. Piaget, *Six Psychological Studies*, p. 48.

74. Ibid., p. 49.

75. Ibid., p. 80.
76. Piaget and Inhelder, Psychology of the Child, p. 98.
77. Piaget, "Developmental Psychology," p. 143.
78. Piaget and Inhelder, Psychology of the Child, p. 99.
79. Piaget, Six Psychological Studies, p. 46.
80. Ibid., p. 79.
81. Flavell, Developmental Psychology, p. 203.
82. Jean Piaget and Bärbel Inhelder, The Growth of Logical Thinking from Childhood to Adolescence, trans. Anne Parsons and Stanley Milgram (New York: Basic Books, 1958; original French, 1956), p. 248.
83. Flavell, Developmental Psychology, p. 203.
84. Piaget and Inhelder, Growth of Logical Thinking, p. 250.
85. Flavell, Developmental Psychology, p. 203.
86. Piaget and Inhelder, Growth of Logical Thinking, p. 251.
87. Flavell, Developmental Psychology, pp. 203–204.
88. Piaget and Inhelder, Growth of Logical Thinking, pp. 250–251.
89. Flavell, Developmental Psychology, p. 204.
90. Ibid.
91. Piaget, Six Psychological Studies, p. 55.
92. Piaget and Inhelder, Psychology of the Child, p. 114.
93. Piaget, Six Psychological Studies, p. 55.
94. Piaget and Inhelder, Psychology of the Child, p. 118.
95. Piaget, Six Psychological Studies, pp. 58–59.
96. Piaget and Inhelder, Psychology of the Child, p. 128.
97. Piaget, Six Psychological Studies, pp. xiv–xv.
98. Jean Piaget, The Moral Judgment of the Child, trans. Marjorie Gabain (New York: Free Press, 1965; original French, 1932).
99. William Kay, Moral Development (New York: Schocken Books, 1968), pp. 150, 172.
100. Ibid., pp. 150, 173.
101. See Lawrence Kohlberg, "Moral Development," International Encyclopedia of the Social Sciences, 17 vols. (New York: Macmillan and Free Press, 1968), 10:483–494, at 489; and Lawrence Kohlberg, "The Claim to Moral Adequacy of a Highest Stage of Moral Judgment," The Journal of Philosophy 70/18 (October 1973): 630–646, at 631–632.
Kohlberg has also suggested the "purely metaphorical notion of a Stage 7 as pointing to some meaningful solutions" to the questions "Why be moral?", "Why be just in a universe full of injustice?", which ultimately entail the ontological or religious question "Why live?" See, for example, Lawrence Kohlberg, "Stages and Aging in Moral Development—Some Speculations," The Gerontologist 13 (Winter 1973): 497–502. Directly connected with this aspect of Kohlberg's thought, and pertinent to the concerns of the present interpretation of conscience in a theological context, is the Piaget-Kohlberg inspired research and theoretical work of James Fowler on faith development; see, for example, James W. Fowler, "Towards a Developmental Perspective on Faith," Religious Education 69/2 (1974): 207–219.
102. Lawrence Kohlberg, "The Development of Children's Orientations Toward a Moral Order: I. Sequence in the Development of Moral Thought," Vita Humana 6 (1963): 11–33 at 18.
103. Lawrence Kohlberg, "Development of Moral Character and Moral Ideology" in Martin Hoffman and Lois Hoffman (eds.), Review of Child Development Research, Vol. 1 (New York: Russell Sage Foundation, 1964), pp. 383–431, at 396.
104. Kohlberg, "Moral Development," p. 488.
105. Kohlberg, "Development of Moral Character," pp. 396–399.
106. Kohlberg, "Moral Development," pp. 488–489.
107. Ibid.

108. Ibid.

109. Lawrence Kohlberg and Carol Gilligan, "The Adolescent as a Philosopher: The Discovery of the Self in a Postconventional World," *Daedalus* 100 (Fall 1971): 1051–1086, at 1066.

110. Lawrence Kohlberg, "Moral Stages and Moralization: The Cognitive-Developmental Approach" in Thomas Lickona (ed.), *Moral Development and Behavior* (New York: Holt, Rinehart and Winston, 1976), pp. 31–53, at 33, 34.

111. Ibid., p. 34.

112. Erikson, *Childhood and Society*, p. 261. On the concept of identity, see Erik Erikson, "Identity, Psychosocial," *International Encyclopedia of the Social Sciences*, 17 vols. (New York: Macmillan and Free Press, 1968), 7:61–65. For a detailed analysis of identity, especially of the relation of ego, self, and conscious I, see my "Erikson's 'Identity': An Essay on the Psychological Foundations of Religious Ethics," *Zygon* 14/2 (June 1979): 125–134.

113. Erikson, *Identity*, p. 128.

114. Ibid., pp. 128–129.

115. Ibid., p. 129.

116. Ibid.

117. Ibid.

118. Ibid., p. 130.

119. Erikson, *Childhood and Society*, pp. 261–262; see also Erikson, "Life Cycle," p. 290.

120. Erikson, "Life Cycle," p. 290.

121. Erikson, *Insight and Responsibility*, p. 125.

122. Erikson, "Life Cycle," p. 290.

123. Erikson, *Insight and Responsibility*, p. 125.

124. Richard Evans, *Dialogue with Erik Erikson* (New York: E. P. Dutton, 1969), pp. 36, 37.

125. Erikson, *Insight and Responsibility*, p. 125.

126. Ibid., pp. 125–126.

127. Erikson, *Childhood and Society*, p. 263.

128. Ibid.

129. Erikson, "Life Cycle," p. 290.

130. Erikson, *Childhood and Society*, p. 263.

131. Evans, *Dialogue with Erik Erikson*, p. 48.

132. Erikson, "Life Cycle," p. 290.

133. Erikson, *Identity*, p. 136.

134. Erikson, *Insight and Responsibility*, p. 130.

135. Ibid., pp. 127–128.

136. Erikson, "Life Cycle," pp. 290–291.

137. Erikson, *Identity*, pp. 136, 137.

138. Erikson, "Life Cycle," p. 290.

139. Erikson, *Identity*, pp. 137, 138.

140. Erikson, *Childhood and Society*, p. 265.

141. Evans, *Dialogue with Erik Erikson*, p. 51.

142. Erikson, "Life Cycle," p. 291.

143. Erikson, *Insight and Responsibility*, p. 130.

144. Erikson, "Life Cycle," p. 291.

145. Erikson, *Identity*, p. 139.

146. Erikson, *Childhood and Society*, p. 268.

147. Erikson, *Identity*, p. 139.

148. Erikson, "Life Cycle," p. 291.

149. Erikson, *Identity*, p. 140.

150. Erikson, "Life Cycle," p. 291.

151. Ibid.

152. Erikson, *Insight and Responsibility*, p. 133.
153. Erikson, *Childhood and Society*, p. 269.
154. Erik Erikson, "Reflections on the Dissent of Contemporary Youth," *International Journal of Psycho-Analysis* 51 (1970): 11–22, at 16.
155. Ibid.
156. Evans, *Dialogue with Erik Erikson*, p. 34.
157. Erikson, "Dissent of Contemporary Youth," p. 16.
158. Ibid.
159. *Webster's New World Dictionary of the American Language*, College Edition, 1958.
160. Erikson, *Insight and Responsibility*, p. 222.
161. Ibid.
162. Ibid., pp. 224, 225.
163. Erikson, *Identity*, pp. 39, 222.
164. Erikson, "Dissent of Contemporary Youth," p. 16.
165. Erik Erikson, "Autobiographic Notes on the Identity Crisis," *Daedalus* 99 (Fall 1970): 730–759, at 753.
166. Erikson, "Dissent of Contemporary Youth," p. 16.
167. Erikson, *Insight and Responsibility*, p. 222.
168. See reference to Luther's "Self-Transcendence" in Erik Erikson, *Young Man Luther* (New York: Norton, 1958). p. 104.
169. Erikson, *Identity and the Life Cycle*, pp. 52–53.
170. Erik Erikson, *Gandhi's Truth: On the Origins of Militant Nonviolence* (New York: Norton, 1969), p. 233.
171. Erikson, *Insight and Responsibility*, pp. 225, 171, 172.
172. Erikson, *Identity*, p. 247.
173. Erikson, *Insight and Responsibility*, p. 171.
174. Erikson, *Identity*, p. 245.
175. Piaget, *Six Psychological Studies*, p. 61.
176. Piaget and Inhelder, *Psychology of the Child*, pp. 130–131.
177. Flavell, *Developmental Psychology*, p. 204; see Piaget and Inhelder, *Growth of Logical Thinking*, pp. 254–266.
178. Flavell, *Developmental Psychology*, pp. 204–205.
179. Ibid., p. 205.
180. Piaget and Inhelder, *Psychology of the Child*, p. 132.
181. Flavell, *Developmental Psychology*, pp. 205–206.
182. Piaget, *Six Psychological Studies*, p. 63.
183. Flavell, *Developmental Psychology*, p. 205.
184. Ibid., pp. 205–206.
185. Piaget and Inhelder, *Psychology of the Child*, pp. 135–136.
186. Flavell, *Developmental Psychology*, p. 206.
187. Ibid., p. 211.
188. Ibid.
189. Ibid., p. 224.
190. Piaget, *Six Psychological Studies*, p. 64.
191. Flavell, *Developmental Psychology*, p. 224.
192. Piaget and Inhelder, *Growth of Logical Thinking*, pp. 345–346.
193. Ibid., p. 346.
194. Ibid., pp. 346–347.
195. Ibid., p. 347.
196. Piaget, *Six Psychological Studies*, p. 64.
197. Piaget and Inhelder, *Psychology of the Child*, pp. 149, 150, 151.
198. Ibid.
199. Piaget and Inhelder, *Growth of Logical Thinking*, p. 349.
200. Piaget, *Six Psychological Studies*, pp. 64, 65.
201. Ibid.

202. Ibid., p. xv.

203. Piaget and Inhelder, *Growth of Logical Thinking*, p. 350.

204. Piaget, *Six Psychological Studies*, p. 66.

205. Ibid., pp. 69–70.

206. Ibid., p. xv.

207. Erikson, *Identity*, p. 245.

208. Erikson, *Childhood and Society*, p. 261.

209. Erikson, *Identity*, pp. 158, 159, 163.

210. Ibid., p. 19.

211. Kohlberg and Gilligan, "Adolescent as a Philosopher," p. 1066.

212. Ibid., p. 1067.

213. Ibid.

214. Kohlberg, "Moral Stages and Moralization," p. 35.

215. Kohlberg and Gilligan, "Adolescent as a Philosopher," pp. 1062–1064.

216. Ibid., pp. 1064–1065.

217. Ibid., pp. 1068, 1071–1072.

218. Ibid., p. 1072.

219. Ibid., p. 1073.

220. Ibid., p. 1074.

221. Ibid.

222. Lawrence Kohlberg, "Continuities in Childhood and Adult Moral Development Revisited" in P. B. Baltes and K. Warner Schaie (eds.), *Life-Span Developmental Psychology: Personality and Socialization* (New York: Academic Press, 1973), pp. 179–204, at 195.

223. Lawrence Kohlberg, "From Is to Ought: How to Commit the Naturalistic Fallacy and Get Away with It in the Study of Moral Development," in Theodore Mischel (ed.), *Cognitive Development and Epistemology* (New York: Academic Press, 1971), pp. 151–235, at 180.

224. Kohlberg and Gilligan, "Adolescent as a Philosopher," pp. 1069–1071.

225. Ibid., p. 1071. Kohlberg's text has "normal" development, but I judge this to be a typographical error.

226. Ibid.

227. Kohlberg, "Continuities Revisited," p. 196.

228. Kohlberg and Gilligan, "Adolescent as a Philosopher," pp. 1066, 1067.

229. Ibid., p. 1067.

230. Ibid., p. 1068.

231. Ibid.

232. Kohlberg, "Moral Development," p. 489.

233. Ibid., pp. 489–490.

234. Kohlberg and Gilligan, "Adolescent as a Philosopher," pp. 1068–1069.

235. Ibid., p. 1069.

236. Lawrence Kohlberg, "Education for Justice: A Modern Statement of the Platonic View" in Nancy F. Sizer and Theodore R. Sizer (eds.), *Moral Education* (Cambridge: Harvard University Press, 1970), pp. 56–83, at 72.

237. Lawrence Kohlberg, "Moral Education in the Schools: A Developmental View," *The School Review* 74 (1966): 1–30, at 21.

238. Ibid., pp. 21, 30.

239. Ibid., p. 21.

240. Kohlberg, "Moral Development," p. 490.

241. Ibid.

242. Quoted in Kohlberg, "Moral Education in the Schools," p. 22, from R. M. Hare, *The Language of Morals* (New York: Oxford University Press, 1952).

243. Kohlberg, "Moral Education in the Schools," p. 20.

244. Kohlberg, "Education for Justice," p. 70. For his understanding of justice, Kohlberg relies heavily on John Rawls.

245. Kohlberg, "Moral Development," p. 490.

246. Quoted in Kohlberg, "Education for Justice," pp. 76–77.

247. Ibid., p. 77.

248. Kohlberg, "Moral Development," p. 490.

249. Lawrence Kohlberg and Richard Kramer, "Continuities and Discontinuities in Childhood and Adult Moral Development," *Human Development* 12 (1969): 93–120, at 106.

250. Ibid., pp. 106, 119, 98–99.

251. Ibid., p. 99.

252. Kohlberg, "From Is to Ought," pp. 188–189.

253. Ibid., p. 189.

254. Kenneth Keniston, "Moral Development, Youthful Activism, and Modern Society," *The Critic*, September-October 1969, pp. 17–24, at 22.

255. Ibid.

256. Lawrence Kohlberg, "The Child as a Moral Philosopher," *Psychology Today*, September 1968, pp. 25–30, at 28.

257. Keniston, "Youthful Activism," p. 23.

258. See Kohlberg, "Continuities Revisited," esp. pp. 193–201.

259. Piaget, *Origins of Intelligence*, p. 367.

260. Flavell, *Developmental Psychology*, p. 61.

261. Piaget, *Construction of Reality*, p. xii.

262. Kohlberg and Gilligan, "Adolescent as a Philosopher," p. 1084.

263. Kohlberg and Kramer, "Continuities and Discontinuities," pp. 119–120.

3

Self-Transcending Subjectivity and Conversion in Lonergan

Chapter two was devoted to the construction of a model of self-transcendence in developmental psychology to serve as a critical context for our analysis of the personal subject and conscience. We arrived, in this way, at a notion of self-transcending subjectivity, and found that a truly ethical orientation of principled conscience implies a conversion that is both intellectual and moral.

In this third chapter, we turn to a philosophical analysis of the personal subject, now considered precisely as self-transcending, and especially in those paramount instances of self-transcendence named conversions.

My strategy here will be to consider first several key elements in Lonergan's notion of subjectivity or, more concretely, the personal subject. The most important points will be Lonergan's distinctive understanding of consciousness and the concept of horizon. Secondly, I will consider the self-transcendence of the personal subject, with special emphasis on cognitional theory. Finally, I will reflect upon the notions of conversion, objectivity, and related ethical questions of a foundational nature.

The scope of Lonergan's thought—in areas philosophical, theological, and methodological—is even more extensive than the other authors we have considered, and thus anything like a comprehensive examination is obviously out of the question. Of necessity, therefore, we will focus only on the selected foundational issues I have already indicated, keeping in mind that they are only parts—though indeed key parts—of an ongoing, open-ended foundational enterprise that is being carried out within the context of theological method. Since it will be impossible to develop this entire context here, the reader is reminded that, among the many bibliographical references, the principal locus for Lonergan's philosophical reflection is his *Insight*, [1] while his most developed exposition of the fundamental issues of theological method is found in his *Method in Theology*; [2] both areas are treated with

clarity and reasonable brevity by David Tracy in his excellent introduction, *The Achievement of Bernard Lonergan.* [3]

Before plunging in, one final prefatory note in the form of a *caveat.*
Lonergan's basic philosophical method is one of self-appropriation.
One may read about it, but for persuasive results, one must *engage* in
it. No summary, let alone the present exposition of selected questions,
can do any more than indicate the approach in a general way and
present certain conclusions. The personal achievement of self-
appropriation does not coincide with the last page of a book or essay; it
is the fruit of rigorous philosophical reflection. Lonergan himself offers
the same *caveat* when in presenting a summary of the basic pattern of
operations in the first chapter of *Method in Theology,* he warns: "Please
observe that I am offering only a summary, that the summary can do
no more than present a general idea, that the process of self-
appropriation occurs only slowly, and, usually, only through a struggle
with some such book as *Insight.* "[4]

We begin this chapter with a consideration of Lonergan's understanding of consciousness because it is central to his notion of the
personal subject or subjectivity, and, therefore, fundamental to his
concept of conscience.

A. SUBJECTIVITY AND HORIZON

1. Consciousness

In English we have come to use two words to designate the moral
and nonmoral meanings of the Latin *conscientia:* "conscience" for the
specifically moral meaning and "consciousness" for the more general
meaning of "awareness."[5] In this way "conscience" has often taken on
the meaning of a special faculty, judging power, or act without any
particular reference to its original intimate connection with "awareness" or "consciousness."

With Lonergan, however, there is something of a return to the
original close relationship between the moral and nonmoral meanings
located in one word—the Greek συνείδησις or the Latin *conscientia*
(a relationship maintained in a single locus in the French *conscience*).
For with Lonergan conscience is consciousness or awareness, but it is
to be understood as a distinctive kind of consciousness, *moral consciousness,* which, as we shall see in detail, is the consciousness of the
responsible, existential subject, clearly differentiated in an explan-

atory theory (but not separated) from the other forms or dimensions of awareness (empirical, intelligent, reasonable) which characterize the conscious subject.

We shall explore with Lonergan, then, this intimate relationship between the notions of consciousness, conscience, and the personal subject. Indeed, we shall see that the very meaning of personal subjectivity is radically constituted by consciousness, and especially by consciousness in its specifically moral dimension, i.e., conscience.

Lonergan's usual strategy in discussing the notion of the personal subject is to begin by contrasting it to the more traditional philosophical conceptions of the human person as essentially substance or soul.

When one is in a coma or dreamless sleep, Lonergan says, "one is actually a substance and only potentially a subject." In order to be a subject, he says, one must at least be dreaming. "But the dreamer is only the minimal subject: one is more a subject when one is awake, still more when one is actively intelligent, still more when one actively is reasonable, still more in one's deliberations and decisions when one actively is responsible and free."[6]

From the viewpoint of a philosophy of human substance, says Lonergan, ". . . human nature is always the same; a man is a man whether he is awake or asleep, young or old, sane or crazy, sober or drunk, a genius or a moron, a saint or a sinner." From this viewpoint, those differences are "merely accidental," he says. "But they are not accidental to the subject, for the subject is not an abstraction; he is a concrete reality, all of him, a being in the luminousness of being." Thus, whereas "substance prescinds from the difference between the opaque being that is merely substance and the luminous being that is conscious," says Lonergan, "subject denotes the luminous being."[7]

From the methodological angle, Lonergan contrasts the study of the personal subject to the metaphysical study of the soul, which he sees as a primary cause of the centuries-long neglect of the subject until the modern period. According to the metaphysical account, humans, like plants and animals, have souls, and "as in plants and animals, so in men the soul is the first act of an organic body." Still, Lonergan points out, "the souls of plants differ essentially from the souls of animals, and the souls of both differ essentially from the souls of men." To discover these differences, the metaphysical method turns "from the soul to its potencies, habits, acts, objects." Acts are known through objects, habits are known through acts, potencies through habits, and through potencies the essence of the soul. The metaphysical study of the soul, Lonergan concludes, is "totally objective. One and the same method is applied to study of plants, animals, and men. The results are completely universal."[8] For, as from the perspective of substance, human nature is always the same, so, from the metaphysical viewpoint all humans have souls, whatever their accidental differences, and that is the important point.

But, on the other hand, Lonergan tells us, "the study of the subject is quite different," for, as we have seen, "it is the study of oneself inasmuch as one is conscious."[9] The study of the personal subject, Lonergan continues,

> prescinds from the soul, its essence, its potencies, its habits, for none of these are given in consciousness. It attends to operations and to their center and source which is the self. It discerns the different levels of consciousness, the consciousness of the dreamer, of the waking subject, of the intelligently inquiring subject, of the rationally reflecting subject, of the responsibly deliberating subject. It examines the different operations on the several levels and their relations to one another.[10]

It is precisely such a study of the conscious personal subject that we will be pursuing in the pages of this chapter. But our first task is to determine exactly what Lonergan means by consciousness, for this is the crux of the issue on which any study of the personal subject succeeds (in some measure) or fails.

The operations to which a study of the subject attends are listed by Lonergan as "seeing, hearing, touching, smelling, tasting, inquiring, imagining, understanding, conceiving, formulating, reflecting, marshaling and weighing the evidence, judging, deliberating, evaluating, deciding, speaking, writing." These operations are transitive, that is, they have objects, Lonergan points out, and "not merely in the grammatical sense that they are denoted by transitive verbs but also in the psychological sense that by the operation one becomes aware of the object." And for Lonergan, this "psychological sense is what is meant by the verb, intend, the adjective, intentional, the noun, intentionality." To say that operations intend objects, in other words, means that by seeing or hearing or imagining there becomes *present* what is seen or heard or imagined; and so for the other operations, "where in each case the presence in question is a psychological event."[11]

Further, the above listed operations are the operations of an operator, of a subject, a subject, says Lonergan, "not merely in the grammatical sense that he is denoted by a noun that is subject of the verbs that in the active voice refer to the operations," but also in the important "psychological sense that he operates consciously." In other words, and this is the tricky and elusive quality of consciousness, "whenever any of the operations are performed, the subject is aware of himself operating, present to himself operating, experiencing himself operating." The important point, then, is that operations not only intend objects, but have the further psychological dimension of occurring consciously, and thereby render the operating subject conscious. Thus, "just as operations by their intentionality make objects present to the subject, so also by their consciousness they make the operating subject present to himself."[12] Such is Lonergan's basic theorem on *conscious intentionality* or *intentional consciousness*.

This theorem is, however, not without its ambiguity, an ambiguity, as Lonergan himself points out, that resides in the admittedly equivocal use of the term "presence." Besides material presence, which does not involve knowing (the presence of grandfather's portrait *in* the living room over the fireplace), there is also psychological or cognitional presence (presence *to*), and it is of two distinct kinds. First, there is the *presence of the object to the subject*, the presence of the film *to* the viewer. The object is present as what is viewed, attended to, intended. But, secondly, and simultaneously, there is also the *presence of the subject to her or himself*, and this self-presence of the subject resides in the viewing, the attending, the intending. Lonergan emphasizes that this self-presence of the subject is *not* "the presence of another object dividing his attention, of another spectacle distracting the spectator; it is presence in, as it were, another dimension, presence concomitant and correlative and opposite to the presence of the object." Objects, as we have noted, are "present by being attended to; but subjects are present as subjects, not by being attended to, but by attending."[13]

Thus, using the image of spectators at a parade, Lonergan tells us that "as the parade of objects marches by, spectators do not have to slip into the parade to become present to themselves; [rather] they have to be present to themselves for anything to be present to them; and they are present to themselves by the same watching that, as it were, at its other pole makes the parade present to them."[14]

And this is why, says Lonergan, "the subject can be conscious, as attending, and yet give his whole attention to the object as attended to."[15] It is this particular nature of intentional consciousness that makes it possible for us to be most present to ourselves, to experience ourselves with an intensely heightened awareness, at the very time, for example, that we are completely absorbed by, "lost" in some especially engrossing book or film (this is *not* the reflexive "self-consciousness" of introspection, which may likely occur as we put down the book or leave the theater).

To put it still another way, we may say that in experiencing herself operating, the subject is not performing yet another operation to be added to the list of operations, "for this experiencing is not intending but being conscious. It is not another operation over and above the operation that is experienced. It is that very operation which, besides being intrinsically intentional, also is intrinsically conscious."[16] The assertion of phenomenologists that "consciousness is always consciousness of an object," therefore, is true enough as far as it goes in emphasizing the *intentional* aspect of consciousness, but it seems to miss the distinctive quality of consciousness by which the subject is also aware of, present to, herself.

A further dimension of this distinctive understanding of consciousness is presented by Lonergan in his monograph *De constitutione Christi*[17] and the later article he wrote in its defense and explication, "Christ as Subject: A Reply."[18] Here Lonergan presents and draws a sharp distinction between two opposed notions of consciousness: *conscientia-experientia* on the one hand, and on the other *conscientia-perceptio*.[19] The basic point here, and Lonergan's main argument, is "that if consciousness is conceived as an experience [*conscientia-experientia*] there is a psychological subject, while if consciousness is conceived as the perception of an object [*conscientia-perceptio*] there is no psychological subject."[20] Our concern with this point is not to prove the existence of the psychological subject, but to try to understand with the help of this distinction the precise nature of the consciousness of the subject.

Perhaps we can best understand Lonergan's point if we begin by puzzling through an explanation of consciousness presented by Lonergan from the viewpoint of *conscientia-perceptio:*

> Consider, then, the two propositions, John knows his dog, John knows himself. In both, the subject is John. In the first, the object is John's dog. In the second, the object is John himself. It follows that knowing is of two kinds: there is direct knowing in which the object is not the subject; there is reflexive knowing in which the object is the subject. Name reflexive knowing consciousness. Define the subject as the object of consciousness. Then it cannot be disputed, it seems, that consciousness is a reflexive knowing, for in consciousness the knower himself is known; and it cannot be disputed, it seems, that the subject is the object of consciousness, for whatever is known is an object. Nothing, it seems, could be simpler or clearer or more evident.[21]

We have here, then, a rather typical interpretation of consciousness as reflexive knowing. Despite its simplicity, clarity, and self-evidentness,

Lonergan suggests that a difficulty could be raised by considering that properly "a cognitive act exercises no constitutive effect upon its object; it simply reveals what the object already is; it exercises no transforming power over the object in its proper reality, but simply and solely manifests what that proper reality is." Following out this suggestion, Lonergan concludes that "if consciousness is knowledge of an object, it can have no constitutive effect upon its object; it can only reveal its object as it was in its proper reality prior to the occurrence of the cognitive act or function named consciousness."[22] To illustrate this aspect of the *conscientia-perceptio* interpretation of consciousness, Lonergan offers the following analytical passage:

> ... If without consciousness John is simply a prime substance (such as this man or this horse) then by consciousness John is merely revealed to himself as a prime substance. Again, if without consciousness John has no other psychological unity beyond the unity found in the objects of his knowledge, then by consciousness John is merely manifested as having no psychological unity beyond the unity found in the objects of his knowledge. Again, if without consciousness John cannot possibly be the conscious subject of physical pain, then by consciousness John is merely manifested as being incapable of suffering. Similarly, if without consciousness John cannot be the consciously intelligent or the consciously rational or the consciously free or the consciously responsible principle of his own intelligent, rational, free, or responsible acts, then by consciousness as knowledge of an object John merely knows himself as neither consciously intelligent, nor consciously rational, nor consciously free, nor consciously responsible.[23]

On the basis of this analysis Lonergan declares that the simple, clear, evident interpretation of consciousness as perception of an object or reflexive knowing (*conscientia-perceptio*) is "*simpliste.*" For while "it takes account of the fact that by consciousness the subject is known by the subject," yet "it overlooks the fact that *consciousness is not merely cognitive but also constitutive.* It overlooks as well the subtler fact that consciousness is cognitive, not of what exists without consciousness, but of what is constituted by consciousness."[24] For, Lonergan continues,

> consciousness does not reveal a prime substance; it reveals a psychological subject that subsequently may be subsumed, and subsumed correctly, under the category of prime substance. Similarly, consciousness does not reveal the psychological unity that is known in the field of objects; it constitutes and reveals the basic psychological unity of the subject as subject. In like manner, consciousness not merely reveals us as suffering but also makes us

capable of suffering; and similarly it pertains to the constitution of the consciously intelligent subject of intelligent acts, the consciously rational subject of rational acts, the consciously free subject of free acts, and the consciously responsible subject of responsible acts.[25]

Given this negative judgment on the *conscientia-perceptio* view of consciousness as the perception of an object or reflexive knowing, then, the question for Lonergan becomes one of accounting for the constitutive function of consciousness without rejecting the principle that knowing simply reveals its object, without admitting, that is, that knowing exercises a constitutive effect on its object.

Lonergan's response, which attempts to do justice to both the cognitive and constitutive aspects of consciousness, is formulated in the following paragraph, which, because of its technical nature and complexity, I will quote in full:

> The alternative [to the *conscientia-perceptio* view], I suggest, is to deny that consciousness is a matter of knowing an object; the alternative is to deny that only objects are known; the alternative is to reject the tacit assumption that *unumquodque cognoscitur secundum quod est obiectum* (everything that is known, is known insofar as it is an object), and to put in its place the familiar axiom that *unumquodque cognoscitur secundum quod est actu* (everything that is known, is known insofar as it is in act). On the basis of this axiom, one can assert that whenever there is a *sensible actu* or an *intelligibile actu*, an object is known; and whenever there is a *sensus actu* or an *intellectus actu*, the subject and his act are known. On this view the subject in act and his act are constituted and, as well, they are known simultaneously and concomitantly with the knowledge of objects; for the *sensibile actu* is the *sensus actu*, and the *intelligibile actu* is the *intellectus actu*. Again, on this view the object is known as *id quod intenditur* (what is intended), the subject is known as *is qui intendit* (he who intends), and the act is known both as the *intendere* (intending) of the subject and the *intendi* (being intended) that regards the object.[26]

This interpretation does justice to both the cognitive and constitutive aspects of consciousness, in Lonergan's mind, because, according to it, cognitive acts not only "constitute a prime substance as actually knowing sensible and intelligible objects," but "they also constitute the prime substance as consciously sentient, consciously intelligent, consciously the one principle of many acts, consciously rational when one act supplies the known reason that motivates another act, consciously free when one act is the principle of other alternative acts, consciously responsible when the consciously free subject knows by other acts the consequences of his free choices."[27]

The main point here, it seems worth repeating, is Lonergan's criti-

lectures or analyzing language. It is a matter of heightening one's consciousness by objectifying it, and that is something that each one, ultimately, has to do in himself and for himself."[36]

Most fundamentally, the objectification involved in transcendental method consists in "applying the operations as intentional to the operations as conscious." By condensing the various conscious and intentional operations of the four levels into the shorthand of "experiencing, understanding, judging, and deciding," we can say that the application of the operations as intentional to the operations as conscious is

> a fourfold matter of (1) experiencing one's experiencing, understanding, judging, and deciding, (2) understanding the unity and relations of one's experienced experiencing, understanding, judging, deciding, (3) affirming the reality of one's experienced and understood experiencing, understanding, judging, deciding and (4) deciding to operate in accord with the norms immanent in the spontaneous relatedness of one's experienced, understood, affirmed experiencing, understanding, judging and deciding.[37]

We can derive from this construction a distinction between consciousness and self-knowledge or (more fully) self-appropriation. Self-appropriation is the reduplicated structure: experiencing, understanding, judging, and deciding with respect to experiencing, understanding, judging, and deciding. Consciousness, on the other hand, is not the fully human knowing (i.e., experiencing, understanding, and judging) and choosing of oneself as one who experiences, understands, judges, and decides, but the basic *experiencing* of oneself in one's experiencing, understanding, judging, and deciding.

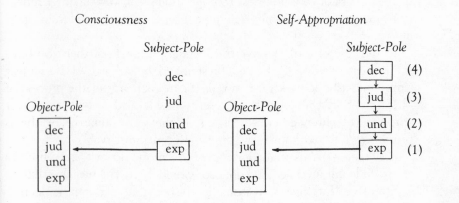

We have such consciousness whenever we experience, or understand, or judge, or decide. But our attention, says Lonergan, "is apt to be

cal and fundamental *distinction* between *consciousness* on the one hand and a *reflexive knowing of the self* on the other. Lonergan draws some of the fine lines of this distinction—as well as of the relationship between consciousness and reflexive knowing—in the following explanatory note:

> Consciousness is not to be confused with reflexive activity. The ordinary operations of intellect are attending, inquiring, understanding, conceiving, doubting, weighing the evidence, judging. Their objects may be either the self or other things. In the former case they are named reflexive; in the latter, direct.... Now by both direct and reflexive operations the subject in act is constituted and known, not as object, but as subject; this constitutive knowing and being known is consciousness. Hence in direct activity the subject is known once, and as subject; but in reflexive activity the subject is known twice, as subject by consciousness, and as object by reflexive activity. Finally, there is a functional relation between consciousness and reflexive activity: just as the data for direct activity are supplied by sense, so the data for reflexive activity are supplied by consciousness. Hence, just as I think of "this" by a backward reference to sense, so I think of "I" by a backward reference to the conscious subject; in both cases one is thinking of the particular; and we think of particulars, not because we understand particularity, but because our inquiry and understanding suppose and regard data. Similarly, just as our judgments about material things involve a verification of concepts in the data of sense, so our judgments about our feelings, our minds, our wills involve a verification of concepts in the data of consciousness.[28]

Such, then, is Lonergan's distinction between consciousness and reflexive knowing, and such the correlative distinction between subject-as-subject and subject-as-object. Consciousness, "an awareness immanent in cognitional acts,"[29] both constitutes the subject and renders the subject present to her or himself, not as object, but *as subject*. Conscious operations are, as we noted above, also intentional, in that they refer to objects, making them present to the subject. As intentional, these conscious operations can refer to, intend the subject, who then becomes present to herself under two quite distinct modalities: through consciousness she is present to herself *as subject*, and by intentionality she is present *as object*.

I have dwelt at length on Lonergan's understanding of consciousness for two primary reasons: first, it is absolutely central to a correct interpretation of his notion of the personal subject, and thus of conscience; and, second, it is one of the key factors in the combination that unlocks the complexities of transcendental method (self-affirmation, self-appropriation).

2. Transcendental Method

With this much said about consciousness, it seems appropriate at this point, since I have put forth the transcendental method of self-appropriation as a way of personally verifying my thesis on self-transcending subjectivity, to sketch out briefly the broad lines and a few distinctive features of Lonergan's transcendental method.[30] In order to do this with any significant degree of clarity, however, it is necessary that we first come to grips with the deceptive, because myth-bound, notion of introspection. And we shall do this by relying on the distinction between consciousness and reflexive knowing worked out above.

First, there is the subject-as-subject to consider. We have seen that the subject is present to him or herself and known as subject through consciousness, even as an object is simultaneously present to the subject as intended. Such consciousness, or presence of the subject to himself as subject is, we have noted, "an awareness immanent in cognitional acts," it is not "some sort of inward look."[31] Neither is it introspection. In discussing the subject's presence to himself as subject, Lonergan warns us that "the reader, if he tries to find himself as subject, to reach back and, as it were, uncover his subjectivity, cannot succeed. Any such effort," he says, "is introspecting, attending to the subject; and what is found is, not the subject as subject, but only the subject as object; it is the subject as subject that does the finding."[32] In describing just how one does increase one's experience of oneself as subject, Lonergan, in the following passage, also reviews for us the various different *levels* of consciousness and intentionality—and thus subjectivity. "In our dream states consciousness and intentionality commonly are fragmentary and incoherent," he says. But, "when we awake, they take on a different hue to expand on four successive, related, but qualitatively different levels":[33]

> To heighten one's presence to oneself [he says], one does not introspect; one raises the level of one's activity. If one sleeps and dreams, one is present to oneself as the frightened dreamer. If one wakes, one becomes present to oneself, not as moved but as moving, not as felt but as feeling, not as seen but as seeing. If one is puzzled and wonders and inquires, the empirical subject becomes an intellectual subject as well. If one reflects and considers the evidence, the empirical and intellectual subject becomes a rational subject, an incarnate reasonableness. If one deliberates and chooses, one has moved to the level of the rationally conscious, free, responsible subject that by his choices makes himself what he is to be and his world what it is to be.[34]

This heightening of one's presence to oneself, this increasing of [con]scious subjectivity, however, is not transcendental method, beca[use it] is not introspective, whereas transcendental method is precise[ly a] technical form of introspection. It is, rather, merely consciou[sly] constituting and revealing the subject-as-subject, not reflexive in[ten]tionality presenting the subject-as-object. Such heightening of [con]scious subjectivity, however, *is* a prerequisite for the fruitful exe[rcise] of transcendental method. For this method, as introspective, att[ends] to the data of consciousness, data which will be unrepresentati[ve of] fully human subjectivity if the subject doing the introspecting i[s not] operating, and thus not present to self, on the highest level of [con]scious intentionality.

Still, the term "introspection" is "misleading inasmuch as it sug[gests] an inward inspection," which, according to Lonergan, is no more [than] a myth whose "origin lies in the mistaken analogy that all cognit[ive] events are to be conceived on the analogy of ocular vision." Th[ey] have consciousness confused with the inward inspection of ob[jects] and identified—as in the *conscientia-perceptio* view—with ref[lexive] knowing. Once, however, we distinguish introspection from [con]sciousness, and go on to understand it not as taking a look, bu[t as a] form of the fundamental process of intelligent inquiry (attendi[ng to] the data of consciousness rather than to the data of sense as i[n the] direct mode of inquiry), we can use it critically to mean "the p[rocess] of objectifying the contents of consciousness." And this, bas[ically,] is the strategy of transcendental method, the objectificatio[n and] critical understanding of key data of consciousness. "Just as we [move] from the data of sense through inquiry, insight, reflection, judg[ment] to statements about sensible things," says Lonergan, "so too we [move] from the data of consciousness through inquiry, understanding, [reflec]tion, judgment, to statements about conscious subjects and their [oper]ations."[35]

In the case of introspective transcendental method, then, w[e have] the primary example of the dual presence of the subject, of the s[ubject] simultaneously being known twice, for in each act of the proc[ess of] objectification the subject is present to self and known *as s[ubject]* through (heightened) consciousness at the same time he or [she is] present to self and known *as object* by intentionality.

Lonergan tells us that "in a sense everyone knows and ob[serves] transcendental method" and does so "precisely in the measure t[hat he] is attentive, intelligent, reasonable, responsible." But in a d[eeper] systematic sense, "it is quite difficult to be at home in transce[ndental] method, for that is not to be achieved by reading books, or listen[ing]

focused on the object, while our conscious operating remains peripheral." We must enlarge our interest, then, says Lonergan, and discover in ourselves the concrete truth of the general statement that "the same operation not only intends an object but also reveals an intending subject." Lonergan continually emphasizes that this discovery is "not a matter of looking, inspecting, gazing upon. It is an awareness, not of what is intended, but of the intending," and of the intending subject.[38]

This discovery, however, is not made without difficulty, for all the conscious and intentional operations are not equally accessible. "Experience is of the given. Experience of seeing is to be had only when one is actually seeing. Experience of insight is to be had only when one actually is having an insight. But one has only to open one's eyes and one will see; one has only to open and close one's eyes a number of times to alternate the experience of seeing and not seeing. Insights, on the other hand," says Lonergan, "cannot be turned on and off in that fashion."[39] Not a little forethought and ingenuity are required, he says, if we are to advert to and become familiar with our experience of inquiry, insight, formulation, critical reflection, weighing the evidence, judging, deliberating, deciding. "One has to know the meaning of each of these words. One has to produce in oneself the corresponding operation. One has to keep producing it until one gets beyond the object intended to the consciously operating subject. One has to do all this within the appropriate context, which is a matter not of inward inspection but of inquiry, enlarged interest, discernment, comparison, distinction, identification, naming."[40] Such, says Lonergan, are the basic conditions of transcendental method.

But such experience, inquiry, and objectification must be of the operations "not only singly, but in their relations, for there are not merely conscious operations," but they occur within a conscious process, a "process that is formally dynamic, that calls forth and assembles its own components, that does so intelligently, rationally, responsibly."[41]

The self-appropriation peculiar to transcendental method is a matter, then, first, of experiencing the operations and attending to them, secondly, of inquiring into and understanding their unity and relations, and thirdly, of raising and answering the critical questions for reflection: "Do these operations occur? Do they occur in the described pattern?" Most of Insight is devoted to these questions. We certainly cannot answer them here. The main point, indeed, is that each person must ask and answer these questions for him or herself. As for Lonergan, he has no doubts. ". . . Conscious and intentional operations exist," he says, "and anyone that cares to deny their existence is merely disqualifying himself as a nonresponsible, nonreasonable, nonintelligent somnambulist."[42] But though empirically, intelligently, rationally, and responsibly conscious subjects exist, "not all know themselves as such, for consciousness is not human knowing but only a potential component in the structured whole that is human knowing. But all can know themselves as such," he says, "for they have only to attend to what they are already conscious of, and understand what they attend to, and pass judgment on the correctness of their understanding."[43]

As to the *pattern* in which empirically, intelligently, rationally, and responsibly conscious subjects operate, Lonergan distinguishes between the pattern as immanent and spontaneously operative and the pattern as objectified. Before inquiry brings the pattern to light, says Lonergan, it is already conscious and operative. Thus, once the unity and relations of the pattern given in consciousness are formulated, "they are not found to express surprising novelties but simply prove to be objectifications of the routines of our conscious living and doing."[44]

But as self-knowledge keeps developing, Lonergan asks himself, will not the pattern of operations need constant revision? His answer is "yes and no," with a very important qualification on the "yes." For revision can affect only the *objectification* of the normative pattern of our conscious and intentional operations, not the pattern itself. Revision "cannot change the dynamic structure of human consciousness. All it can do is bring about a more adequate account of that structure." And this is where the qualification enters the picture, for any revision by definition requires that certain conditions be fulfilled. Briefly, any possible revision of any theory consists basically in the *responsible* claim that a new explanation is a better and *more probable understanding* of *data* that the opinion under review either overlooked or misapprehended. Revision, then, consists of operations in accord with the very objectification of the normative pattern, "so that a revision rejecting the pattern would be rejecting itself." In this basic sense, then, "the objectification of the normative pattern of our conscious and intentional operations does not admit revision."[45]

Thus, while "any theory, description, account of our conscious and intentional operations is bound to be incomplete and to admit of further clarifications and extensions," there is, as Lonergan says, "a rock on which one can build."[46] For, he continues,

. . . all such clarifications and extensions are to be derived from the conscious and intentional operations themselves. They as given in consciousness are the rock; they confirm every exact account; they refute every inexact or incomplete account. The rock, then, is the subject in his conscious, unobjectified attentiveness, intelligence, reasonableness, responsibility. The point to the labor of objectifying the subject and his conscious operations is that thereby one begins to learn what these are and that they are.[47]

But so much for our brief excursus on the nature of transcendental method. We must return now to a direct consideration of what Lonergan calls its rock, the conscious subject. And we shall do this in the context of the notion of horizon.

3. Horizon of Personal Subject

"The being of the subject," Lonergan tells us, "is becoming. One becomes oneself."[48] The subject's "existing lies in developing."[49] Further, "as the subject develops, his world changes."[50] In referring to this world of the subject, Lonergan calls our attention to the distinction between "the world" and "the subject's world." "The world," he says, "is what is there to be known and that is unchanged by its being known." In contrast, "the subject's world is correlative to the subject: it may be a world that is mostly fantasy; it may be the real world; but its *differentia* is that it is the world in which the subject actually lives and develops."[51]

We have, then, a developing subject and his or her correlative world, a world that is defined—at each point of development—by a specific horizon.[52]

Horizon, in its literal sense, says Lonergan, "denotes the bounding circle, the line at which earth and sky appear to meet. This line is the limit of one's field of vision. As one moves about, it recedes in front and closes in behind so that, for different standpoints, there are different horizons." Objects within a given horizon can be seen, while those lying beyond the horizon are, at least for the time, invisible. Now, Lonergan goes on, "as our field of vision, so too the scope of our knowledge, and the range of our interests are bounded."[53] And this horizon is most significantly set by the range of *questions* a person can seriously raise. For a person's world is constituted not only by what one knows (the questions one can raise and answer—the *known*), but also by what one can meaningfully question (the *known-unknown*). In these terms, the *unknown-unknown* is the area about which the subject cannot even raise meaningful questions, the area, that is, that lies beyond one's present horizon, outside one's world. [54] In other words, defined by the process of raising and answering questions, the horizon is the limit, the boundary between the *known-unknown* (what the subject can question) and the *unknown-unknown* (what the subject cannot question); the image of concentric circles with the *known* in the center and *unknown-unknown* lying outside the widest circumference might be helpful in grasping the point here.

Also, Lonergan tells us, "as fields of vision vary with one's standpoint, so too the scope of one's knowledge and the range of one's interests vary with the period in which one lives, one's social background and milieu, one's education and personal development." So, then, we have, derived from the primary visual image, an analogous meaning of horizon as a generalized model for personal consciousness and its development. In this generalized sense, "what lies beyond one's horizon is simply outside the range of one's knowledge and interests: one neither knows nor cares. But what lies within one's horizon is in some measure, great or small, an object of interest and of knowledge."[55] In this sense, says Lonergan, "a horizon is specified by two poles, one objective [the subject's world] and the other subjective [the standpoint of the consciously operating subject], with each pole conditioning the other."[56]

So defined, different horizons can be understood to be related to each other in complementary, genetic, or dialectic ways. The functional specialization of labor in a developed civilization is perhaps a good example of complementary horizons. The parts of a biography might be examples of genetic horizons—that is, they are related to one another as successive stages in some process of development, the later includes the earlier but develops from it, dropping some elements, transforming others, adding still others. Horizons, finally, are related dialectically when each has some awareness of others but are opposed—the inclusion of the other in awareness is also its negation, rejection, even condemnation. "Both astrology and genocide," says Lonergan, "are beyond the pale, but the former is ridiculed, the latter is execrated."[57]

Lonergan also explains how horizons, in their concreteness, are related to past and future:

> Horizons are the structured resultant of past achievement and, as well, both the condition and the limitation of further development. They are structured. All learning is, not a mere addition to previous learning, but rather an organic growth out of it. So all our intentions, statements, deeds stand within contexts. To such contexts we appeal when we clarify,

amplify, qualify our statements, or when we explain our deeds. Within such contexts must be fitted each new item of knowledge and each new factor in our attitudes. What does not fit, will not be noticed or, if forced on our attention, it will seem irrelevant or unimportant. Horizons then are the sweep of our interests and of our knowledge; they are the fertile source of further knowledge and care; but they also are the boundaries that limit our capacities for assimilating more than we already have attained.[58]

As concrete and developing, then, horizons are rooted in a past and oriented toward the future. Michael Novak, an informed and perceptive commentator on Lonergan's work, has noted that "horizon indicates a dynamic orientation, for the human subject is not stationary. He moves through many and varied experiences, gains new insights, sometimes is led by experience to shift those criteria of relevance and evidence that guide his judgment, and regularly 'tries to do' projects that carry his view into the future."[59] Emphasizing that a person's horizon is distinctive because it develops in time, Novak points out three key aspects of the concept:

It calls attention to the symbolic dimension of human action (including inquiry). Different men discern different significance in a given action or invest the same acts with different significance.

It highlights the fact that the subject and all the objects or persons to whom he is related fall within the same symbolic framework. The dualism of the subject and the object is finally untenable, for objects are known by subjects only insofar as they fall within the horizontal of the subject.

It emphasizes that knowing and acting are not exhaustively analyzed into the categories either of classical rationalism or of naturalistic pragmatism. The horizon of a subject is influenced by all the experiences, emotions, memories, tendencies, interests, desires, insights, and judgments of the subject. There is no pure isolated ego, no atom of consciousness confronting pure objects "objectively out there now." Nor is the dualism of the emotive and the cognitive tenable.[60]

It should not be difficult to notice in Lonergan's formulation of horizon an influence from Piaget's understanding of the relationship of the individual to the environment in terms of the adaptive processes of assimilation and accommodation. Operations—more and more differentiated and complexly organized in group and lattice structures—relate from the subject-pole to their appropriate objects. Thus, for example, the world of music for a given pianist is defined in terms of the complexity and sophistication of her organized operations. In the most general sense, then, we have at the subjective pole, specifying horizon, the subject and her conscious operations, and at the objective pole the complex of "worlds" in which she dwells.

From this consideration of the conscious subject in terms of his or her concrete horizon we shall make a twofold movement: first we shall attend to the question of horizon and personal development in the general terms of self-transcendence, discussing Lonergan's structural analysis of knowing and deciding and their related world dimensions—the world of immediacy as well as the worlds mediated and constituted by meaning; then we shall turn our attention to the special instances of self-transcendence named conversions and the different realms of meaning they define in response to the fundamental exigences of the human spirit. Our main concern throughout, of course, will be Lonergan's understanding of moral consciousness, moral conversion, and, in this context, the meaning of conscience.

B. SELF-TRANSCENDENCE AND VALUE

1. Self-Transcendence: Questions, Operations, Worlds

We have noted that as the personal subject develops, his or her world changes. We shall now consider the basic structural dimensions of the subject's world which emerge in this development.[61]

The first dimension Lonergan has named the world of immediacy. This is the infant's world of the nursery. It is "the world of what is felt, touched, grasped, sucked, seen, heard—it is the world to which the adult returns [or attempts to return] when with an empty head he lies in the sun—it is the world of immediate experience, of the given as given, of image and affect without any perceptible intrusion from insight or concept, reflection or judgment, deliberation or choice."[62] It is, he says, "the world of pleasure and pain, hunger and thirst, food and drink, rage and satisfaction and sleep."[63]

A further and vastly more expansive dimension of the subject's world emerges as the command of language develops. For, as Lonergan says, "words denote not only what is present but also what is absent or past or future, not only what is factual but also the possible, the ideal, the normative."[64] More than what we have discovered for ourselves, language expresses the learning and wisdom of the human community. If this larger world mediated by meaning is at first only an extension of the world of immediacy, "the revelation," as Lonergan says, "of a larger world than the nursery that comes through pictures, speech, stories, that is of incredible extent and variety," there gradually occurs the "discovery of the difference between fact and fiction, between what is just a story and what really and truly is so."⁶⁵ And, as Lonergan puts it, the "necessity of that distinction" reveals with a definite clarity that, far from lying within anyone's immediate experience, the world mediated by meaning transcends the totality of all worlds of immediate experience. "For meaning is an act that does not merely repeat but goes beyond experiencing. For what is meant is what is intended in questioning and is determined not only by experience but also by understanding, and, commonly, by judgment as well." And it is precisely understanding and judgment that make this world mediated by meaning possible. "In this larger world," says Lonergan, "we live out our lives. To it we refer when we speak of the real world. But because it is mediated by meaning, because meaning can go astray, because there is myth as well as science, fiction as well as fact, deceit as well as honesty, error as well as truth, that larger real world is insecure."⁶⁶

But beyond this world that we know, there is the world that in our creativity we construct. Most obviously, there is "man's transformation of his environment, a transformation that is effected through the intentional acts that envisage ends, select means, secure collaborators, direct operations."⁶⁷ Thus we have the humanly constructed, artificial world of technology that now stands between us and a prior world of nature, the whole of which is the product of human acts of meaning.

But if this world of cities and industries and jet airliners is the most obvious of human constructions, it is far from the most significant. For beyond our transformation of nature, there is our transformation of ourselves. There is, in other words, a world of the subject that is not only mediated or directed but also *constituted* by meaning.

It is most conspicuous [Lonergan says] in the educational process, in the difference between the child beginning kindergarten and the doctoral candidate writing his dissertation. But the difference produced by the education of individuals is only a recapitulation of the longer process of the education of mankind, of the evolution of social institutions and of the development of cultures. Religions and art forms, languages and literatures, sciences, philosophies, the writing of history, all had their rude beginnings, slowly developed, reached their peak, perhaps went into decline and later underwent a renaissance in another milieu. And what is true of cultural achievements, also, though less conspicuously, is true of social institutions. The family, the state, the law, and the economy are not fixed and immutable entities. They adapt to changing circumstance; they can be reconceived in the light of new ideas; they can be subjected to revolutionary change. Moreover, and this is my present point, all such change is in its essence a change of meaning—a change of idea or concept, a change of judgment or evaluation, a change of the order or the request. The state can be changed by rewriting its constitution; more subtly but no less effectively it can be changed by reinterpreting the constitution or, again, by working on men's minds and hearts to change the objects that command their respect, hold their allegiance, fire their loyalty. Community is a matter of a common field of experience, a common mode of understanding, a common measure of judgment, and a common consent. Such community is the possibility, the source, the ground of common meaning; and it is this common meaning that is the form and act that finds expression in family and polity, in the legal and economic system, in customary morals and educational arrangements, in language and literature, art and religion, philosophy, science, and the writing of history.[68]

In summing up his consideration of the different dimensions of the subject's world, Lonergan returns to the concrete subject in the full consciousness of his or her being:

I have spoken of the self-constituting subject and his world. The two are correlative, not only by definition inasmuch as I have distinguished *the* world and *his* world, but also because the free and responsible self-constituting subject can exist only in a freely constituted world. The world of immediacy is not freely constituted; the world mediated by meaning is not freely constituted; but the world constituted by meaning, the properly human world, the world of community is the product of freely self-constituting subjects.

For it is in the field where meaning is constitutive that man's freedom reaches its high point. There too his responsibility is greatest. There there occurs the emergence of the existential subject, finding out for himself that he has to decide for himself what he is to make of himself. It is there that individuals become alienated from community, that communities split into factions, that cultures flower and decline, that historical causality exerts its sway.[69]

Now that we have discussed the several dimensions of the subject's world that form the objective correlative to the subject in his or her basic development from infancy to adulthood, we can take a closer look at the structure of basic operations that constitute the core of the concrete subject in his or her conscious intentionality. Since we have already had occasion earlier in the chapter to attend to the operations themselves, we may concentrate now on the fashion in which they are *structured* by the radical dynamism of *questioning*. Central to our concern here, of course, will be the issue of self-transcendence. For self-transcendence is Lonergan's criterion for distinguishing between authentic and inauthentic realizations of human potentiality. The basic question for a contemporary ethic, he says, is "What is authentic or genuine realization of human potentiality?" And his answer, quite simply, is that "authentic realization is a self-transcending realization."[70] So we must determine as exactly as possible the full range of what Lonergan means by self-transcendence.

And first of all, here, as in our study of the psychological theories of development, two different but related forms of self-transcendence must be distinguished. The most obvious form was apparent in our consideration of the various dimensions of the subject's world, dimensions which successively transcended but incorporated each other in something of a hierarchical manner, with the world constituted by meaning at the top. But even there we could discern a hint of the more important form of self-transcendence, for one dimension was seen as transcending another precisely insofar as it constituted a qualitatively distinct expansion of the depth and range of the subject's world. In the same way now, as we advert to the structure of operations at the subject-pole, we will notice that in response to successive, qualitatively different kinds of questions there are successive levels of operations in the process of knowing and deciding related in such a way that the higher level transcends the lower even as it presupposes, complements and incorporates it (sublation). But again, what is really important in this successive transcendence of levels of operations is the criterion of self-transcendence (in which the objective operation takes the subject beyond her or himself) that is normatively definitive for each level. And to this notion of self-transcendence we shall now return.

"Man's transcendental subjectivity," Lonergan says, "is mutilated or abolished, unless he is stretching forth towards the intelligible, the unconditioned, the good of value." For "man achieves authenticity in self-transcendence."[71]

> One can live in a world, have a horizon, just in the measure that one is not locked up in oneself. A first step towards this liberation is the sensitivity we share with the higher animals. But they are confined to a habitat, while man lives in a universe. Beyond sensitivity man asks questions, and his questioning is unrestricted.[72]

First, of course, there are questions for intelligence. We ask what, why, how, how often, what for, and so forth, about our experience. Our understanding (specifically the activities of insight and formulating) attempts to respond to these questions, according to Lonergan, by unifying and relating, classifying and constructing, serializing and generalizing. Thus, "from the narrow strip of space-time accessible to immediate experience we move towards the construction of a world-view and towards the exploration of what we ourselves could be and could do."[73]

We noted in chapter two that insights are always into images, that, in other words, and more generally, understanding is always of experience. Because the human good is always concrete and not to be captured alive in abstract definitions,[74] a full appreciation of the concrete-universal nature of insight is indispensable for ethical theory. For since insight is always in touch with the concreteness and particularity of experience, it transcends the specific situation in its search for the meaning of that situation in a universal context, without losing itself in the emptiness of merely abstract concepts. The activity of insight, in other words, is the crucial pivot between the concrete and the universal on which the vitality of moral understanding radically depends.

If we have so far stressed the concrete quality of insight, we now see how questions for intelligence specify two distinct levels of operations in the cognitive process, a level of experiencing that presents data to be questioned, and a level of understanding that responds to questions with possible answers (each level of operations in the entire cognitional process is thus defined implicitly through its relation with the other levels). But the questions for intelligence and the insights that answer them not only create a qualitatively distinct level which transcends the level of experiencing, they constitute a major step in the subject's process of self-transcendence by moving the subject out of his or her own small world of immediate experience into, as Lonergan says, a universe of meaning beyond him or herself. And this normative process of self-transcendence, of liberating oneself from one's own self and needs, can ultimately constitute the subject, as we shall see, as a principle of the fidelity, love, and care that Erikson finds definitive of human authenticity.

We also noted in chapter two that insight tends to operate in either of two basic patterns: in a concrete, symbolic pattern of common sense, insight is not only into images, but illuminates their meaning by dwelling in them; while in a more abstract, theoretical pattern, insight uses images only as necessary springboards to its own level of conceptual understanding that is not intrinsically tied to the imagination.[75] Both general patterns are important: the theoretical is proper for ethics; the practical, symbolic pattern for moral living. In chapter two

I stressed the symbolic, but in the present context I must point out
that cognitional analysis, and especially intellectual conversion, depend on insight that operates on its own level of conceptual understanding, and not only on the level of imagination, for the objects of
such study—insight, conceptualization, reflection, judgment, decision
—are *not* objects that can be imagined, and one will miss the point
of such analysis and fail at intellectual conversion as long as he or she
remains tied to the imaginative level. No one, in other words, has ever
imagined—let alone seen—intelligibility, sufficient evidence, or value,
and unless a person discovers his or her own understanding as distinct
from imagination, and operates on its proper level, his or her understanding of knowing will never transcend the myth that knowing is
like looking and that reality is already-out-there-now to be seen. (We
shall return to this point later.)

But insights, or merely possible answers to questions for intelligence, are a "dime a dozen" according to Lonergan.[76] In its radical
thrust toward self-transcendence, the questioning dynamism of the
mind is not satisfied with what possibly may be so. Intelligibility or
meaning is not enough, the drive of human inquiry demands correct
meaning, verified intelligibility. Upon questions for intelligence,
then, says Lonergan, follow questions for reflection. "We move beyond imagination and guesswork, idea and hypothesis, theory and
system, to ask whether or not this really is so or that really could be."[77]
As Lonergan puts it in *Insight*,

. . . the level of intelligence, besides presupposing and complementing an
initial level, is itself presupposed and complemented by a further level of
reflection.

The formulations of understanding yield concepts, definitions, objects of
thought, suppositions, considerations. But man demands more. Every answer to a question for intelligence raises a further question for reflection.
There is an ulterior motive to conceiving and defining, thinking and
considering, forming suppositions, hypotheses, theories, systems. That
motive appears when such activities are followed by the question, "Is it
so?" We conceive in order to judge. As questions for intelligence, What?
and Why? and How often?, stand to insights and formulations, so questions for reflection stand to a further kind of insight and to judgment. It is
on this third level that there emerge the notions of truth and falsity, of
certitude and the probability that is not a frequency but a quality of judgment. It is within this third level that there is involved the personal
commitment that makes one responsible for one's judgments. It is from this
third level that come utterances to express one's affirming or denying,
assenting or dissenting, agreeing or disagreeing.[78]

"Now self-transcendence takes on a new meaning" on this third level, Lonergan asserts. "Not only does it go beyond the subject but also it seeks what is independent of the subject. For a judgment that this or that is so reports," he continues, "not what appears to me, not what I imagine, not what I think, not what I wish, not what I would be inclined to say, not what seems to me, but what is so."[79]

"What is so," then, according to Lonergan, is the determination of reflective understanding, of judgment. The issue of the nature of judgment is a vastly complex one, and we can hope for no more here than a general first approximation. Let us look again to *Insight*:

> Like the acts of direct and introspective understanding, the act of reflective understanding is an insight. As they meet questions for intelligence, it meets questions for reflection. As they lead to definitions and formulations, it leads to judgments. As they grasp unity, or system, or ideal frequency, it grasps the sufficiency of the evidence for a prospective judgment.[80]

Now, for Lonergan, "to grasp evidence as sufficient for a prospective judgment is to grasp the prospective judgment as virtually unconditioned."[81] In outline, Lonergan puts the issue this way:

> By the mere fact that a question for reflection has been put, the prospective judgment is conditioned; it stands in need of evidence sufficient for reasonable pronouncement. The function of reflective understanding is to meet the question for reflection by transforming the prospective judgment from the status of a conditioned to the status of a virtually unconditioned; and reflective understanding effects this transformation by grasping the conditions of the conditioned and their fulfillment.[82]

In other words, as Lonergan summarizes the point in *Method in Theology*:

> Judgment proceeds rationally from a grasp of a virtually unconditioned. By an unconditioned is meant any "x" that has no conditions. By a virtually unconditioned is meant any "x" that has no unfulfilled conditions. In other words, a virtually unconditioned is a conditioned whose conditions are fulfilled. To marshall the evidence is to ascertain whether all the conditions are fulfilled. To weigh the evidence is to ascertain whether the fulfillment of the conditions certainly or probably involves the existence or occurrence of the conditioned.[83]

Accordingly, in Lonergan's view, to take possession of oneself in a critical fashion, "one has to discover that man's intellectual and rational operations involve a transcendence of the operating subject, that the real is what we come to know through a grasp of a certain type of virtually unconditioned."[84] In his article on "Cognitional Structure" Lonergan explains quite directly that

> Because human knowing reaches such an unconditioned, it transcends itself. For the unconditioned *qua* unconditioned cannot be restricted, qualified, limited; and so we all distinguish sharply between what is and, on the other hand, what appears, what seems to be, what is imagined or thought or might possibly or probably be affirmed; in the latter cases the object is still tied down by relativity to the subject; in the former the self-transcendence of human knowing has come to its term; when we say that something is, we mean that its reality does not depend upon our cognitional activity.[85]

Still, we must recognize, says Lonergan, that "such self-transcendence is only cognitive. It is in the order not of doing but only of knowing." There is a further dimension of self-transcendence, for "on the final level of questions for deliberation, self-transcendence becomes moral."[86] This is the sphere of responsible action, and in *Insight* Lonergan discusses this fourth level of conscious questions and operations in terms of an extension of the fundamental dynamism of inquiry into the field of human action:

> The detached, disinterested, unrestricted desire to know grasps intelligently and affirms reasonably not only the facts of the universe of being but also its practical possibilities. Such practical possibilities include intelligent transformations not only of the environment in which man lives but also of man's own spontaneous living. For that living exhibits an otherwise coincidental manifold into which man can introduce a higher system by his own understanding of himself and his own deliberate choices. So it is that the detached and disinterested desire extends its sphere of influence from the field of cognitional activities through the field of knowledge into the field of deliberate human acts. So it is that the empirically, intelligently, rationally conscious subject of self-affirmation becomes a morally self-conscious subject. Man is not only a knower but also a doer; the same intelligent and rational consciousness grounds the doing as well as the knowing; and from that identity of consciousness there springs inevitably an exigence for self-consistency in knowing and doing.[87]

Most fundamentally, then, the radical dynamism that thrusts the personal subject toward self-transcendence reveals itself on this level of moral consciousness as an exigence for self-consistency, for conformity between deciding and judging; and this demand for self-consistency,

for conformity, is, as we see in the following passage, insistently concrete:

> For "not to choose" is not the object of a possible choice and, while one's
> choices can be reasonable or not, while they can be more reasonable or
> less, still one's own rational consciousness is an accomplished fact in the
> field of knowing and it demands in the name of its own consistency its
> extension into the field of doing. Such is the dynamic exigence, the
> operative, moral imperative. But as it concretely exists and functions in
> consciousness, it is immanent in its own concrete presuppositions and
> implications. It demands, not consistency in the abstract, but consistency
> in my consciousness, not the superficial consistency purchased by the flight
> from self-consciousness nor the illusory consistency obtained by self-
> deception and rationalization nor the inadequate consistency that is con-
> tent to be no worse than the next fellow, but the penetrating, honest,
> complete consistency that alone meets the requirements of the detached,
> disinterested, unrestricted desire to know.[88]

Choosing or deciding, then, is clearly the key operation of the fourth
level of consciousness. And this choice or decision is made always
under the imperious shadow of the personal subject's exigence for
self-consistency, for making one's decisions, one's choices in accord
with one's best judgment about what he or she should do.

The subject's judgments about what he or she should do, of course,
occur within a pattern of knowing that is oriented in a practical
direction. Lonergan points out that "while speculative and factual
insights are concerned to lead to knowledge of being, practical insights
are concerned to lead to the making of being. Their objective is not
what is but what is to be done. [They presuppose, of course, factual
insights and judgments about what is.] They reveal, not the unities
and relations of things as they are, but the unities and relations of
possible courses of action."[89]

But, as Lonergan says, "the grasp of a possible course of action need
not result automatically and blindly in its execution." Thus the role of
practical reflection, for further questions arise as to "whether the unity
is going to be made to exist or whether the correlation is going to be
made to govern events." Further questions may regard the course of
action itself, its various features, successive steps, probable consequences, etc. Insofar as practical reflection is a kind of knowing, it can
reach a virtually unconditioned regarding "the possibility of a proposed course of action, or its agreeableness, or its utility, or its ob-
ligatoriness." But, says Lonergan, "insofar as this knowing is practical,
insofar as its concern is with something to be done and with the

reasons for doing it, the reflection has not an internal term [a virtually unconditioned] but an external term; for the reflection is just knowing, but the term is an ulterior deciding and doing."[90]

Paramount among the further questions that practical reflection regards is what Lonergan has more recently referred to as questions for deliberation, questions, that is, which concern *value*. For beyond questions about the concrete possibility and factual consequences of some proposed course of action that can be met by virtually unconditioneds, there are questions about the goodness, the worthwhileness, the value of a possible course of action. And it is these questions for deliberation which specify the fourth level of responsible consciousness, which transform rational consciousness into specifically moral consciousness. "When we ask whether this or that is worthwhile, whether it is not just apparently good but truly good, then we are inquiring," says Lonergan, "not about pleasure or pain, not about comfort or ill ease, not about sensitive spontaneity, not about individual or group advantage, but about objective value." Because, he continues, "we can ask such questions, and answer them, and live by the answers, we can effect in our living a moral self-transcendence."[91]

In the tripartite structure of this last sentence Lonergan specifies for us the three key features of moral consciousness: first there are the questions about value, secondly these questions are answered in judgments of value, and, finally, to "live by the answers" means that decisions must conform to the judgments of value. In the practically oriented pattern of operations, therefore, specifically *moral* concerns about *value* follow upon the practical insights and reflection of the second and third levels.

Judgments of value, according to Lonergan's analysis, are either simple or comparative. "They affirm or deny that some x is truly good or only apparently good. Or," he says, "they compare distinct instances of the truly good to affirm or deny that one is better or more important, or more urgent than the other."[92]

Perhaps most important for the purpose of our thesis is Lonergan's assertion that judgments of value are "objective or merely subjective inasmuch as they proceed or do not proceed from a self-transcending subject. Their truth or falsity, accordingly, has its criterion in the authenticity or lack of authenticity of the subject's being." If the *criterion* of value judgments lies in the authenticity of the subject, however, their *meaning* is objective. Lonergan puts his understanding of the value judgment's meaning this way: "To say that an affirmative judgment of value is true is to say what objectively is or would be good or better. To say that an affirmative judgment of value is false is to say what objectively is not or would not be good or better." Lonergan's comparison of judgments of value with judgments of fact in the following passage should help to further clarify the nature of the value judgment:

> Judgments of value differ in content but not in structure from judgments of fact. They differ in content, for one can approve of what does not exist, and one can disapprove of what does. They do not differ in structure, inasmuch as in both there is the distinction between criterion and meaning. In both, the criterion is the self-transcendence of the subject, which, however, is only cognitive in judgments of fact but is heading towards moral self-transcendence in judgments of value. In both, the meaning is or claims to be independent of the subject: judgments of fact state or purport to state what is or is not so; judgments of value state or purport to state what is or is not truly good or really better.[93]

In saying that the self-transcendence of the subject is "heading toward moral self-transcendence in judgments of value," Lonergan means that "true judgments of value go beyond merely intentional [or cognitive] self-transcendence without reaching the fullness of moral self-transcendence." For in his analysis, "that fullness is not merely knowing but also doing, and man can know what is right without doing it."[94]

Clearly, then, a sharp distinction must be drawn not only between the fourth level and its predecessors on the basis of value, but also between two different phases of self-transcendence within the fourth level itself on the basis of the differences between judgment of value and decision. For the judgment of value "is itself a reality in the moral order. By it the subject is constituting himself as proximately capable of moral self-transcendence, of benevolence and beneficence, of true loving."[95] But the proximate capacity for the fullness of moral self-transcendence is not that fullness itself, just as judgment is not decision. So we distinguish two phases within the level of moral consciousness, but we also recognize that the two phases are intimately linked by the dynamic thrust for self-transcendence which makes itself felt here as an exigence for self-consistency, for conforming decision to the judgment of value. Inasmuch as operations respond to questions, we may say that decision responds to the question provoked by the judgment of value: Now that I have judged that course z is valuable, worthwhile, and something *I* should pursue, what am I going to *do* about it?[96]

"On the topmost level of human consciousness," then, according to

Lonergan, "the subject deliberates, evaluates, decides, controls, acts. At once he is practical and existential: practical inasmuch as he is concerned with concrete courses of action; existential inasmuch as control includes self-control, and the possibility of self-control involves responsibility for the effects of his actions on others and, more basically, on himself. The topmost level of human consciousness is conscience."[97]

Such, then, in outline, according to Lonergan's analysis, is the structure of the personal subject's basic operations and the dynamic questions which thrust him or her toward self-transcendence. Such an outline could be filled out in many ways, as only a brief glance at *Insight* or *Method in Theology* will show. Here, however, we must restrict ourselves to some brief comments on the transcendental notions (especially that of value) and on the relationship between value and feeling.

2. Transcendental Notion of Value

The fundamental difference in modes of intending, and thus also the principal division of sources of meaning, according to Lonergan, lies between the categorial and the transcendental. Categories are involved in asking determinate questions and giving determinate answers through experiencing, understanding, judging, deciding. Transcendentals, on the other hand, "are contained in questions prior to the answers," they "ground questioning." Transcendentals are, in fact, "the radical intending that moves us from ignorance to knowledge. They are *a priori* because they go beyond what we know to seek what we do not know yet. They are unrestricted because answers are never complete and so only give rise to still further questions. They are comprehensive because they intend the unknown whole or totality of which our answers reveal only part."[98]

Most importantly for our interests, however, "the transcendental notions, that is, our questions for intelligence, for reflection, and for deliberation, constitute our capacity for self-transcendence." In the following passage Lonergan further clarifies the meaning of this radical thrust for self-transcendence by distinguishing between transcendental concepts and transcendental notions:

> . . . Intelligence takes us beyond experiencing to ask what and why and how and what for. Reasonableness takes us beyond the answers of intelligence to ask whether the answers are true and whether what they mean really is so. Responsibility goes beyond fact and desire and possibility to

discern between what truly is good and what only apparently is good. So if we objectify the content of intelligent intending, we form the transcendental concept of the intelligible. If we objectify the content of reasonable intending, we form the transcendental concepts of the true and the real. If we objectify the content of responsible intending, we get the transcendental concept of value, of the truly good. But quite distinct from such transcendental concepts, which can be misconceived and often are, there are the prior transcendental notions that constitute the very dynamism of our conscious intending, promoting us from mere experiencing toward understanding, from mere understanding toward truth and reality, from factual knowledge to responsible action.[99]

We have already noted that the subject operates on different levels of consciousness. Besides their distinctiveness and functional interdependence, we can now understand, I think, how these "levels of consciousness are united by the unfolding of a single transcendental intending of plural, interchangeable objectives." Lonergan formulates the dynamic movement this way:

> What promotes the subject from experiential to intellectual consciousness is the desire to understand, the intention of intelligibility. What next promotes him from intellectual to rational consciousness, is a fuller unfolding of the same intention: for the desire to understand once understanding is reached, becomes the desire to understand correctly; in other words, the intention of intelligibility, once an intelligible is reached, becomes the intention of the right intelligible, of the true and, through truth, of reality. Finally, the intention of the intelligible, the true, the real, becomes also the intention of the good, the question of value, of what is worth while, when the already acting subject confronts his world and adverts to his own acting in it.[100]

The many levels of conscious intentionality, then, are, as Lonergan says, just "successive stages in the unfolding of a single thrust, the eros of the human spirit."[101] And this single, radical drive is the principle of the relation and interdependence between the levels of consciousness. For the image of "levels" of consciousness is no more than a metaphor denoting the successive and sublating enlargements of consciousness that occur with the unfolding of the subject's fundamental drive for transcendence. These successive enlargements and sublations of consciousness are brought out clearly in the following passage as Lonergan first runs through the "levels" from "top to bottom," then reverses the direction:

> To know the good [the human spirit] must know the real; to know the real, it must know the true; to know the true, it must know the intelligible; to

know the intelligible, it must attend to the data. So from slumber, we awake to attend. Observing lets intelligence be puzzled, and we inquire. Inquiry leads to the delight of insight, but insights are a dime a dozen, so critical reasonableness doubts, checks, makes sure. Alternative courses of action present themselves and we wonder whether the more attractive is truly good. Indeed, so intimate is the relation between the successive transcendental notions, that it is only by a specialized differentiation of consciousness that we withdraw from more ordinary ways of living to devote ourselves to a moral pursuit of goodness, a philosophic pursuit of truth, a scientific pursuit of understanding, an artistic pursuit of beauty.[102]

Lonergan further suggests that the transcendental notions not only promote the subject to full consciousness and direct him or her to appropriate goals, but they also

provide the criteria that reveal whether the goals are being reached. The drive to understand is satisfied when understanding is reached but it is dissatisfied with every incomplete attainment and so it is the source of ever further questions. The drive to truth compels rationality to assent when evidence is sufficient but refuses assent and demands doubt whenever evidence is insufficient. The drive to value rewards success in self-transcendence with a happy conscience and saddens failures with an unhappy conscience.[103]

Value, then, in this analysis, is a transcendental notion, that is, it is "what is intended in questions for deliberation, just as the intelligible is what is intended in questions for intelligence, and just as truth and being are what are intended in questions for reflection." But we must emphasize again, with Lonergan, that "such intending is not knowing." "When I ask what, or why, or how, or what for," he says, "I do not know the answers, but already I am intending what would be known if I knew the answers." Likewise, "when I ask whether this or that is so, I do not as yet know whether or not either is so, but already I am intending what would be known if I did know the answers." And so, "when I ask whether this is truly and not merely apparently good, whether this is or is not worth while, I do not yet know value but I am intending value."[104]

Again, to repeat a fundamental point, just "as the notion of being is the dynamic principle that keeps us moving toward ever fuller knowledge of being, so the notion of value is the fuller flowering of the same dynamic principle that now keeps us moving toward ever fuller realization of the good, of what is worthwhile."[105]

Readers of Insight will recognize that the analysis of value I have outlined here does not correspond to the treatment given in Insight under the title, "The Notion of Value." The fact is that Lonergan had not yet worked out a *transcendental* notion of value at the *Insight* period of his development. In *Insight*, value is the good of order with its concrete contents as a possible object of rational choice that comes to light in moral consciousness.[106] Ten years later, however, in *The Subject* (1968), Lonergan presents an explicit consideration of the notion of value as transcendental. Here, however, the transcendental notion *seems* simply to replace the former notion of value developed in *Insight* as part of a threefold division of the good: the particular good as object of desire, the good of order, and value. For in *The Subject* Lonergan says that the transcendental notion of value is "distinct from the particular good that satisfies individual appetite, such as the appetite for food and drink, the appetite for union and communion, the appetite for knowledge, or virtue, or pleasure." Further, he says, the transcendental notion of value is "distinct from the good of order, the objective arrangement or institution that ensures for a group of people the regular recurrence of particular goods. As appetite wants breakfast," he says, "so an economic system is to ensure breakfast every morning. As appetite wants union, so marriage is to ensure lifelong union. As appetite wants knowledge," Lonergan continues, "so an educational system ensures the imparting of knowledge to each successive generation."[107] So far, what Lonergan has said here about particular goods as objects of desire and those objects as ordered corresponds exactly to his position in *Insight*.[108] He continues in *The Subject*, however, by saying that "beyond the particular good and the good of order, there is the good of value."[109] But this value that is beyond the particular good and good of order is the transcendental notion of value, not the good of order itself with its concrete contents as a possible object of rational choice, as in *Insight*.[110] This transcendental notion of value in *The Subject* functions as a norm, for Lonergan says that "it is by appealing to value or values that we satisfy some appetites and do not satisfy others, that we approve some systems for achieving the good of order and disapprove of others, that we praise or blame human persons as good or evil and their actions as right or wrong."[111] But while introducing this transcendental notion of value, *The Subject* does not explicitly discuss the notion of value worked out in *Insight*, and by discussing the transcendental notion of value in the context of and in relation to the particular good and the good of order, *The Subject* has the effect of allowing the reader to confuse the two notions of value, or to think that the concept of value of *Insight* has simply been replaced by the new transcendental notion of value.

Method in Theology finally introduces some measure of clarity to this question, but while both notions of value are treated here, the discussions are separate and not explicitly linked. Further, as we have noticed, *Method in Theology* adds the issue of judgments of value to the whole question. So while there is some degree of clarity to this latest work, it is in something of a potential form that needs to be actualized through some direct explicating and relating.

Three key terms central to our question occur at various places in *Method in Theology*: judgments of value, terminal value (as in *Insight*), and the transcendental notion of value (as in *The Subject*). We have already noticed how judgments of value are related to questions for deliberation and to decisions. And we shall soon consider their relation to feelings in the pattern of operations. Judgments of value are related to terminal values through decisions or choices, inasmuch as terminal values are objects of possible choice or are, indeed, actually chosen;[112] and choices, when they are responsible, conform to judgments of value. Terminal values, indeed, are the primary and basic instances of value discussed in *Insight* under the title "The Notion of Value," in relation to the particular good and the good of order, a threefold division that is maintained in *Method in Theology*.[113] In *Insight*, Lonergan explains that these values may be true or false, insofar as they are or are not the objects of reasonable choice.[114] In *Method*, however, he emphasizes true values, describing terminal values as "true instances of the particular good, a true good of order, a true scale of preferences regarding values and satisfactions."[115]

As we have seen above, *Method* also discusses the transcendental notion of value, but without explicitly and clearly relating it to the notion of terminal value. We may recall, however, that in discussing the transcendental notion of value, Lonergan likens it to the notion of being. "Just as the notion of being intends but, of itself, does not know being," he says, "so too the [transcendental] notion of value intends but, of itself, does not know value."[116] There are further similarities between the transcendental notions of being and value that Lonergan points out which will, I think, be helpful to note here:

Just as the notion of being functions in one's knowing and it is by reflecting on that functioning that one comes to know what the notion of being is, so also the notion or intention of the good functions within one's human acting and it is by reflection on that functioning that one comes to know what the notion of good is. Again, just as the functioning of the notion of being brings about our limited knowledge of being, so too the functioning of the notion of the good brings about our limited achievement of the good. Finally, as our knowledge of being is, not knowledge of essence, but only knowledge of this and that and other beings, so too the only good, to which we have first-hand access, is found in instances of the good realized in themselves or produced beyond themselves by good men.[117]

The first point in the above passage will be especially important in helping us to understand the relation between *Insight's* notion of terminal value and the later transcendental notion of value. Just as we can distinguish the being or reality *intended* in questions for reflection from the being or reality *known* through true judgments, so we can distinguish the value *intended* in questions for deliberation from the value *known* in true judgments of value and *realized* in reasonable, responsible decisions or choices which conform to those true judgments. There are, in other words, the reality and value which are intended in questioning (the transcendental notions) and the concrete instances of reality and value which are known and realized in correct judgments and authentic choices. We may say, then, that the transcendental notion of value stands to the notion of being as terminal values stand to the reality known through true judgments, or, in more direct response to our original question, that terminal values stand to the transcendental notion of value as the reality known through true judgments stands to the notion of being. As the notion of being functions as a criterion for the judgments through which reality is known, so the transcendental notion of value functions as a criterion for the decisions and choices through which terminal values are realized.

3. Value and Feelings

We have considered several aspects of the question of value thus far, but we must now turn our attention to one aspect that is central to our thesis, the relation of value to feelings. For while we have discussed judgments and choices of values in relation to cognitive operations, Lonergan makes a point of the fact that "the apprehension of values and disvalues is the task not of understanding but of intentional response." And "such response is all the fuller, all the more discriminating," Lonergan says, "the better a man one is, the more refined one's sensibility, the more delicate one's feelings." Briefly, and quite simply, Lonergan puts the matter this way: "Intermediate between judgments of fact and judgments in value lie apprehensions of value. Such apprehensions are given of feelings."[118]

Lonergan's most interesting consideration of feelings, perhaps, is in connection with his analysis of symbolic meaning, through which "mind and body, mind and heart, heart and body communicate." Because of "internal tensions, incompatibilities, conflicts, struggles, destructions," the need for this internal communication is basic, and symbols, obeying "the laws not of logic but of image and feeling," have the power of recognizing and expressing the internal tensions and conflicts which logical discourse abhors. "Organic and psychic vitality," says Lonergan, "have to reveal themselves to intentional consciousness and, inversely, intentional consciousness has to secure the collaboration of organism and psyche. Again," he says, "our apprehensions of values occur in intentional responses, in feelings: here too it is necessary for feelings to reveal their objects and, inversely, for objects to awaken feelings." Most basically, according to Lonergan, "a symbol is an image of a real or imaginary object that evokes a feeling or is evoked by a feeling."[119] Though we will not pursue Lonergan's analysis of symbolic meaning here, we should remember that this is the primary context in which his discussion of value and feeling must be interpreted, the issue which we must now consider directly.

Relying on the phenomenological analyses of Max Scheler and Dietrich von Hildebrand, Lonergan distinguishes in the realm of feelings between "nonintentional states and trends" and "intentional responses." Nonintentional states are fatigue, anxiety, bad humor. Trends or urges are, for example, hunger, thirst, sexual discomfort. Such states and trends have causes or goals, and the feeling is related to the cause or goal simply as effect to cause, as trend to goal. "The feeling itself," says Lonergan, "does not presuppose and arise out of perceiving, imagining, representing the cause or goal. Rather, one first feels tired and, perhaps belatedly, one discovers that what one needs is a rest. Or first one feels hungry and then one diagnoses the trouble as a lack of food." Now values are apprehended not in these states and trends, says Lonergan, but rather in the intentional responses which he contrasts to them in the following description:

Intentional responses, on the other hand, answer to what is intended, apprehended, represented. The feeling relates us, not just to a cause or an end, but to an object. Such feeling gives intentional consciousness its mass, momentum, drive, power. Without these feelings our knowing and deciding would be paper thin. Because of our feelings, our desires and our fears, our hope or despair, our joys and sorrows, our enthusiasm and indignation, our esteem and contempt, our trust and distrust, our love and hatred, our tenderness and wrath, our admiration, veneration, reverence, our dread, horror, terror, we are oriented massively and dynamically in a world mediated by meaning. We have feelings about other persons, we feel for them, we feel with them. We have feelings about our respective situations, about the past, about the future, about evils to be lamented or remedied, about the good that can, might, must be accomplished.[120]

But, further, intentional responses are not all of a kind, and values are not to be apprehended in every intentional response. For, as Lonergan explains, "feelings that are intentional responses regard two main classes of objects: on the one hand, the agreeable or disagreeable, the satisfying or dissatisfying; on the other hand, values, whether the ontic value of persons or the qualitative value of beauty, understanding, truth, virtuous acts, noble deeds."[121]

Response to the agreeable or disagreeable, the satisfying or dissatisfying is, unfortunately, ambiguous. "What is agreeable," says Lonergan, "may very well be what is a true good. But it also happens that what is a true good may be disagreeable. Most good men," he says, "have to accept unpleasant work, privations, pain, and their virtue is a matter of doing so without excessive self-centered lamentation." In contrast, according to Lonergan, "response to value both carries us toward self-transcendence and selects an object for the sake of whom or of which we transcend ourselves." For, he says, "we are so endowed that we not only ask questions leading to self-transcendence, not only can recognize correct answers constitutive of intentional self-transcendence, but also respond with the stirring of our very being when we glimpse the possibility or the actuality of moral self-transcendence."[122]

Feelings, then, in Lonergan's analysis, respond to values, but they do not respond simply; rather, they respond in accord with a scale of preference. So Lonergan suggests that we may distinguish "vital, social, cultural, personal, and religious values in an ascending order." He sketches the character of these various types of values in the following passage:

Vital values, such as health and strength, grace and vigor, normally are preferred to avoiding the work, privations, pains involved in acquiring, maintaining, restoring them. Social values, such as the good of order which conditions the vital values of the whole community, have to be preferred to the vital values of individual members of the community. Cultural values do not exist without the underpinning of vital and social values, but none the less they rank higher. Not on bread alone doth man live. Over and above mere living and operating, men have to find a meaning and value in their living and operating. It is the function of culture to discover, express, validate, criticize, correct, develop, improve such meaning and value. Personal value is the person in his self-transcendence, as loving and being loved, as originator of values in himself and in his milieu, as an inspiration and invitation to others to do likewise. Religious values, finally, are at the heart of the meaning and value of man's living and man's world....[123]

It is also important for the ethical theorist to note, as Lonergan does, that feelings develop. Feelings, of course, are fundamentally spontaneous in their origin, not lying at the beck and call of decision. Once arisen, however, feelings "may be reinforced by advertance and approval, and they may be curtailed by disapproval and distraction." Lonergan continues by pointing out that

> such reinforcement and curtailment not only will encourage some feelings and discourage others but also will modify one's spontaneous scale of preferences. Again, feelings are enriched and refined by attentive study of the wealth and variety of the objects that arouse them, and so no small part of education lies in fostering and developing a climate of discernment and taste, of discriminating praise and carefully worded disapproval, that will conspire with the pupil's or student's own capacities and tendencies, enlarge and deepen his apprehension of values, and help him toward self-transcendence.[124]

Before returning more directly to the question of value, we should note with Lonergan that feelings are not merely transient, that while some easily aroused feelings just as easily pass away and while some feelings are repressed into an unhappy subterranean life, still

> there are in full consciousness feelings so deep and strong, especially when deliberately reinforced, that they channel attention, shape one's horizon, direct one's life. Here [says Lonergan] the supreme illustration is loving. A man or woman that falls in love is engaged in loving not only when attending to the beloved but at all times. Besides particular acts of loving, there is the prior state of being in love, and that prior state is, as it were, the fount of all one's actions. So mutual love is the intertwining of two lives. It transforms an "I" and "thou" into a "we" so intimate, so secure, so permanent, that each attends, imagines, thinks, plans, feels, speaks, acts in concern for both.[125]

Lonergan concludes his brief consideration of feelings by noting that besides development there are also aberrations of feelings, and that "it is much better to take full cognizance of one's feelings, however deplorable they may be, than to brush them aside, overrule them, ignore them." This issue, which has received so little consideration from moralists, seems to lie at the heart of the question about an adequate ethical theory, for such a theory must be able to come to grips in a satisfactory way with the nature of personal authenticity, itself intrinsically dependent on genuine self-knowledge. And, as Lonergan says,

> to take cognizance of [one's feelings] makes it possible for one to know oneself, to uncover the inattention, obtuseness, silliness, irresponsibility that gave rise to the feeling one does not want, and to correct the aberrant attitude. On the other hand, not to take cognizance of them is to leave them in the twilight of what is conscious but not objectified [what Lonergan thinks at least some psychiatrists mean by the unconscious]. In the long run there results a conflict between the self as conscious and, on the other hand, the self as objectified.
>
> Just as transcendental method rests on a self-appropriation, on attending to, inquiring about, understanding, conceiving, affirming one's attending, inquiring, understanding, conceiving, affirming, so too therapy is an appropriation of one's own feelings. As the former task is blocked by misconceptions of human knowing, so too the latter is blocked by misconceptions of what one spontaneously is.[126]

To conclude, now, our discussion of value, we may point out with Lonergan that in judgments of value three components unite. First, says Lonergan, "there is knowledge of reality and especially of human reality. Secondly, there are intentional responses to values. Thirdly, there is the initial thrust toward moral self-transcendence constituted by the judgment of value itself." This is simply a more explicit and systematic way of saying what we have already noted with Lonergan, that "intermediate between judgments of fact and judgments in value lie apprehensions of value." There are, in other words, first the issues on which practical reflection itself can reach virtually unconditioneds. Thus Lonergan says that "the judgment of value presupposes knowledge of human life, of human possibilities proximate and remote, of the probable consequences of projected courses of action." In this regard, Lonergan notes that "when knowledge is deficient, then fine feelings are apt to be expressed in what is called moral idealism, i.e., lovely proposals that don't work out and often do more harm than good." But, as our consideration of value and feeling has indicated, "knowledge alone is not enough," and, Lonergan says, "while everyone has some measure of moral feeling for, as the saying is, there is honor among thieves, still moral feelings have to be cultivated, enlightened, strengthened, refined, criticized, and pruned of oddities."[127]

Finally, says Lonergan, "the development of knowledge and the development of moral feeling head to the existential discovery, the discovery of oneself as a moral being, the realization that one not only chooses between courses of action but also thereby makes oneself an authentic human being or an unauthentic one. With that discovery," he states, "there emerges in consciousness the significance of personal value and the meaning of personal responsibility."[128] But this brings us to the question of conversion, the topic of our next section. Here we have restricted our consideration to the various degrees of self-transcendence that the conscious subject can effect through the response of conscious operations to the fundamental human dynamism expressed in questions for intelligence, reflection, deliberation, and decision. Although the issue of objectivity is intimately connected with the question of self-transcendence, we shall reserve our reflections on it until after we have discussed the special instance of self-transcendence called intellectual conversion. For while objectivity is achieved in every instance of self-transcendence, its reality is properly understood only from the standpoint of the converted subject.

We may bring this section to an appropriate close, while anticipating our discussion of conversion in the next section, by pointing out with Lonergan that "it is by the transcendental notion of value [the fullest manifestation of the personal subject's radical exigence for self-transcendence] and its expression in a good and uneasy conscience that man can develop morally. But a rounded moral judgment is ever the work of a fully developed self-transcending subject or, as Aristotle would put it, of a virtuous man."[129] To the conversions from which such subjects emerge, then, we now turn.

C. CONVERSION AND OBJECTIVITY

1. Conversions and Realms of Meaning

In our earlier discussion of the conscious subject and his or her horizon we considered the various dimensions of the subject's world—a world not only of immediate experience but mediated and constituted by meaning. We must now complicate that account by introducing the distinct human exigences that, by giving rise to different modes of conscious and intentional operation, ground the various basic world possibilities or realms of meaning which Lonergan groups in three sets: common sense/theoretical; exterior/interior; profane/sacred.

First of all, there is the "systematic exigence that separates the

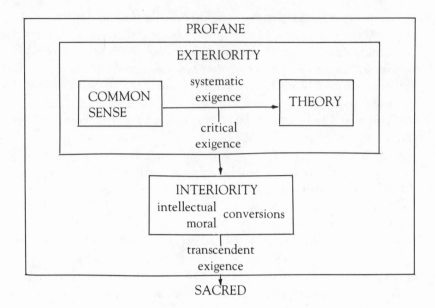

realm of common sense from the realm of theory." While the same real objects are the concern of these two realms, their standpoints are so different that the objects can be related only by shifting back and forth between the standpoints.[130] The realm of common sense meaning is the visible, everyday, practical world of persons and things in their relations to us. We come to know it, says Lonergan, "not by applying some scientific method, but by a self-correcting process of learning, in which insights gradually accumulate, coalesce, qualify and correct one another, until a point is reached where we are able to meet situations as they arise, size them up by adding a few more insights to the acquired store, and so deal with them in an appropriate fashion."[131] Thus one gradually becomes a master of some field, at home with the familiar and quick to recognize and attack the unfamiliar (if not unexpected) problem, whether one's art be repairing autos, teaching first grade reading, or hosting a television talk show.

Lonergan proposes Plato's early dialogues as an excellent illustration of the systematic exigence's intrusion into the realm of common sense. There Socrates asks his fellow Athenians for the definition of a specific virtue: What is justice? What is courage? And while everyone claims to recognize and know the meaning of the virtue in its particular, concrete instance, no one is able to give Socrates the kind of answer he wants: universal, *omni et soli* definitions that fit every case of justice and nothing but justice, that apply to each and every instance of courage and only to courage.[132] If, from Plato's dialogues, says Lonergan, "one shifts to Aristotle's *Nicomachean Ethics*, one can find definitions worked out both for virtue and vice in general and for a series of virtues each flanked by two opposite vices, one sinning by excess, and the other by defect."[133] These definitions answer Socrates' question, but that is not Aristotle's only objective. For, as Lonergan explains,

> the systematic exigence not merely raises questions that common sense cannot answer but also demands a context for its answers, a context that common sense cannot supply or comprehend. This context is theory, and the objects to which it refers are in the realm of theory. To these objects one can ascend from commonsense starting-points, but they are properly known, not by this ascent, but by their internal relations, their congruences, and differences, the functions they fulfill in their interactions.[134]

Lonergan's illustration of the systematic exigence and realm of theory here is the philosophical one from Plato and Aristotle, but examples abound in many fields. The obvious ones, of course, are in physics, where, as Lonergan points out, "mass, temperature, the electromagnetic field are not objects in the world of common sense. Mass is neither weight nor momentum. A metal object will feel colder than a wooden one beside it, but both will be of the same temperature." And, Lonergan continues, "Maxwell's equations for the electromagnetic field are magnificent in their abstruseness."[135]

So we have a realm of descriptive, commonsense knowing and a distinct and seemingly opposed realm of explanatory theory resulting from the systematic or theoretical exigence; each has its own method of coming to know, its own criteria for the relevance of further questions, its own language and, indeed, community. The confusion resulting from these two apparently opposed "stories" about the world is well illustrated in Eddington's classic example of the two tables: "the bulky, solid, colored desk at which he worked, and the manifold of colorless 'wavicles' so minute that the desk was mostly empty space."[136] But our own language exemplifies the problem everytime we speak about the sun rising and setting.[137] Sally Brown deals with this problem in her own way one day while she and Linus are sitting under their favorite tree, conversing. She mentions that some morning she is going to "get up real early and watch the sun rise." Linus, with a professorial gesture, points out that "actually, as you probably know, the sun doesn't rise. . . . The earth turns. . . ." After a moment of reflection, Sally rephrases her plan: "Some morning I'm going to get up real early and watch the earth turn. . . ."

And if one takes the disparity between the two accounts of the world seriously, if one allows the systematic exigence its full run and tries to spell out the relationship between the two realms in an explanatory fashion, one comes face to face with the demands of the *critical* exigence.

And so questions are now asked, as Lonegan points out, about common sense, theory, and, indeed, knowing themselves. "Is common sense just primitive ignorance to be brushed aside with an acclaim to science as the dawn of intelligence and reason?" "Or is science of merely pragmatic value, teaching us to control nature, but failing to reveal what nature is?" "Or, for that matter, is there any such thing as human knowing?" And thus, through some such series of questions arising from the differences between theory and common sense, one is confronted with what Lonergan calls the three basic philosophical questions: "What am I doing when I am knowing?" (cognitional theory); "Why is doing that knowing?" (epistemology); and "What do I know when I do it?" (metaphysics).[138]

Far from being merely three more in an endless series of human questions, these basic philosophical questions—like Socrates' probings for universal definitions—create the possibility of a deeper realm of meaning, a larger and far richer human world. For, as one began a movement from common sense to theory with Socrates' testy questions, with these fundamental questions one turns, as Lonergan puts it, "from the outer realms of common sense and theory to the appropriation of one's own interiority, one's subjectivity, one's operations, their structure, their norms, their potentialities."[139]

This shift in response to the critical exigence, difficult and necessarily gradual in achieving a measure of fullness (intellectual conversion), is one of what Lonergan calls *basic* horizon factors. While these basic horizon factors—or conversions—are central in the study of philosophy and theology, they are not without import also in the human sciences. For while these sciences are concerned with the study of *relative* horizon factors, their standpoints are defined—at least implicitly—by basic horizon factors, that is, by the presence or absence of conversion in the scientist. Even the natural sciences with their precisely limited questions are not entirely immune from these basic horizon factors, as the debates in the philosophy of science over the past century have clearly shown.[140] Even so, it seems obvious that a basic horizon factor such as intellectual conversion has its greatest import in the human sciences, philosophy, and theology, for here, unlike the natural sciences, a new horizon on the object, as Lonergan says, requires a new horizon on the personal subject, for in these fields the subject is one of the objects.[141] And such a new horizon on the

3 Subjectivity and Conversion in Lonergan

personal subject, according to Lonergan, demands not only new concepts, postulates, axioms, methods, and techniques, but also a conversion of the subject, a reorganization, a reorientation. For without this
conversion of the subject the new ideas will not only be inoperative in
one's own living, they will also remain rather insignificant, without
urgent meaning, without any vital expansiveness even in the domain
of objects. The grasp of the new ideas, then, as Newman would put it,
is only notional, without any real foundation in the personal experience of the subject. In other words, as Lonergan sums up the problem,
inasmuch as there is a need for conversion, there exists what he calls
an existential gap—and this gap is the difference, however large or
small, between one's horizon on oneself and what one really is. The
reality of the personal subject, in other words, can be beyond the
horizon of the subject. The subject can suffer from an unknown-
unknown regarding her or himself. And when basic horizon factors are
at stake, the unknown-unknown is not some erudite aspect of the
human sciences that a person could well be excused from knowing; it
is, rather, a matter of the subject's own intelligence and reasonableness, of his or her own freedom and responsibility. On the one hand,
says Lonergan, a person might manifest these realities, assert them,
and repudiate any suggestion that they are wanting in him or herself,
and yet at the same time it may be true in a very real sense that these
realities stand beyond the person's horizon. So now we must consider
the conversions which effect basic shifts in the subject's horizon. We
shall begin with intellectual conversion. But, first, a brief word about
the general notion of conversion.

In explaining his understanding of the basic reality of conversion,
Lonergan notes the distinction drawn by Joseph de Finance between a
horizontal and a vertical exercise of freedom. A horizontal exercise of
freedom, says Lonergan, is a "decision or choice that occurs within an
established horizon" and "from the basis of a corresponding existential
stance." A vertical exercise of freedom, on the other hand, is "the set
of judgments and decisions by which we move from one horizon to
another." Lonergan explains that there may be "a sequence of such
vertical exercises of freedom, and in each case the new horizon,
though notably deeper and broader and richer, none the less is con-
sonant with the old and a development out of its potentialities." But,
Lonergan continues, it is "also possible that the movement into a new
horizon involves an about-face; it comes out of the old by repudiating
characteristic features; it begins a new sequence that can keep revealing ever greater depth and breadth and wealth. Such an about-face
and new beginning is what is meant by a conversion."[142]

2. Intellectual Conversion

We have already touched upon intellectual conversion in our discussion of transcendental method, for intellectual conversion lies at
the heart of that method. Without conversion, one can have only a
lifeless, notional apprehension of transcendental method. We shall
now examine this intellectual conversion directly in some detail. But
even this treatment is merely a summary, of course, in no way intended to replace the rigorous self-scrutiny encouraged by a book like
Insight.

In *Method in Theology* Lonergan says that "intellectual conversion is
a radical clarification and, consequently, the elimination of an ex-
ceedingly stubborn and misleading myth concerning reality, objectivity, and human knowledge. The myth is that knowing is like looking,
that objectivity is seeing what is there to be seen and not seeing what
is not there, and that the real is what is out there to be looked at."[143]

Put most simply, this fundamental myth about knowing overlooks,
according to Lonergan, the distinction we have already noted between
the world of immediacy and the world mediated by meaning. "The
world of immediacy," as we have seen, "is the sum of what is seen,
heard, touched, tasted, smelt, felt. It conforms well enough," says
Lonergan, "to the myth's view of reality, objectivity, knowledge. But
it is but a tiny fragment of the world mediated by meaning. For the
world mediated by meaning," Lonergan emphasizes, "is a world known
not by the sense experience of an individual but by the external and
internal experience of a cultural community, and by the continuously
checked and rechecked judgments of the community." Through intellectual conversion, then, one realizes that an adequate account of
human knowing, of its criteria of objectivity, and of the thus known
universe, must take account not only of the world of immediacy but of
that world and also of the complex process from it to the world
mediated by meaning. For knowing, from Lonergan's standpoint, is
not just seeing, taking a look: "it is experiencing, understanding,
judging, and believing." And thus "the criteria of objectivity are not
just the criteria of ocular vision; they are the compound criteria of
experiencing, of understanding, of judging, and of believing." And, in
the same way, "the reality known is not just looked at; it is given in
experience, organized and extrapolated by understanding, posited by
judgment and belief."[144]

In contrast to this position of Lonergan, and, as he says, as consequences of the myth, are the various viewpoints Lonergan names
counterpositions:

The naive realist knows the world mediated by meaning but thinks he knows it by looking. The empiricist restricts objective knowledge to sense experience; for him, understanding and conceiving, judging and believing are merely subjective activities. The idealist insists that human knowing always includes understanding as well as sense; but he retains the empiricist's notion of reality, and so he thinks of the world mediated by meaning as not real but ideal.[145]

In Lonergan's view, "only the critical realist can acknowledge the facts of human knowing and pronounce the world mediated by meaning to be the real world; and he can do so only inasmuch as he shows that the process of experiencing, understanding, and judging is a process of self-transcendence."[146]

For Lonergan the difference between empiricism, idealism, and critical realism involves more than a merely technical point in philosophy, for they constitute "three totally different horizons with no common identical objects." An idealist, he says, "never means what an empiricist means, and a realist never means what either of them means." For example, "an empiricist may argue that quantum theory cannot be about physical reality; it cannot because it deals only with relations between phenomena. An idealist would concur and add that, of course, the same is true of all science and, indeed, of the whole of human knowing. The critical realist," says Lonergan, "will disagree with both: a verified hypothesis is probably true; and what probably is true refers to what in reality probably is so."[147] Such examples are endless, for basic "philosophical issues are universal in scope, and some form of naive realism seems to appear utterly unquestionable to very many" people. And, Lonergan continues,

as soon as they begin to speak of knowing, of objectivity, of reality, there crops up the assumption that all knowing must be something like looking. To be liberated from that blunder, to discover the self-transcendence proper to the human process of coming to know, is to break often long-ingrained habits of thought and speech. It is to acquire the mastery in one's own house that is to be had only when one knows precisely what one is doing when one is knowing. It is a conversion, a new beginning, a fresh start. It opens the way to ever further clarifications and developments.[148]

As Lonergan puts it in his introduction to *Insight,* intellectual conversion, or "the appropriation of one's own rational self-consciousness,"

is not an end in itself but rather a beginning. It is a necessary beginning, for unless one breaks the duality in one's knowing, one doubts that understanding correctly is knowing. Under the pressure of that doubt, either one will sink into the bog of a knowing that is without understanding, or else one will cling to understanding but sacrifice knowing on the altar of an immanentism, an idealism, a relativism. From the horns of that dilemma one escapes only through the discovery (and one has not made it yet if one has no clear memory of its startling strangeness) that there are two quite different realisms, that there is an incoherent realism, half animal and half human, that poses as a halfway house between materialism and idealism and, on the other hand, that there is an intelligent and reasonable realism between which and materialism the halfway house is idealism.[149]

This passage does have a certain (almost systematic) obscurity about it, but from one point of view its very value lies in that obscurity, for it seems to be something of a touchstone or litmus paper for intellectual conversion as Lonergan conceives it: certainly, anyone who has read and understood *Insight* finds the passage a model of clarity. For intellectual conversion, indeed, is the primary and central goal of *Insight*.

But if intellectual conversion results in the elimination of this fundamental myth about knowing, it consists essentially of the possession one takes of one self as a knower, and in the realization, specifically, that the criterion of the real is the virtually unconditioned of one's own judgment. As Lonergan puts it in *Insight*, "the aim of the book is to issue an invitation to a personal, decisive act," i.e., conversion. And the crucial issue involved in this invitation is an experimental issue, but, says Lonergan, "the experiment will be performed not publicly but privately."[150] It will consist, he says, in "one's own rational self-consciousness clearly and distinctly taking possession of itself as rational self-consciousness. Up to that decisive achievement," Lonergan says, "all leads. From it, all follows. No one else, no matter what his knowledge or his eloquence, no matter what his logical rigor or persuasiveness, can do it for you." For, as Lonergan points out, "the dynamic, cognitional structure to be reached is not the transcendental *ego* of Fichtean speculation, nor the abstract pattern of relations verifiable in any Tom and Dick and Harry, but the personally appropriated structure of one's own experiencing, one's own intelligent inquiry and insights, one's own critical reflection and judging and deciding." Again, he says that the point at issue is personal appropriation: "the point is to discover, to identify, to become familiar with the activities of one's own intelligence; the point is to become able to discriminate with ease and from personal conviction between one's purely intellectual activities and the manifold of other, 'existential' concerns that invade and mix and blend with the operations of intellect to render it ambivalent and its pronouncements ambiguous."[151]

In chapter eleven of *Insight*, Lonergan has concretized intellectual conversion in the affirmation of oneself as a knower according to the basic pattern of (cognitional) operations that we have already considered in our discussion of transcendental method (minus "decision"). Lonergan says that affirmation of oneself as a knower is a judgment not of necessity but of fact, and like other judgments, rests upon a grasp of the unconditioned.[152] Further, says Lonergan, as in other judgments of fact,

> the unconditioned is the combination of
>   (1) a conditioned,
>   (2) a link between the conditioned and its conditions, and
>   (3) the fulfillment of the conditions.
> The relevant conditioned is the statement, I am a knower. The link between the conditioned and its conditions may be cast in the proposition, I am a knower, if I am a concrete and intelligible unity-identity-whole, characterized by acts of sensing, perceiving, imagining, inquiring, understanding, formulating, reflecting, grasping the unconditioned, and judging. The fulfillment of the conditions is given in consciousness.[153]

Here the conditioned, "I am a knower," is merely the expression of what is to be affirmed—not an epistemological theorem, but simply a claim by the subject that he or she performs certain acts, spelled out in the "link" and already familiar to us, and these are what is meant by "knowing."[154] And Lonergan says that the fulfillment of the conditions is "given in consciousness." We have already considered Lonergan's understanding of consciousness in general; now, therefore, we will examine this crucial element only as it functions in the judgment of self-affirmation as a knower.

In our earlier discussion of consciousness we examined Lonergan's account in some detail, but such an *account* of consciousness, Lonergan insists, is not itself consciousness. Rather, "the account supposes consciousness as its data for inquiry, for insight, for formulation, for reflection, for grasp of the unconditioned, for judgment." Lonergan says that "giving the account is the formulating and the judging, while the account itself is what is formulated and affirmed." But "consciousness as given is neither formulated nor affirmed. Consciousness is given independently of its being formulated or affirmed."[155]

By experiential fulfillment, then, Lonergan "does not mean the conditioned, nor the link between the conditioned and its conditions,

160 Conscience: Development and Self-Transcendence

nor the conditions as formulated, let alone as affirmed." He means, rather, the conditions, which are formulated, as they are "found in a more rudimentary state within cognitional process." For "just as inquiry brings about the advance from the perceived and not understood to the perceived and understood, so there is a reverse shift," says Lonergan, "by which one moves from the perceived and understood to the merely perceived. It is this reverse shift that commonly is meant by verification." In other words, for Lonergan, "verification is an appropriate pattern of acts of checking [which] are reversals from formulations of what would be perceived to the corresponding but more rudimentary cognitional contents of acts of perceiving or sensing." Thus, though "in the formulation there always are elements derived from inquiry, insight, conceiving," Lonergan asserts that "in virtue of the checking one can say that the formulation is not pure theory, that it is not merely supposed or merely postulated or merely inferred, that its sensible component is given."[156]

Now, with regard to the affirmation of oneself as a knower, says Lonergan, "just as there is reversal to what is given sensibly, so there is reversal to what is given consciously." And, he goes on to explain, "just as the former reversal is away from the understood as understood, the formulated as formulated, the affirmed as affirmed, and to the merely sensed, so also the latter reversal is from the understood, formulated, affirmed as such, to the merely given."[157] Therefore, Lonergan summarizes,

in the self-affirmation of the knower, the conditioned is the statement, I am a knower. The link between the conditioned and its conditions is cast in the proposition, I am a knower if I am a unity performing certain kinds of acts. The conditions as formulated are the unity-identity-whole to be grasped in data as individual and the kinds of acts to be grasped as similar. But the fulfillment of the conditions in consciousness is to be had by reverting from such formulations to the more rudimentary state of the formulated where there is no formulation but merely experience.[158]

Now, just as we noted earlier in our discussion of the impossibility of a radical revision of the basis of transcendental method, there is here, too, in the judgment of self-affirmation a logic that places the merely factual affirmation of self as knower in a context of necessity, for, as Lonergan points out, if the contingent is supposed as a fact, it becomes conditionally necessary. Thus, there is a peculiar logical character to the question "Am I a knower?" that renders a negative answer intrinsically contradictory, not in the words of the negation but between them and the very performance itself. The negative answer, then, is "incoherent, for if I am not a knower, how could the question be raised and answered by me?" For the negative answer is an answer; it is an affirmation which, when its implicit performance is explicated, is equivalent to "It is true that..." or "I know that I am not a knower." Likewise, says Lonergan, "the hedging answer, I do not know, is incoherent. For if I know that I do not know, then I am a knower; and if I do not know that I do not know, then I should not answer."[159]

Now Lonergan explains further that it is not only the conditional necessity of contingent fact that succeeds in leading the talking sceptic into contradiction, but that the Aristotelian prescription depends also on "the nature, the natural spontaneities and natural inevitabilities, that go with that fact." The personal subject, in short, is empirically, intelligently, and rationally conscious, and he or she has no choice in the matter. Sensations, percepts, images cannot be escaped. And just as the personal subject cannot escape them, neither can he nor she be content with them. Spontaneously the subject tries to understand. He or she enters, "without questioning, the dynamic state that is revealed in questions for intelligence." The subject "can question everything else, but to question questioning is self-destructive." Lonergan says that "I might call upon intelligence for the conception of a plan to escape intelligence, but the effort to escape would only reveal my present involvement and, strangely enough, I would want to go about the business intelligently and I would want to claim that escaping was the intelligent thing to do."[160]

But as the personal subject is not content with the flow of presentations and representations, so he or she cannot be content with inquiry, understanding, formulation. If, above all, the subject wants to understand, says Lonergan, still he or she wants to understand the facts. For, Lonergan goes on,

> inevitably, the achievement of understanding, however stupendous, only gives rise to the further question, Is it so? Inevitably, the progress of understanding is interrupted by the check of judgment. Intelligence may be a thoroughbred exulting in the race; but there is a rider on its back; and, without the rider, the best of horses is a poor bet. The insistence that modern science envisages an indefinite future of repeated revisions does not imply an indifference to fact. On the contrary, it is fact that will force the revisions, that will toss into the wastebasket the brilliant theories of previous understanding, that will make each new theory better because it is closer to the facts.[161]

Fact, then, quite simply, is the criterion of cognitional self-transcendence. Thus, in delineating what he means by fact, Lonergan summarizes the essential points of his cognitional theory. Clearly, he says,

> fact is concrete as is sense or consciousness. Again, fact is intelligible: if it is independent of all doubtful theory, it is not independent of the modest insight and formulation necessary to give it its precision and its accuracy. Finally, fact is virtually unconditioned: it might not have been; it might have been other than it is; but as things stand, it possesses conditional necessity, and nothing can possibly alter it now. Fact, then, combines the concreteness of experience, the determinateness of accurate intelligence, and the absoluteness of rational judgment. It is the natural objective of human cognitional process. It is the anticipated unity to which sensation, perception, imagination, inquiry, insight, formulation, reflection, grasp of the unconditioned, and judgment make their several complementary contributions.[162]

And, indeed, the fundamental power of transcendental method, the radical realization of intellectual conversion, is that we are committed, inexorably, to the realm of fact. We are committed, says Lonergan, "not by knowing what it is and that it is worthwhile, but by an inability to avoid experience, by the subtle conquest in us of the Eros that would understand, by the inevitable aftermath of that sweet adventure when a rationality identical with us demands the absolute, refuses unreserved assent to less than the unconditioned and, when that is attained, imposes upon us a commitment in which we bow to an immanent Anagke."[163]

Now just as the intellectually converted subject discovers rational consciousness' virtually unconditioned as the criterion of the real, so he or she also discovers that while rational consciousness criticizes everything, including the achievement of science, it cannot criticize itself. For the subject discovers, as Lonergan says, that "the critical spirit can weigh all else in the balance, only on the condition that it does not criticize itself. It is a self-assertive spontaneity that demands sufficient reason for all else but offers no justification for its demanding." And this rational consciousness that the subject discovers is his or her own; it is not some item on sale at the discount center which momentarily attracts one's curiosity; the subject is already involved, engaged, committed. For, as Lonergan says, "the disjunction between rationality and non-rationality is an abstract alternative but not a concrete choice. Rationality," he continues, "is my very dignity, and so closely to it do I cling, that I would want the very best of reasons for abandoning it. Indeed, I am so much one with my reasonableness that, when I lapse from its high standards, I am compelled either to repent my folly or to rationalize it."[164]

Self-affirmation, then, as one concrete form of intellectual conversion, is a judgment of fact. In it the subject affirms that, in fact, he or she does perform certain operations within a definite pattern, and that this pattern of operations is knowing. And because the evidence for this judgment is given and grasped in the immediacy of consciousness, it is, on the most basic level, unrevisable and, indeed, finally inescapable, as we have seen in the contradiction of self-negation. Through the judgment of self-affirmation, then, Lonergan helps the subject to discover and realize the natural spontaneities and inevitabilities that constitute the possibility and nature of knowing, not by demonstrating in some abstract, "objective" way that one can know, but by concretely and pragmatically engaging him or her in the process of knowing. And, concludes Lonergan, in the last resort one cannot "reach a deeper foundation than that pragmatic engagement. Even to seek it involves one in a vicious circle; for if one seeks such a foundation, one employs one's cognitional process; and the foundation to be reached will be no more secure or solid than the inquiry utilized to reach it."[165]

The central aim of *Insight*, then, is the self-appropriation of the subject as a knower, the study of human understanding (as the subtitle indicates) in the concrete, existential instance of one's own understanding; in short, the intellectual conversion of the subject. And the affirmation of oneself as a knower—one who experiences, understands, and judges—in which such appropriation or conversion concretely occurs (at least for those who follow the *Insight* route), is, as we have noted, a judgment of fact. In fact, the experimenting subject may positively realize, I *do* perform the various operations in the pattern Lonergan specifies. And further reflection on that fact reveals still more, as we have seen, about the nature and very possibility of knowing.

One of the first and most important questions that arises from a reflection on the meaning of fact has to do with the issue of objectivity, an issue from which Lonergan deliberately and explicitly prescinds in his analysis of cognitional process. For Lonergan, as we noted above, carefully differentiates between cognitional theory and epistemology, between, in other words, the questions "What am I doing when I am knowing?" and "Why is doing that knowing?" While the first question excludes the issue of objectivity, once answered, it provides a context in which through the second question one can come to grips with the epistemological issue of objectivity in a direct and adequate way.

Thus, while forcing the question of objectivity upon us, self-affirmation as a judgment of fact at the same time supplies the proper framework in which to meet it. To this question, then, we must now turn, not only because of the immediate demand of the nature of fact, but because it is fundamental to any attempt to develop an understanding of conscience rooted in self-transcending subjectivity. For subjectivity transcends itself only insofar as it is objective, or, to put it the other way, as I have already claimed, subjectivity is objective only inasmuch as it transcends itself. Thus it is imperative that I clarify exactly what is meant by objectivity in the claim of this thesis, and that I explain how, according to Lonergan, authentic (i.e., self-transcending) subjectivity can be identified with objectivity.

3. Objectivity

Objectivity is a common enough, if controversial, notion. It occurs not only in philosophical treatises, but in discussions on an extremely broad spectrum of topics ranging from scientific method to the reporting of news events on television. Thus the meaning of the word is not univocal, despite Webster's rather deceptively simple definition of it as "the state or quality of being objective." The multiplicity of meanings appears as soon as we turn to "objective," however. Here we find, for example: "without bias or prejudice; detached; impersonal," which seems to be what discussions regarding journalism are about. And this meaning seems to follow from "objective" in the sense of "determined by and emphasizing the features and characteristics of the object, or thing dealt with, rather than the thoughts, feelings, etc., of the artist, writer, or speaker: as an *objective* description, painting, etc.," which seems to be at least one of the senses of objectivity involved in critical discussions about scientific method. And little reflection is required, I think, to realize that this meaning presupposes the meaning of "objective" as "of or having to do with a known or perceived object as distinguished from something existing only in the mind of the subject, or person thinking," hence, "being, or regarded as being, independent of the mind; real; actual."[166] This last definition seems to be the basic meaning philosophers usually have in mind when they discuss the problem of "objectivity."

If there are different meanings of objectivity, however, it also seems true that these meanings interconnect, overlap, and share a common denominator. Indeed, our discussion of objectivity in Piaget's theory of cognitional development involved each of the above meanings to some degree, usually a combination of the first and second as a result of a process of development in which objectivity in the third, or basic, sense gradually emerges through ever greater differentiation and inte‑ gration of operations.

The common denominator among these various meanings of objec‑ tivity, I suggest, is correct judgment or, simply, truth. Clearly, objec‑ tivity as a journalistic ideal is an attempt to eradicate bias, prejudice, etc., for the sake of reporting events—as far as humanly possible—as they happened, in as full and balanced a context as the best available understanding allows; for the sake, in other words, of reporting the truth. For the scientist, too, the ideal of objectivity rests in a complete understanding of the universe as it is, and this notwithstanding the truncated philosophies of science which, as Michael Polanyi has ar‑ gued, mistakenly try to exclude the role of the scientist, pretending an account of a science without the understanding of a scientist, an account that would give a picture of the universe as understood, really, by nobody.[167] But there are scientists, and they are interested in understanding the facts, in truth.

Finally, there is the "objectivity" that philosophers discuss. And at first glance this meaning of objectivity would not seem to be con‑ nected necessarily with truth or correct judgment, for it would seem that a reality independent of the mind exists—by definition—without dependence on true judgments and in spite of false judgments. But objectivity is a concern only to subjects, and, as such, arises as a question only to subjects who know themselves to be subjects distinct from known objects. Objectivity, in other words, is a function of judgment, a point we shall consider in the course of our examination of Lonergan's understanding of objectivity, to which we must now turn our attention.

We may begin our consideration of Lonergan's notion of objectivity most effectively, perhaps, by recalling his distinction between the world of immediacy and the world mediated by meaning. For to each of these worlds, according to Lonergan, there belongs a quite distinct meaning of the term "object," and thus, as we shall soon see, of the word "objectivity." As we have noted, the world of immediacy is "a world quite apart from questions and answers, a world in which we lived before we spoke and while we were learning to speak, a world into which we try to withdraw when we would forget the world mediated by meaning, when we relax, play, rest."[168] In this world without questions and answers, of course, the object of immediate experience is neither understood, nor described, nor even named. But the object of this world can be reflected upon in the world mediated by meaning, and from this standpoint we can understand that the object of immediate experience is related not to intelligent procedure, but to "merely biological and nonintelligent response...."[169] It is an "already, out, there, now, real," Lonergan says:

> It is *already:* it is given prior to any questions about it. It is *out:* for it is the object of extraverted consciousness. It is *there:* as sense organs, so too sensed objects are spatial. It is *now:* for the time of sensing runs along with the time of what is sensed. It is *real:* for it is bound up with one's living and acting and so must be just as real as they are.[170]

But in addition to this "already, out, there, now, real" object of biologically extraverted consciousness, there is also the object in the world mediated by meaning, the object not simply of immediate experience that is common to both animals and humans, but of fully human knowing. It is, as Lonergan says, "what is intended by the question, and it is what becomes understood, affirmed, decided by the answer. To this type of object we are related immediately by our questions and only mediately by the operations relevant to answers, for the answers refer to objects only because they are answers to questions."[171]

There are, then, two basically different meanings of "object"; and correlative to them are two distinct meanings of "objectivity." For, as Lonergan puts it, "in the world of immediacy the necessary and sufficient condition of objectivity is to be a successfully functioning animal."[172] And this, indeed, is a real objectivity, but it is not the objectivity of fully human knowing. It is, however, a particularly alluring form of objectivity, for, as Lonergan says, humans, "besides being intelligent and reasonable, also are animals. To them as animals, a verified hypothesis is just a jumble of words or symbols. What they want is an elementary knowing of the 'really real,' if not through sense, at least by imagination." And it is from this confusion between the objectivity of immediate experience and the objectivity of intelligence and reasonableness that the most basic epistemological difficulties arise. For, as Lonergan reveals to us, "animals have no epistemological problems." And, he claims, "neither do scientists as long as they stick to their task of observing, forming hypotheses, and verifying. The perennial source of nonsense," he says, is that even scientists, after verifying their hypotheses, are "likely to go a little further and tell the layman what, approximately, scientific reality looks like!"[173]

Thus, as there are two types of knowing, an elementary type constituted completely on the level of experience in which questions play no part, and a fully human type of intelligent and reasonable knowing in which experience functions merely as the supplier of data for the questions which essentially constitute it, so also there are two corresponding and fundamental meanings of "object," the "already, out, there, now, real" body of immediate, biologically oriented experience on the one hand, and on the other the object that is intended by questions, understood by intelligence, and affirmed by judgment. And, further, there are also two basic meanings of objectivity, and these, like the types of knowing and object, are opposed, for one is rooted in intelligent and reasonable questions and answers, and the other is not. Again, like the two types of knowing and object, the two basic and opposed meanings of objectivity are "linked together in man who, at once, is an animal, intelligent, and reasonable. Unless they are distinguished sharply by a critical theory of knowledge," says Lonergan, "they become confused to generate aberrations that affect not only scientific thought but far more conspicuously the thought of philosophers."[174]

Inasmuch as the two types of knowing, objects, and objectivity are valid in themselves, the epistemological problem is not one of elimination but of critical distinction. For, as Lonergan puts it, the difficulty lies not in either type of knowing, object, or objectivity by itself, "but in the confusion that arises when one shifts unconsciously from one type to the other."[175] Therefore, having specified the objectivity that is proper to the world of immediacy, and having explicitly distinguished it from the fully human knowing that in response to the dynamism of questioning is intelligent and reasonable as well as experiential, I will now explain the nature of the latter, properly human objectivity in greater depth and detail. My treatment, however, must be only a summary statement of conclusions derived from Lonergan's position on objectivity inasmuch as that position is itself rooted in a cognitional theory essentially dependent on self-appropriation or intellectual conversion for its justification. I can, in other words, explain the conceptual elements of Lonergan's position on objectivity, as I have done in the case of his cognitional theory, but the persuasive force and justification for such a position lies only in the personal experiment of self-appropriation which each person must perform for her or himself. This disclaimer, I must emphasize, derives not from a limitation of my own explanatory powers (however limited they may be), but from the philosophical necessity of personal, existential appropriation that lies at the very heart of Lonergan's method. Such a disclaimer is not an appeal to the mystical, visionary gnosis of an elite group of *illuminati,* but a simple recognition of the unhappy fact that philosophical understanding is not part of our birthright but the fruit of a long and arduous struggle. Its requirement of exact scholarship, rigorous analysis, and relentless personal reflection is no more unreasonable than the sciences' prerequisite of mathematical facility.

The possibility of human knowing, as we have noted, lies in an "unrestricted intention that intends the transcendent, and a process of self-transcendence that reaches it." And it is this intentionality, according to Lonergan, that constitutes the "intrinsic objectivity of human cognitional activity."[176] The dynamic structure of human knowing, says Lonergan, pressed on by the ceaseless questions of inquiring intelligence and critical reflection, intends being.[177] Now this intention is unrestricted, for, as Lonergan points out, "there is nothing that we cannot at least question." Furthermore, for Lonergan, this

> intention is comprehensive, for questioning probes every aspect of everything; its ultimate goal is the universe in its full concreteness. Being in that sense is identical with reality: as apart from being there is nothing, so apart from reality there is nothing; as being embraces the concrete totality of everything, so too does reality.[178]

Primarily, the "intrinsic relation of the dynamic structure of human knowing to being and so to reality," is, according to Lonergan, "the originating drive of human knowing" (not *"pensée pensée* but *pensée pensante,* not *intentio intenta* but *intentio intendens,* not *noêma* but *noêsis"*). But, as answers stand to questions, says Lonergan, so cognitional activities stand to this originating drive of knowing, to the intention of being, of reality. But, further, Lonergan points out that "an answer is *to* a question, because it and the question have the same object." Thus, he says, the intrinsic relation of the dynamic structure of knowing to reality "passes from the side of the subject to the side of the object," the *"intentio intendens* of being becomes the *intentio intenta* of this or that being." In summary, then, according to Lonergan,

> the *intentio intendens* of the subject summons forth and unites cognitional activities to objectify itself in an *intentio intenta* that unites and is determined by the partial objects of the partial activities. As the *intentio intendens* of the dynamic structure, so the corresponding *intentio intenta* of the structured cognitional activities is intrinsically related to being and reality.[179]

It remains that the two relations are not identical. The *intentio intendens* is not knowing but merely intending: it is objectivity in potency. But the *intentio intenta* resides not in mere intending but in structured activities of knowing: it is objectivity in act.[180]

But we must note that this "objectivity in act," constituted, according to Lonergan's cognitional analysis, not by a single operation but by a structured manifold of operations, is, in this perspective, "not some single property of human knowing but a compound of quite different properties." Lonergan reminds us that "empiricists have tried to find the ground of objectivity in experience, rationalists have tried to place it in necessity, idealists have had recourse to coherence." In Lonergan's mind, these views are correct in what they affirm, but mistaken in what they exclude. For as human knowing is a structured manifold of operations, its objectivity is a triple cord: first, there is an "experiential component that resides in the givenness of relevant data"; secondly, there is a "normative component that resides in the exigences of intelligence and rationality guiding the process of human knowing from data to judging"; thirdly and finally, there is an "absolute component that is reached when reflective understanding combines the normative and the experiential elements into a virtually unconditioned, i.e., a conditioned whose conditions are fulfilled."[181]

I think this summary, however brief, should give some indication of how Lonergan's understanding of objectivity is intimately related to and dependent upon his analysis of the dynamic structure of cognitional operations. For, as we have seen, the objectivity of human knowing, in Lonergan's position, rests upon both an unrestricted intention which directs the process to reality and an unconditioned result which grasps it. Without the preciseness of a personally appropriated cognitional theory that grasps the dynamism of knowing, one very easily can not only lose the "needle" that intends reality in the haystack of static concepts, ideas, and even affirmations of being, but also, on the object side, overlook the fact that the objectivity of human knowing consists of three distinct components, the third of which results from a reflective understanding of the other two. With a grasp of the dynamic structure of knowing, however, one can appreciate with Lonergan that

the empiricists are right in their insistence on data, for in the givenness of data resides the experiential component of objectivity; [that] there is something to the idealist insistence on coherence, for in the directive exigences of intelligence and rationality there resides the normative component of objectivity; and [that] there is something to the rationalist insistence on necessity, for a conditioned whose conditions are fulfilled is virtually an

unconditioned, and reflective understanding grasps such a virtually unconditioned whenever it finds the fulfillment of conditions in the data of sense
or consciousness and, at the same time, derives from normative objectivity
the link that binds conditions with conditioned.[182]

By now I hope it is clear that for Lonergan the epistemological
problem of objectivity, though complex, consists essentially of making
explicit and clarifying the objectivity that is intrinsic to human knowing, not in solving the misleading puzzle of how one "bridges the gap"
between the knowing subject and the known object.

For, as Lonergan explains it, "principally the notion of objectivity is
contained within a patterned context of judgments which serve as
implicit definitions of the terms, object, subject." For example, one
may define a subject as an object who affirms her or himself as a
knower. Further, to the judgment, "I am a knower," may be added
"This is a typewriter," and, yet further, "I am not this typewriter."
Further objects may be added through additional positive and negative
judgments. Finally, says Lonergan, "insofar as one can intelligently
grasp and reasonably affirm the existence of other knowers besides
oneself, one can add to the list objects that are also subjects."[183]

Now, for Lonergan, the principal notion of objectivity emerges only
from the context of such a definite pattern of judgments (not from any
single judgment or any part of a single judgment), and, as he says, the
validity of this notion of objectivity is "the same as the validity of the
set of judgments that contain it; if the judgments are correct, then it is
correct that there are objects and subjects in the defined sense, for the
sense defined is simply the correctness of the appropriate pattern of
judgments." Most simply, then, "there is objectivity if there are distinct beings, some of which know themselves and know others as
others." For, as being (reality) is divided from within, there being
nothing apart from being (reality), it follows, argues Lonergan,

> that there cannot be a subject that stands outside being and looks at it; the
> subject has to be before he can look; and, once he is, then he is not outside
> being but either the whole of it or some part. If he is the whole of it, then
> he is the sole object. If he is only a part, then he has to begin by knowing a
> multiplicity of parts (A is; B is; A is not B) and add that one part knows
> others ("I" am A).[184]

Such an analysis, I suggest, solves the impossible, because illusory,
epistemological problem of transcendence by identifying and eliminat-
ing the misleading question of how a subject gets beyond her or himself to a known object. While this deceptive question "supposes the

knower to know himself and asks how he can know anything else," Lonergan contends that though "the knower may experience himself or think about himself without judging, still he cannot know himself until he makes the correct affirmation, I am." Further, he contends that "other judgments are equally possible and reasonable, so that through experience, inquiry, and reflection there arises knowledge of other objects both as beings and as being other than the knower." Therefore, Lonergan places "transcendence, not in going beyond a known knower, but in heading for being within which there are positive differences, and among such differences, the difference between object and subject." And inasmuch as such judgments occur, he maintains, "there are in fact objectivity and transcendence."[185]

Such, then, are the main elements of Lonergan's position on objectivity. It is the objectivity of the world mediated by meaning, a world that includes the world of immediacy, but through inquiry, understanding, and judgment also goes beyond it. Commonly, though, by "objectivity" is meant the spontaneous, instinctive objectivity of the world of immediacy. For the meaning of objectivity proper to the world mediated by meaning is reached only through a long and rigorous process of reflective inquiry pursued within a detached, disinterested intellectual pattern of experience which few are prepared to undertake. And if that meaning is difficult to reach, it is also difficult to maintain, for no one lives exclusively within the intellectual pattern. Lonergan has formulated the basic, underlying problem of philosophical inquiry in terms of this situation in the following key passage:

> Against the objectivity that is based on intelligent inquiry and critical reflection, there stands the unquestioning orientation of extroverted biological consciousness and its uncritical survival not only in dramatic and practical living but also in much of philosophic thought. Against the concrete universe of being, of all that can be intelligently grasped and reasonably affirmed, there stands in a prior completeness the world of sense, in which the "real" and the "apparent" are subdivisions within a vitally anticipated "already out there now." Against the self-affirmation of a consciousness that at once is empirical, intellectual, and rational, there stands the native bewilderment of the existential subject, revolted by mere animality, unsure of his way through the maze of philosophies, trying to live without a known purpose, suffering despite an unmotivated will, threatened with inevitable death and, before death, with disease and even insanity.
>
> The peculiarity of these antitheses is not to be overlooked. They are not mere conflicting propositions. They are not pure logical alternatives, of which one is simply true and the other is utterly false. But in each case both the thesis and the antithesis have their ground in the concrete unity-

in-tension that is man. For human consciousness is polymorphic. The pattern in which it flows may be biological, aesthetic, artistic, dramatic, practical, intellectual, or mystical. These patterns alternate; they blend or mix; they can interfere, conflict, lose their way, break down. The intellectual pattern of experience is supposed and expressed by our account of self-affirmation, of being, of objectivity. But no man is born in that pattern; no one reaches it easily; no one remains in it permanently; and when some other pattern is dominant, then the self of our self-affirmation seems quite different from one's actual self, the universe of being seems as unreal as Plato's noetic heaven, and objectivity spontaneously becomes a matter of meeting persons and dealing with things that are "really out there."[186]

Since philosophers, too, are human, it should not be surprising that "objectivity" has had a turbulent history. Though the naive realist, like everyone else, knows the world mediated by meaning, he or she is persuaded, and would persuade us, that it is known merely by "taking a good look at what is going on out there now," in one's immediate experience. A more rigorous and thoroughgoing empiricist, like Hume, regarding understanding and judging as merely subjective activities, restricts objective knowledge to sense experience, and "eliminates from the world mediated by meaning everything that is not given in the world of immediacy." The critical idealist, like Kant, correctly refutes the claim that the whole objectivity of human knowing is located in its experiential component. But while "the idealist insists that human knowing always includes understanding as well as sense," still "he retains the empiricist's notion of reality, and so he thinks of the world mediated by meaning as not real but ideal." For the critical idealist claims to know not reality but only appearances; only the limiting concept brings one to talk about the unknowable reality of things themselves. From here it is only a short step to the absolute idealism of a Hegel and, finally, to the natural reaction which it invited, in Kierkegaard, who found no room in the system for the self-determining freedom that is existence, but only for the idea of existence.[187]

According to Lonergan, "Kierkegaard marks a trend. Where he was concerned with faith, Nietzsche was with power, Dilthey with concrete human living, Husserl with the constitution of our intending, Bergson with his *élan vital*, Blondel with action, . . . European existentialists with authentic subjectivity." Thus, from something like a forgetfulness of being on the part of naive realists, empiricists, and idealists alike, there has come about a semantic reversal, "not so much a clarification as a shift in the meaning of the terms, objective and subjective."[188]

Whereas subjectivity was once an entirely perjorative term, denoting a "violation of the normative exigences of intelligence and rationality," says Lonergan, it has come, as a result of the trend noted above, to denote a rejection of the misconceived objectivity of the positivists and behaviorists who would restrict objective (valid) knowledge to those areas in which investigators commonly agree, principally mathematics and the sciences. The lack of common agreement in other areas, such as philosophy, ethics, and religion, says Lonergan, is usually "explained by the subjectivity of philosophers, moralists, religious people," as if, according to Polanyi's complaint, they alone, and not mathematicians and scientists, exercised subjectivity. "But whether subjectivity is always mistaken, wrong, evil," says Lonergan, "is a further question." While positivists and behaviorists would tend to say that it is, Lonergan points out that others "would insist on distinguishing between an authentic and an unauthentic subjectivity." According to this view, "what results from the former is neither mistaken nor wrong nor evil. It just is something quite different from the objective knowledge attainable in mathematics and in science."[189] In other words, even the promoters of subjectivity surrender to the empiricist definition of objective knowledge and satisfy themselves by claiming that subjectivity is something quite different from objectivity, and are content that the twain shall never meet. And, except for the occasional and only mildly embarrassing thrust of a Polanyi who reminds us that scientists, too, like philosophers, have minds and use them, so the story about objectivity and subjectivity goes. Those who despise subjectivity do so in the name of a misconceived objectivity, while supporters of subjectivity content themselves with the exegesis of its many facets, conceding the field of "objective" knowledge to the occupiers.

It is in such a context, Lonergan points out, that a philosopher like Karl Jaspers, who combines existential concerns with an idealist inheritance, would contend that a clarification of the reality of one's own subjectivity (such as self-appropriation), however authentic, is not objective knowledge. For Lonergan, however, while "self-appropriation occurs through a heightening of consciousness" that "reveals not the subject as object but the subject as subject," it is nevertheless true that "this heightening of consciousness proceeds to an objectification of the subject, to an intelligent and reasonable affirmation of the subject, and so to a transition from the subject as

subject to the subject as object. Such a transition," Lonergan contends, "yields objective knowledge of the subject just as much as does
any valid transition from the data of sense through inquiry and understanding, reflection, and judgment." Without such an appropriation
of self the ambiguities underlying such counterpositions as naive
realism, empiricism and idealism not only survive but flourish. But
"once an adequate self-appropriation is effected," and those ambiguities are removed, one can develop an entirely different context of
critical realism by distinguishing, as we have seen, between "object
and objectivity in the world of immediacy and, on the other hand,
object and objectivity in the world mediated by meaning and
motivated by value . . . ."[190] For once it is recognized that the world
mediated by meaning and motivated by value is the real world, it
becomes apparent that, as Lonergan puts it, "*objectivity is simply the
consequence of authentic subjectivity,* of genuine attention, genuine intelligence, genuine reasonableness, genuine responsibility."[191]

These are the key features of the normative structure of our conscious intentionality. In claiming the structure to be normative, of
course, Lonergan does not mean that it cannot be violated. For our
conscious and intentional acts may be "directed, not to the truth that
is affirmed because a virtually unconditioned has been grasped, but to
any of the misconceptions of truth that have been systematized in
sundry philosophies . . . ." Or, as he further points out, "they may be
directed, not to increasing human understanding, but to satisfying the
'objective' or the 'scientific' or the 'meaningful' norms set up by some
logic or method that finds it convenient to leave human understanding out of the picture."[192]

Thus, for example, as Lonergan points out, if one holds logical
proof as basic, one is looking for an objectivity that is independent of
the concrete existing subject. But, as he explains, "the fact of the
matter is that proof becomes rigorous only within a systematically
formulated horizon, that the formulation of horizons varies with the
presence and absence of intellectual, moral, religious conversion, and
that conversion is never the logical consequence of one's previous
position but, on the contrary, a radical revision of that position."
Thus, it is essential to recognize the fundamental point that "while
objectivity reaches what is independent of the concrete existing subject, objectivity itself is not reached by what is independent of the
concrete existing subject." On the contrary, as Lonergan emphasizes,
"objectivity is reached through the self-transcendence of the concrete
existing subject, and the fundamental forms of self-transcendence are
intellectual, moral, and religious conversion." And to attempt to

guarantee objectivity apart from self-transcendence by some "objective" criterion or test or control only generates illusions, for that meaning of "objective" is itself mere delusion.[193]

To repeat, for Lonergan's critical realism of self-appropriation, "genuine objectivity is the fruit of authentic subjectivity," and "it is to be attained only by attaining authentic subjectivity." And apart from such authenticity of the concrete subject, the use of any "alternative prop or crutch invariably leads to some measure of reductionism," says Lonergan, for "as Hans-Georg Gadamer has contended at length in his *Wahrheit und Methode,* there are no satisfactory methodical criteria that prescind from the criteria of truth." In the last analysis, then, while "mathematics, science, philosophy, ethics, theology differ in many manners," one of Lonergan's fundamental points is to insist that "they have the common feature that their objectivity is the fruit of attentiveness, intelligence, reasonableness, and responsibility."[194]

I have dwelt at some length on this point because it is essential to the book's thesis to clarify as fully and precisely as possible the various and conflicting meanings of subjectivity and objectivity, to uncover the epistemological source of the confusing conflict, and to indicate how valid meanings of both, grounded in cognitional analysis, rather than undercut, condemn, or merely ignore each other, indeed require each other's intimate complementarity. They are, to be sure, only two aspects of the one authentic human reality. But that reality is more than knowing, for, as Lonergan says, authentic human existence is also, and especially, the original creation and perpetual novelty of the concrete subject's self-constitution, of the free choices by which she makes herself what she is. While it is "quite true that objective knowing is not yet authentic human living," it is also true that "without objective knowing there is no authentic living." For "authentic living includes objective knowing;"[195] its responsible decisions have no other ground than the objective judgments of the intelligently inquiring and critically reflecting subject.

Thus any ethical theory that aims at adequacy must confront the epistemological question of objectivity head-on; and having done so, it must consider the implications of that objectivity for responsible decision and action. So, we must turn now to a consideration of the fundamental question of how the affirmation of one's self not only as a knower, but also as a responsible decision maker and chooser expands on the fourth level of consciousness into the issue of choosing, appropriating, taking possession of oneself precisely as a free, responsible subject: the question, quite simply, of moral conversion.

Before shifting our attention from the issue of objectivity to the question of moral conversion, however, we might briefly consider again the objectivity of value judgments. We have already noted that for Lonergan the criterion of objective value judgments lies in authentic subjectivity, but there is also inauthentic subjectivity, which is opposed to objectivity. Thus, Lonergan says that

> there are true and there are false value-judgments. The former are objective in the sense that they result from a moral self-transcendence. The latter are subjective in the sense that they represent a failure to effect moral self-transcendence. False value-judgments are an intrusion of [inauthentic] subjectivity. True value-judgments are the achievement of a moral objectivity, of an objectivity that, so far from being opposed to the objectivity of true judgments of fact, presupposes them and completes them by adding to mere cognitional self-transcendence a moral self-transcendence.[196]

4. Moral Conversion

We have seen that the affirmation of oneself as an empirically, intelligently, and rationally conscious subject is a special and crucial instance of cognitional self-transcendence, a precise formulation of intellectual conversion in which the criterion of the real is recognized in the virtually unconditioned judgment. In the same way, the further affirmation and appropriation of oneself as not only an empirically, intelligently, and rationally but also morally (or rationally self-) conscious subject is the central and strategic instance of moral self-transcendence, the recognition and choice of oneself as a free and responsible originator of value. Such is the substance, the issue at stake in moral conversion. While the precise meaning of "self-appropriation" is not always clear with Lonergan, it does seem certain that even in *Insight*, where his principal concern is intellectual conversion, the "self-appropriation" to which Lonergan invites his readers is the appropriation of one's rational self-consciousness; the crucial, experimental issue, he says there, consists "in one's own rational self-consciousness clearly and distinctly taking possession of itself as rational self-consciousness." Now, as Lonergan makes clear in chapter eighteen of *Insight*, "rational self-consciousness" is the consciousness of a subject on the level of deliberating and deciding. The subject on this level is also referred to as being "morally self-conscious." And even while the larger context of the above quote from *Insight's* introduction seems to be that of intellectual conversion, i.e., the appropriation or taking possession of oneself as an experiencer, understander, and judger, its more immediate context seems to include oneself as a decider, also, for the quote follows directly upon a reference to "the personally appropriated structure of one's own experiencing, one's own intelligent inquiry and insights, one's own critical reflection and judging and deciding."[197] And whereas Lonergan speaks of reduplicating the structure of experiencing, understanding, and judging as "self-knowledge" in *Collection's* "Cognitional Structure,"[198] the "self-appropriation" that constitutes the transcendental method of *Method in Theology* also includes deciding in the structure of operations to be reduplicated.[199] So it seems that while by "self-appropriation" Lonergan sometimes means the possession one takes of oneself in intellectual conversion, "self-appropriation" more consistently and properly means the possession, beyond self-knowledge, that the conscious subject takes of her or himself not only as experiencer, understander, and judger, but also and especially as decider. In this sense "self-appropriation" is equivalent to critical moral conversion, and it is in this sense that I will use it here.

Structurally, if self-knowledge (self-affirmation as knower) is the "conjuction of (1) experiencing experience, understanding, and judging, (2) understanding one's experience of experience, understanding, and judging, and (3) judging one's understanding of experience, understanding, and judging to be correct,"[200] then a methodical approach to self-appropriation may be seen as a "fourfold matter of (1) experiencing one's experiencing, understanding, judging, and deciding, (2) understanding the unity and relations of one's experienced experiencing, understanding, judging, and deciding, (3) affirming the reality of one's experienced and understood experiencing, understanding, judging, deciding, and (4) deciding to operate in accord with the norms immanent in the spontaneous relatedness of one's experienced, understood, affirmed experiencing, understanding, judging, and deciding."[201]

As these two outlines indicate, self-appropriation adds to the affirmation of one's self as a knower both the affirmation and the choice of oneself as a free and responsible decider as well as knower.[202]

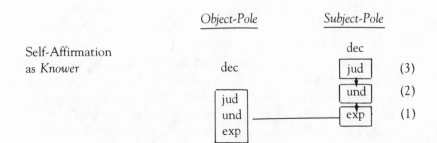

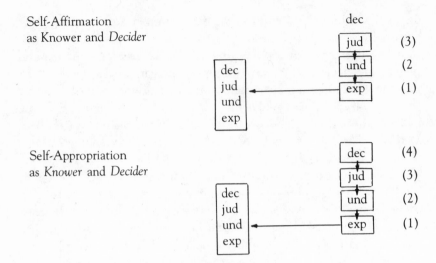

Self-Affirmation
as Knower and *Decider*

Self-Appropriation
as *Knower* and *Decider*

Now the point of this highly formalized elaboration is not to suggest that moral conversion always follows such an explicit form (indeed, we shall want to distinguish between the appropriation of moral conversion simply and its more technically explicit formulation in transcendental method), but merely to indicate the structure (whether it be explicit or merely implicit) of the moral conversion we will be discussing from the standpoint of philosophical analysis. For as moral conversion is an expansion of the appropriation of one's own interiority, one's subjectivity that we analyzed in the affirmation of one's self as a knower, it, like intellectual conversion, resembles theory in its technical expression, though it occurs in the realm of interiority rather than theory.[203]

While the appropriation of one's moral consciousness may be considered as the full goal of the critical exigence that leads initially to the appropriation of one's interiority in the form of intellectual conversion, and as such is included by Lonergan as part of transcendental method, its power, range, and depth are not to be minimized as having to do only with the question of method. For familiarity with transcendental method on a merely conceptual level is not the issue at stake here. At the dynamic heart of transcendental method on every level is a preconceptual performance, a conversion. Just as the intellectual conversion called "self-affirmation as knower," though part of transcendental method, is not something to be just read about in a book, so taking possession of one's moral consciousness, though part of transcendental method, is an existential performance (with a significance outside and beyond the context of transcendental method).

Further, in its full sense, moral conversion is performance not just as discovery, recognition, affirmation of one's moral consciousness in all its implications, but also and especially as the active decision to accept fully the exigence of that moral consciousness, the existential choice of oneself as a free and responsible originator of value in one's judgments, decisions, and choices. Transcendental method in this sense, I repeat, is not attained by simply reading books, listening to lectures, attending courses, following doctoral programs. All these may help, but the full self-appropriation of transcendental method is essentially an entirely personal achievement; each person performs it for her or himself. Further, though part of transcendental method, self-appropriation or moral conversion—like intellectual conversion—must not be thought of as something proper only to philosophy, science, or scholarship; its import and ramifications extend to the whole of concrete living—it is the source, indeed, of authentic subjectivity.

Put most simply, but in a way that gets to the core of the issue, moral conversion, says Lonergan, "changes the criterion of one's decisions and choices from satisfactions to values." We have already considered this differentiation between criteria in our discussion of the transcendental notion of value, value judgments, deliberation, and decision on the fourth level of responsible consciousness. As Lonergan puts it, "by deliberation, evaluation, decision, action, we can know and do, not just what pleases us, but what is truly good, worthwhile."[204] In other words, on the topmost level of consciousness the subject is "at once practical and existential: practical inasmuch as he is concerned with concrete courses of action; existential inasmuch as control includes self-control, and the possibility of self-control involves responsibility for what he makes of himself."[205] As Lonergan points out, however, self-control can be grounded in quite different personal realities. If that ground be mere selfishness, says Lonergan, "then the process of deliberation, evaluation, decision is limited to determining what is most to one's advantage, what best serves one's interests, what on the whole yields a maximum of pleasure and a minimum of pain."[206]

But self-control can, at the opposite pole, also proceed from a concern with value, and in the measure that one's living is a response to value, in that measure one effects a real self-transcendence.[207] In every decision, every action, every achievement that is a response to value and not the mere gratification of personal desire, in other words, one moves beyond, transcends her or himself in a real way. And to the degree that one achieves such self-transcendence, one becomes a source, a principle, as Lonergan puts it, of "benevolence and beneficence, capable of genuine collaboration and of true love." But, as Lonergan is quick to add, it is one thing to transcend oneself in response to value "occasionally, by fits and starts. It is another to do it regularly, easily, spontaneously."[208] For only from a long process of development involving every facet of the conscious human subject does there emerge the *sustained* self-transcendence of the virtuous person. The crucial factor in this long process of "moral" (or personal, human) development, of course, is the transformation of horizon, the shift in criterion of choice that Lonergan names moral conversion.

While Lonergan calls moral conversion (like the other conversions) a "modality of self-transcendence,"[209] it is neither the only nor just any instance of the self-transcendence that is achieved in response to value. Just as any true judgment (and not only the judgment grounding intellectual conversion) achieves cognitive self-transcendence, so every genuine decision and good act in response to value achieves real self-transcendence. Thus one does not need to be morally converted to realize self-transcendence in particular choices any more than one needs to be intellectually converted to attain cognitive self-transcendence in given instances of true judgment. But, also, as intellectual conversion is a special instance of cognitive self-transcendence, so, too, the choice of oneself as a free and responsible originator of value is a special instance of moral or real self-transcendence—special in the sense that it grounds, provides the programmatic base for the development of the sustained moral self-transcendence of human authenticity.

As we have noticed in our discussion of moral development from the psychological perspective of chapter two, mature moral judgments of a principled conscience require such a complex level of cognitive and affective development that even with the minority of people who reach it, the psychological maturity for such a principled conscience emerges only in young adulthood. Inasmuch as Kohlberg restricted himself for the most part to a consideration of moral judgment, it seems clear that at least such a complex development is required for moral conversion. For moral conversion is a matter of not only a judgment of a principled conscience, but also a choice, and that judgment and choice about not just anything, but about and of the self as a free and responsible subject. If moral conversion, then, is the beginning of a deliberate movement toward an ever more complete authenticity, it is also the end of a process of many years of fundamental developments which constitute the very condition for the possibility of a radical moral conversion.

The fact is that a normative personal conscience is in no way given as an accomplished fact. From the very beginning in the early years of childhood, as we have seen, even the most rudimentary moral sense must be developed. Thus, even the emergence (let alone conversion) of what Lonergan calls the fourth level of responsible consciousness, the level of deliberation, evaluation and choice, is a slow process that only begins to occur between the ages of three and six. It is then, says Lonergan, summarizing the development of the period, that "the child gradually enters the world mediated by meaning and regulated by values and, by the age of seven years, is thought to have attained the use of reason."[210]

Such use of reason is, of course, only a bare minimum, as Piaget and Kohlberg have amply indicated, and is, as Lonergan says, only the beginning of human authenticity. It is a seed that must develop over many years with careful nurture. In childhood, as Lonergan says, we must be "persuaded, cajoled, ordered, compelled to do what is right."[211] But as the very being of the subject is becoming, one slowly and painfully becomes oneself. And as each year, month, day passes, the subject has more and more to do with his or her own becoming. The subject also, of course, *wants* more and more to do with his or her becoming. And because, as Lonergan points out, "development is a matter of increasing the number of things that one does for oneself, that one decides for oneself, that one finds out for oneself,"[212] the young subject, resenting adult interference, wants to do, decide, and discover more and more for her or himself, despite the fact that desire for doing and deciding quickly outruns ability for reasonable judgment and thus responsible deciding. This fact seems responsible for a good measure of the tragic quality of human existence, for, as Lonergan puts it in *Insight*, "man develops biologically to develop psychically, and he develops psychically to develop intellectually and rationally. The higher integrations suffer the disadvantage of emerging later. They are the demands of finality upon us before they are realities in us. They are manifested more commonly in aspiration and in dissatisfaction with oneself than in the rounded achievement of complete genuineness, perfect openness, universal willingness." And during the process of self-development "one has to live and make decisions in the light of one's undeveloped intelligence and under the guidance of one's incomplete willingness."[213] Indeed, it is for this reason that "one has to have passed well beyond the turmoil of puberty before becoming fully responsible in the eyes of the law." But, at the same time, "as our knowledge of human reality increases, as our responses to human values are strengthened and refined," parents and teachers and superiors of one kind or another more and more let us do, decide, and

discover things on our own, leaving "us to ourselves so that our freedom may exercise its ever advancing thrust toward authenticity."²¹⁴

And in such a thrust toward authenticity there is the possibility of
moral conversion, of the concrete human subject reaching that critical
point, that existential moment within a long and gradual process of
development and increasing autonomy when she discovers that her
judging and choosing affect herself, the subject, no less than the
objects of her judgments and choices, and that it is up to herself to
decide for herself what she is to make of herself. Such discovery, such
realization of oneself as an originator of value who creates herself in
every deed, decision, and discovery of life, which all accumulate as
dispositions, habits, and character determining what one's very subjectivity is and is to be, demands that the subject through a radical
exercise of her fundamental, vertical freedom take hold of and responsibly choose herself precisely as the originating value she has realized
herself to be (in which case originating and terminal values coincide).²¹⁵ Such a radical appropriation of oneself as a free and responsible creator of value establishes an entirely new horizon defined by the
choice of value as criterion of decision and choice, a criterion, indeed,
of one's living. Even before this conversion, this discovery and choice
of oneself as responsibly free, and the consequent reorientation and
reorganization of one's priorities and values, the self is its own creator;
the essential point to note about moral conversion is that after conversion the self's creation of itself is open-eyed and deliberate. As Lonergan puts it, "autonomy decides what autonomy is to be."²¹⁶

And even if, before the discovery of ourselves as moral persons, we
have made ourselves what we are without any significant awareness of
what we were doing, still, after that discovery, it is to a large extent
possible to recreate ourselves in the light of better knowledge and
fuller responsibility. To refuse the opportunity of such re-creation of
self offers no escape, for it means, ultimately, the assumption of responsibility, whether we want it or not, for whatever we have inadver-
tantly made of ourselves in the past.²¹⁷ The opposite to the open-
eyed, deliberate control of the self-appropriated autonomy emerging
from moral conversion, is, quite simply, drifting. As Lonergan puts it,

> the drifter has not yet found himself; he has not yet discovered his own
> deed and so is content to do what everyone else is doing; he has not yet
> discovered his own will and so he is content to choose what everyone else
> is choosing; he has not yet discovered a mind of his own and so he is
> content to think and say what everyone else is thinking and saying; and
> others too are apt to be drifters, each of them doing and choosing and
> thinking and saying what others happen to be doing, choosing, thinking,
> saying.²¹⁸

The moral conversion we have discussed here must not be confused, of course, with moral perfection, of which it falls far short. To opt for a new horizon, to choose a new criterion of decision is one thing; to live within that horizon fully, to choose consistently according to that new criterion is another. As Lonergan says, "deciding is one thing, doing another."[219] It is, indeed, difficult enough for one to overcome the resistance that one spontaneously throws up against the possibility of conversion, of moving into a radically new horizon. For horizons define not abstractions but the shape of concrete living. And for anyone to experience, anticipate, or even seriously contemplate a change in the style of concrete living that has up until now more or less successfully synthesized and integrated the key elements of one's personality—unconscious as well as conscious, practical as well as interpersonal—is to invite an experience of anxiety or dread. And the spontaneous and resourceful resistance which this dread releases not only attempts to defend the given horizon that is being challenged, but necessarily does so from within it, employing a logic of common sense based on its own meanings and values that is unimpeachable on its own grounds.[220] From the viewpoint of logic, then, conversion to a radically new horizon is a leap, and such a leap is necessarily effected not by logical argument, but by more concrete and symbolic means which do not attack logical defenses but reach immediately to the very core of horizon, tunneling directly to its imaginative and affective ground, the "heart" of the subject.

As difficult as such a leap of conversion may be, however, it is, as I have already suggested, more a beginning than an end. As Lonergan has put it, "in this life the critical point is never transcended." For, again, "it is one thing to decide what one is to make of oneself; . . . it is another to execute the decision. Today's resolutions do not predetermine the free choice of tomorrow, of next week, or next year, or ten years from now. What has been achieved," says Lonergan, "is always precarious: it can slip, fall, shatter. What is to be achieved can be ever expanding, deepening. To meet one challenge is to effect a development that reveals a further and graver challenge."[221]

Moral conversion is not moral perfection. Still, meeting the challenge of moral conversion not only brings the meaning of personal responsibility into sharp focus, but also highlights in an intensely personal fashion the ideal of authentic human living—as well as the distance between it and one's present achievement. Thus moral conversion is not so much an achievement as a call to commitment. For insofar as through conversion one realizes how drastically one's effective freedom is limited,[222] one must commit oneself to the seemingly endless task of conquering the jungle of one's personal prejudices and biases, of developing one's knowledge of concrete human realities and possibilities, of scrutinizing one's intentional responses to values and their implicit scale of preferences, of listening to criticism and protest, and of learning from others. For, as Lonergan says, "moral knowledge is the proper possession only of morally good men and, until one has merited that title, one has still to advance and to learn."[223] And even after "meriting the title," one must continue to advance and learn, of course. As will be evident when we consider the reality of falling-in-love, the affective conversion that transforms a subject into a being-in-love, the commitment to moral perfection that we have discussed here is not a commitment to perfection for its own sake but for the sake of becoming a more authentic source of love dedicated to the ever greater realization of true value, especially the personal values of communal life: mutuality, peace, forgiveness.

Judgments and decisions sometimes occur in a context of growth, a context in which, says Lonergan, "one's knowledge of human living and operating is increasing in extent, precision, refinement, and in which one's responses are advancing from the agreeable to vital values, from vital to social, from social to cultural, from cultural to personal, from personal to religious. Then there prevails an openness to ever further achievement." In this context "one is responding to the transcendental notion of value, by determining what it would be worthwhile for one to make of oneself, and what it would be worthwhile for one to do for one's fellow men. One works out an ideal of human reality and achievement, and to that ideal one dedicates oneself. As one's knowledge increases, as one's experience is enriched, as one's reach is strengthened or weakened, one's ideal may be revised and the revision may recur many times."[224]

But, as Abraham Maslow points out, such continuous growth is rare.[225] Humans, as Lonergan puts it in *Insight*, are plagued by moral impotence, an impotence measured by the gap between our potential freedom and that which we actually possess. Complete self-development, Lonergan points out, is a long and difficult process, and, as we have noted above, "during that process one has to live and make decisions in the light of one's undeveloped intelligence and under the guidance of one's incomplete willingness." Further, Lonergan reminds us, "the less developed one is, the less one appreciates the need of development and the less one is willing to take time out for one's intellectual and moral education."[226] So we have not only the "deviations occasioned by neurotic need," and the "refusals to keep on taking the plunge from settled routines to an as yet unexperienced but richer mode of living"; but also "mistaken endeavors to quieten an uneasy conscience by ignoring, belittling, denying, rejecting higher values," distortion of preference scales, and soured feelings; as well as the invasion of bias into one's outlook, "rationalization into one's morals, ideology into one's thought." And so, rather than responding to, one ignores the motives that lead to ever fuller authenticity, and one drifts into an ever less authentic selfhood. [227]

Now, Lonergan is a theologian, so it is not surprising that for him the rarity of continuous growth, the incapacity of humans for sustained development, raises religious questions. One's judgments of value, decisions, choices, he says, are revealed by moral conversion as "the door to one's fulfillment or to one's loss." And "experience, especially repeated experience, of one's frailty or wickedness raises the question of one's salvation and, on a more fundamental level, there arises the question of God." [228]

5. Religious Conversion and Love

Thus, according to Lonergan's analysis, beyond intellectual and moral conversion there is—also on the fourth level of responsible, existential consciousness—the possibility of religious conversion. Such religious conversion, in response to the transcendent exigence, [229] moves one beyond the realm of interiority (as well as those of theory and common sense) to the realm of transcendence, of the sacred. By following Lonergan's analysis of religious conversion we can round out his discussion of foundational issues, and provide an explicitly theological context for our interpretation of conscience. Also, Lonergan's analysis of religious conversion includes the essential element of affectivity to which we will want to give special attention. Then, I will indicate some qualifications on the way Lonergan relates religious conversion to moral and intellectual conversion.

But, first, what, according to Lonergan's perspective, is religious conversion? Lonergan's answer is given most simply and directly, I think, in the following passage:

> Religious conversion is being grasped by ultimate concern. It is other-worldly falling in love. It is total and permanent self-surrender without conditions, qualifications, reservations. But it is such a surrender, not as an act, but as a dynamic state that is prior to and principle of subsequent acts. It is revealed in retrospect as an undertow of existential consciousness, as a fated acceptance of a vocation to holiness, as perhaps an increasing simplicity and passivity in prayer. It is interpreted differently in the context of different religious traditions. For Christians it is God's love flooding our

hearts through the Holy Spirit given to us. It is the gift of grace, and since
the days of Augustine, a distinction has been drawn between operative and
cooperative grace. Operative grace is the replacement of the heart of stone
by a heart of flesh, a replacement beyond the horizon of the heart of stone.
Cooperative grace is the heart of flesh becoming effective in good works
through human freedom. Operative grace is religious conversion. Cooperative grace is the effectiveness of conversion, the gradual movement toward
a full and complete transformation of the whole of one's living and feeling,
one's thoughts, words, deeds, and omissions.[230]

Like intellectual and moral conversion, religious conversion is a
special modality, a fundamental form, a crucial instance of self-
transcendence. While intellectual conversion is "to truth attained by
cognitional self-transcendence," and moral conversion is "to values
apprehended, affirmed, and realized by real self-transcendence," religious conversion, for Lonergan, is "to a total being-in-love as the
efficacious ground of all self-transcendence, whether in the pursuit of
truth, or in the realization of human values, or in the orientation man
adopts to the universe, its ground, its goal."[231]

Thus, as forms of self-transcendence, intellectual, moral, and religious conversions, when found within one person's consciousness,
may, says Lonergan, be understood to be related, like the various
self-transcending operations of the different levels of consciousness, in
terms of sublation. Following Karl Rahner's understanding of the
term,[232] Lonergan takes sublation to mean that what sublates—in this
case the higher level conversion—"goes beyond what is sublated, introduces something new and distinct, puts everything on a new basis,
yet so far from interfering with the sublated or destroying it, on the
contrary needs it, includes it, preserves all its proper features and
properties, and carries them forward to a fuller realization within a
richer context."[233]

I think it should be clear from what we have seen of Lonergan's own
words that central to his understanding of religious conversion is the
reality of love, a total, other-worldly, love of God "with all one's heart
and all one's soul and all one's mind and all one's strength."[234] This
love of God, of course, is not the only kind of love, and although
other forms may not be total and other-worldly, they do, as Lonergan
recognizes, have structural likenesses and play functionally similar
roles in the human personality. In "Faith and Beliefs," Lonergan
points out in his introductory remarks on religious involvement that
the human "capacity for self-transcendence" becomes "achievement
when one falls in love." When one falls in love, he says, "one's being
becomes being-in-love." Now while it is true that "such being-in-love

has its antecedents, its causes, its conditions, its occasions," still, once it has occurred and as long as it lasts, it takes over as first principle, and "from it flow one's desires and fears, one's joys and sorrows, one's discernment of values, one's decisions and deeds." All this is true generally of being-in-love, and to this point we shall return quite soon. But, says Lonergan, "being-in-love is of different kinds. There is the love of intimacy, of husband and wife, of parents and children. There is the love of one's fellow men with its fruit in the achievement of human welfare. There is the love of God with one's whole heart and whole soul, with all one's mind and all one's strength." And while all love is self-surrender, being-in-love with God is experienced as being-in-love in an "unrestricted" fashion, "without limits or qualifications or conditions or reservations."[235]

Perhaps because of his particular theological perspective, the earlier Lonergan, while recognizing the existence of nonreligious love, almost never considers the reality of love outside of the religious context, and within that context the all but exclusive emphasis is on the love of God. One must go through nearly all of the almost eight-hundred philosophical pages of *Insight,* for example, before finding a few brief references to love, and then, again, these are to the theological virtue of love as part of a solution—along with hope and faith—to the human condition of moral impotence. Of course, as we noticed above in our discussion of feelings, by the time he wrote *Method in Theology,* Lonergan's appreciation of the reality of love in its many dimensions had become more explicit.

My point here is that while theological ethics will certainly include the reality of religious conversion and the love of God, it can also find great wealth in Lonergan's few very brief remarks on being-in-love as the first principle of a person's horizon and the efficacious ground of all self-transcendence. What I am pointing to, then, is the reality of affective self-transcendence, of being-in-love, "as a dynamic state that is prior to and principle of subsequent acts."[236] Such a being-in-love brings about a transformation of one's horizon, one's world, one's very being, and so a transformation of the source of all one's discoveries, decisions, and deeds. Such being-in-love, then, is a real and basic conversion, and its depth and range are not to be predetermined. It can take many forms, from the gift of oneself to one other person to the gift one makes of oneself to all persons in offering one's total being to God. Unlike theological ethics, a philosophical, humanist perspective in ethics may not wish to presuppose God and his love, but if it is to be authentically open it must be ready to recognize that human self-transcending love has no necessary limits. Indeed, insofar as a religious outlook may be specified by its recognition and acceptance of life as a gift, even the most circumscribed human love, if it be genuine self-surrender, can be considered as the beginning of religious conversion.

The basic point I want to make in this section is the necessity of building into one's ethical perspective an appreciation and analysis of the reality of love and its transforming power over all that humans are and do, of providing a place at the center of one's ethical framework for affective self-transcendence, for the conversion to a being-in-love. For if moral conversion is essentially a challenge to an ever fuller, authentic development, affective conversion seems to constitute the concrete conditions for the possibility of successfully responding to that challenge. Indeed, we may say that in a very real sense only an affectively converted consciousness can truly be morally effective. Such an approach to the reality of love, affective self-transcendence, and affective conversion is clearly suggested by the way Lonergan leads up to a discussion of the other-worldly love of God in this passage from *Method in Theology*:

> We noted that the human subject was self-transcendent intellectually by the achievement of knowledge, that he was self-transcendent morally inasmuch as he sought what was worth while, what was truly good, and thereby became a principle of benevolence and beneficence, that he was self-transcendent affectively when he fell in love, when the isolation of the individual was broken and he spontaneously functioned not just for himself but for others as well.[237]

However, whether the far-reaching transformation of affective self-transcendence be considered as religious conversion to a total, other-worldly being-in-love, or, more generally, as conversion to a being-in-love of a more limited kind, there remains the question of relating this conversion to the intellectual and moral conversions, and, indeed, of relating the intellectual and moral conversions to each other. We have seen that Lonergan explains these relationships—like those between different levels of consciousness—in terms of sublation. There is a difference, however. For, he states, "though religious conversion sublates moral, and moral conversion sublates intellectual, one is not to infer that intellectual comes first and then moral and finally religious" (as is true in the case of the sublating levels of consciousness, where the experiential does come before the intelligent, the intelligent before the rational, etc., and this genetically as well as structurally). Rather, Lonergan claims that usually there first is religious conversion, followed by moral, and then, but only rarely, by intellectual conversion. He states his position this way in *Method in Theology:* "from a causal viewpoint, one would say that first there is God's gift of his love. Next, the eye of this love reveals values in their splendor, while the strength of this love brings about their realization, and that is moral conversion. Finally," he says, "among the values discerned by the eye of love is the value of believing the truths taught by the religious tradition, and in such tradition and belief are the seeds of intellectual conversion." This is, at least, the usual order, says Lonergan.[238]

This position, it seems to me, is not without difficulties. First of all, internally, only two pages before stating this order of religious, moral, and then intellectual conversion, Lonergan, relating them in terms of sublation (with the religious sublating the moral, and the moral the intellectual), said, as we noted, that the sublating conversion not only includes, preserves, and carries the sublated conversion forward to a fuller realization within a richer context, but also *needs* the sublated conversion. Clearly, in the case of the successive levels of consciousness, higher levels *need* lower levels because each level functions only in relation to lower, sublated levels (one can understand only what one has experienced, etc.). So it is not easy to understand how Lonergan can assert an order of occurrence which has religious conversion preceding moral, and moral preceding intellectual, while at the same time claiming that as sublating, religious conversion *needs* the sublated moral and intellectual conversions, and as sublating, moral conversion *needs* the sublated intellectual conversion. (Based on Lonergan's own explication of sublation, this difficulty does not seem to be explained away by his claim that, contrary to the dictum, *nihil amatum nisi praecognitum,* "in religious matters love precedes knowledge.")[239]

Further, in asserting the usual order of occurrence as religious, moral, and then intellectual, Lonergan begins by stating that "from a causal viewpoint, one would say that first there is God's gift of his love."[240] This may be true, but by Lonergan's own definition religious *conversion* seems primarily to be a loving, total self-surrender—in other words, a full *response* to "God's gift of his love." And if, as Lonergan would surely maintain, God offers his loving grace to all persons, then it seems clear that some refuse to fully accept it. The difference between fully accepting and refusing or only partially responding to God's gift of his love, then, seems, on this definition, to distinguish the religiously converted person from others.[241]

Of course, in Lonergan's theological perspective, God's grace plays a key role in moral and intellectual conversion, too. But the love whose "eye" "reveals values in their splendor," and whose strength "brings about their realization," moral conversion, would appear to be the love that responds to God's gift of his love in religious conversion, not the gift itself. Indeed, Lonergan later does speak of "religious conversion as the *fruit* of God's gift of his grace."[242] Moreover, in order for God's gracious love to be involved in intellectual as well as in moral conversion, it does not seem necessary that they follow upon a *total* response to this love, religious conversion. In fact, Lonergan has drawn religious conversion in such full and deep colors that it does not seem to be a common occurrence at all; it seems, indeed, worlds apart from the orientation of very many people who, in some genuine sense of the word, can accurately be described as "religious."

We have been considering religious conversion from two angles, that of cause, and that of effect. From the latter, it seems that, despite the number of religious people, religious conversion in Lonergan's sense is somewhat rare.[243] (I do not mean to imply, of course, that religiously unconverted people in this sense are in no way religious, any more than intellectually and morally unconverted people are in no way reasonable knowers and responsible choosers.) From the viewpoint of cause, then, it may well be that while God's gift of his love is first, a person's total loving response to that gift in religious conversion may be last, following intellectual and moral conversions.

However, it is still true that intellectual conversion is for Lonergan a rare phenomenon;[244] thus to say that religious conversion "needs" intellectual as well as moral conversion would make the religiously converted an elite group indeed. The same problem holds, of course, for the relationship between moral and intellectual conversion; does moral conversion "need" intellectual conversion, or does intellectual conversion normally follow upon moral conversion as its fruit?[245] Moral conversion, like religious, is not, of course, something that one simply falls into, but should we say that it is restricted to the elite of the intellectually converted?

While the solution I will now propose pertains to all three conversions, the religious as well as the moral and intellectual, I will emphasize the relationship between the intellectual and the moral conversions, inasmuch as the nature of the moral conversion is our primary interest. My proposed solution involves, on the one hand, a distinction between a *critical* moral (or religious) conversion and an *uncritical* moral (or religious) conversion, and, on the other, a distinction between a fully *explicit*, philosophical intellectual conversion and a more *implicit* but nonetheless real intellectual conversion.

Most simply, as we have seen, moral conversion is that shift in "criterion of one's decisions and choices from satisfactions to values."[246] But this shift in criterion can be made critically or uncritically; that is, one can *critically* recognize and accept the responsibility of critically discovering and establishing one's own values (in dialogue with one's community), or one may merely turn *uncritically* toward and accept a *given* set of values, be they given by parents, school, church, peers, "society," or whomever. Moral conversion in this second, uncritical sense is a real enough conversion (from satisfaction to values), but it presupposes no intellectual conversion, and could follow very easily, or so it seems, from religious motivation. The second or conventional level of Kohlberg's schema seems to illustrate this kind of uncritical concern for value quite well. Moral consciousness that is converted in this uncritical way sublates the empirical, intelligent, and rational levels of consciousness, but these levels as intellectually unconverted. In general, it seems more accurate to speak of one level (converted or unconverted) sublating another or others (converted or not) than of one "conversion" sublating another "conversion."

If the shift in criterion, however, is rooted in the existential moment when we discover for ourselves "that it is up to each of us to decide for himself what he is to make of himself,"[247] a truly critical moral conversion is involved, for the existential discovery that it is up to each of us to decide for ourselves what we are to make of ourselves presupposes at least what I would call an *implicit* intellectual conversion, that is, a subject's tacit but nonetheless real recognition and choice of him or herself as the criterion of the real and the truly good in his or her own self-transcending judgments and choices of value. I say "at least implicit" because, while a fully critical moral conversion can follow upon a fully articulated philosophical version of intellectual conversion, such an explicit conversion is not necessary, as the implicit or tacit intellectual realization spelled out above is in itself a sufficient (as well as necessary) condition for a critical moral conversion. And given the rarity of philosophically articulated intellectual conversion, this implicit intellectual conversion (which, though hardly a common phenomenon, is less rare, I think, than Lonergan's strictly philosophical conversion) would seem to be the usual basis for a critically grounded moral conversion.

This differentiation between critical and uncritical moral conversion is based on Lonergan's own analysis of the basic structure of conscious operations. For, basically, moral conversion is a decision or choice on the fourth level of consciousness, a choice of value over satisfaction as criterion for decisions, and a choice of oneself as responsible. And this choice, like any other, is just as good—no more, no less—as the understanding and judgment from which it proceeds and on which it depends. We have already noted above that the fourth level of consciousness itself involves two moments, two different kinds of responses: judgments of value, and decisions or choices. While it may not always be easy to distinguish judgments of value from judgments of fact, one can distinguish decisions or choices from judgments, and one's decisions will be critical insofar as they proceed from realistic judgment, authentic insofar as they conform to objective judgment. Thus a moral conversion proceeding from an intelligent grasp and reasonable affirmation of one's own interiority is a truly critical self-appropriation.

Moral conversion as a mere shift in criterion for decision from satisfaction to value, on the other hand, lacks fundamental self-knowledge, and, while adequate perhaps for getting along in untroubled times, is vulnerable to exploitation from every side, and, because its values are held uncritically, is like a ship without a captain during stormy times. The fact of the matter is that in our complex world critical self-appropriation is no luxury; it is an essential part of authentic human living. And insofar as religious conversion has a moral dimension, it too, if uncritical, will be defenseless against a world of challengers, not to mention the internal enemy, the human proclivity to mythmaking. But religious conversion, too, besides being uncritical, may follow upon not only a philosophically articulated intellectual conversion and full self-appropriation, but also upon the critical self-appropriation that involves an implicit intellectual conversion.

While intellectual conversion is of great importance for making fundamental clarifications in fields like philosophy of science, philosophy of history, theological method, to name only a few, its really crucial significance is found in the kind of personal, existential self-appropriation that we have been discussing, the appropriation of oneself as a free, responsible, and self-constituting originator of value, who in one's own self-transcending judgments and choices is the criterion of the real and the truly good. And in this area, the basic realization, more than its technical philosophical expression, is of paramount importance, for the breakthrough that dispels the myth of knowing as taking a look and of reality as the already-out-there-now need be only as technical as the myth's own expression. In most people, the myth is spontaneous and without technical articulation, so the conversion that overcomes it need not match the philosophical sophistication of a Hume or a Kant. For such people, an intellectual conversion implicit within a fuller moral conversion would be sufficient.

Indeed, moral conversion is not only a possible, but also a very natural and highly likely context for such an intellectual conversion. For, clearly, nothing is closer, more personal to the subject than his or her own decisions and choices, and thus the reflection, deliberation, and evaluation leading up to them. And if the choice is more important than the restaurant for tonight's dinner, or of more personal concern than the color of a new automobile, the centrality of one's subjectivity can be exposed in a sometimes all too harsh fashion, for one finds it difficult to surround oneself with the defenses of "objective" criteria when one faces personal decisions about the military draft, aborting a fetus, or withholding the means of life from an incurably sick, elderly parent suffering unendurable pain; or when one decides on a spouse, or a career, or must choose between marriage and career. Because one does not want to decide or choose blindly, without reflection, one usually discovers before too long in his or her attempts at intelligent and reasonable reflection that there are neither easy, simple answers to concrete questions of life and death, nor a predetermined, easy-to-follow program for one's life somewhere "out there" to be hit upon if only one looks long and hard enough. This discovery, what Lonergan calls an "inverse insight,"[248] that no pre-packaged life scripts or solutions to human problems exist, and that the pursuit of them leads one into the maze of endless blind alleys of unauthentic decisions, has the singular power of leading one to the positive discovery of oneself, in the authentic, self-transcending insights, judgments, decisions, and choices of one's own subjectivity, as the only truly objective source and criterion of human meaning and value. I must emphasize that this intellectual conversion is implicit *not* in the sense that one accidentally and almost without noticing falls upon it during the course of life, but in the sense that it occurs along with, within, and as part of a moral conversion upon which attention is focused. Insofar as this happens, the focal conversion is not simply a moral shift, but also a critical self-appropriation.

Such an implicit intellectual conversion forms an adequately critical ground for a full moral conversion whose shift in criteria for decisions will be to the appropriation of personally discovered and developed values rather than to an uncritical conformity with a moral code or set of values given by some external authority. But it is not in any strict sense a philosophical conversion, and would have to be developed and expressed in a technical fashion in order to be employed in the work of philosophical analysis. Despite its non-philosophical character, however, I have departed from Lonergan's analysis of conversion in order to develop this notion of implicit intellectual conversion because it seems necessary for the analysis proper to foundational ethics, where conversion plays a dual role. For intellectual conversion is crucial to foundational ethics not only in the strictly philosophical, systematic, and technical sense, inasmuch as those doing foundational ethics must be critically self-appropriated in order to grasp correct basic philosophical positions, break the fundamental myths on knowing, objectivity, and reality, and establish the ethical enterprise on authentic grounds. It is also crucial in the sense of the implicit intellectual conversion within moral (and affective or religious) conversion which I have introduced, inasmuch as personal conversion is a principal object of analysis in foundational ethics, where conscience is a paramount reality. And it is explicitly to conscience, finally, that we must now turn our attention.

Notes

1. Bernard Lonergan, *Insight: A Study of Human Understanding* (2nd ed.; New York: Philosophical Library, 1958).
2. Bernard Lonergan, *Method in Theology* (New York: Herder and Herder, 1972).
3. David Tracy, *The Achievement of Bernard Lonergan* (New York: Herder and Herder, 1970).
4. Lonergan, *Method*, p. 7.
5. See Eric D'Arcy, *Conscience and Its Right to Freedom* (New York: Sheed and Ward, 1961), p. 4.
6. Bernard Lonergan, *Collection*, ed. F. E. Crowe (New York: Herder and Herder, 1967), p. 241.
7. Ibid.
8. Bernard Lonergan, *The Subject* (Milwaukee: Marquette University Press, 1968), pp. 6-8.
9. Ibid., p. 7.
10. Ibid., pp. 7-8.
11. Lonergan, *Method*, pp. 6-7.
12. Ibid., p. 8.
13. Lonergan, *Collection*, p. 226.
14. Ibid.
15. Lonergan, *Method*, p. 8.
16. Ibid.
17. Bernard Lonergan, *De constitutione Christi ontologica et psychologica* (4th ed.; Rome: Pontificia Universitas Gregoriana, 1964).
18. Bernard Lonergan, "Christ as Subject: A Reply," *Gregorianum* 40 (1959): 242-270; reprinted in *Collection* as chap. 11, pp. 164-197. References below are to *Collection*. In this article on "Christ as Subject," it is all too awkwardly clear that Lonergan is addressing a scholastic audience in scholastic terminology. While this article is, in that respect, uncharacteristic of Lonergan's English works, I have referred to it and quoted from it at length because it is the only English source in which

Lonergan offers such a detailed explanation of his understanding of consciousness. So distinctive and important, in my judgment, is this view of consciousness as constitutive but nonreflexive knowing that the price of struggling through the jungle of scholastic Latinisms is fully justified.
19. See Lonergan, *De constitutione Christi*, pp. 130–134.
20. Lonergan, *Collection*, p. 175.
21. Ibid., pp. 175–176.
22. Ibid., p. 176.
23. Ibid.
24. Ibid., my emphasis.
25. Ibid., pp. 175–176.
26. Ibid., p. 177.
27. Ibid., p. 178.
28. Ibid., pp. 177–178.
29. Lonergan, *Insight*, p. 320.
30. Lonergan says: "I conceive method concretely. I conceive it, not in terms of principles and rules, but as a normative pattern of operations with cumulative and progressive results. I distinguish the methods appropriate to particular fields and, on the other hand, their common core and ground, which I name transcendental method. Here, the word, transcendental, is employed in a sense analogous to Scholastic usage, for it is opposed to the categorial (or predicamental). But my actual procedure also is transcendental in the Kantian sense, inasmuch as it brings to light the conditions of the possibility of knowing an object in so far as that knowledge is *a priori*" (*Method*, p. 14).
31. Lonergan, *Insight*, p. 320.
32. Lonergan, *Collection*, pp. 226–227.
33. Lonergan, *Method*, p. 9.
34. Lonergan, *Collection*, p. 227.
35. Lonergan, *Method*, pp. 8–9.
36. Ibid., p. 14.
37. Ibid., pp. 14–15.
38. Ibid., p. 15.
39. Lonergan, *Collection*, p. 225.
40. Lonergan, *Method*, p. 15.
41. Ibid., pp. 15–16.
42. Ibid., pp. 16–17.
43. Lonergan, *Collection*, p. 227.
44. Lonergan, *Method*, p. 18.
45. Ibid., p. 19.
46. Ibid.
47. Ibid., p. 20.
48. Lonergan, *Collection*, p. 241.
49. Lonergan, *Insight*, p. 625.
50. Lonergan, *Collection*, p. 243.
51. Ibid.
52. The exact relationship between "world" and "horizon" in Lonergan's writings is not easy to determine. Both terms are fairly recent. *Insight* used "viewpoints" and "contexts" which seemed to relate to each other as the later "subject-pole" and "object-pole" of horizon as discussed in "Metaphysics as Horizon" (1963). In relation to this version of horizon, the subject's "world" ("*Existenz* and *Aggiornamento*," 1964) appeared to constitute the "object-pole." As spelled out in *Method in Theology* (1972), however, the concept of horizon seems to conform more exactly to its visual analogue, defining the object-pole (still "world") which is structurally related to a subject-pole now called the "standpoint" of the subject. Actually, the

1963 and 1972 versions seem fundamentally the same insofar as both are rooted in the same image; but while "Metaphysics as Horizon" begins with horizon as a "maximum field of vision from a determinate standpoint," it very quickly turns horizon into a somewhat vague "umbrella" that covers both subjective and objective poles, thus confusing at least the literal image if not the metaphysical meaning. "Horizon" and "world," then, now seem to be practically equivalents; perhaps, for the sake of theoretical distinction, we may say that a subject's world is defined by and lies within the boundary of his or her horizon, both of which refer to the object-pole correlative to the subject's standpoint. "Metaphysics as Horizon," originally published in *Gregorianum* 44 (1963):307–318, and "*Existenz* and *Aggiornamento,*" a 1964 address originally published in *Focus: A Theological Journal* 2 (1965): 5–14, are both reprinted in *Collection* as chapter 13, pp. 202–220, and chapter 15, pp. 240–251 respectively.

53. Lonergan, *Method*, pp. 235, 236.
54. See Bernard Lonergan, "Notes on Existentialism" (mimeographed notes for lectures at Boston College, July, 1957), sec. 4, p. 7.
55. Lonergan, *Method*, p. 236.
56. Lonergan, *Collection*, p. 213.
57. Lonergan, *Method*, pp. 236, 237.
58. Ibid., p. 237.
59. Michael Novak, "The Christian and the Atheist" in Bernard Murchland (ed.), *The Meaning of the Death of God* (New York: Vintage Books, 1967), pp. 70–80, at 77.
60. Ibid.
61. The relationship here to Piaget's developmental scheme should become obvious as we move along; e.g., the correlation between the sensorimotor stage and the world of immediacy; also, greater development (Piaget) equals more complex structure (Lonergan), so first there is only experiencing, then experiencing and understanding, then these plus judging (with all three becoming ever more complex and subtle).
62. Lonergan, *Collection*, p. 243.
63. Lonergan, *Method*, p. 76. Correlating world-dimensions with levels of operations we get: immediacy/experiencing; mediated/understanding and judging; constituted/deciding (each sublating the preceding).
64. Ibid., p. 77.
65. Lonergan, *Collection*, p. 243.
66. Lonergan, *Method*, p. 77.
67. Lonergan, *Collection*, p. 255.
68. Ibid., pp. 254–255.
69. Ibid., pp. 224, 225.
70. Bernard Lonergan, *A Second Collection*, ed. W. F. J. Ryan and B. J. Tyrrell (Philadelphia: Westminster, 1974), p. 166.
71. Lonergan, *Method*, pp. 103, 104.
72. Ibid., p. 104.
73. Ibid.
74. Ibid., p. 27.
75. See Lonergan, *Insight*, pp. 8–10, 533.
76. Lonergan, *Second Collection*, p. 36.
77. Lonergan, *Method*, p. 104.
78. Lonergan, *Insight*, p. 273.
79. Lonergan, *Method*, p. 104.
80. Lonergan, *Insight*, p. 279.
81. Ibid., p. 280.
82. Ibid.
83. Lonergan, *Method*, p. 102.
84. Ibid., p. 76.

85. Lonergan, *Collection,* p. 230.
86. Lonergan, *Method,* p. 104.
87. Lonergan, *Insight,* pp. 598–599.
88. Ibid., p. 602.
89. Ibid., p. 609.
90. Ibid., pp. 609, 610, 611.
91. Lonergan, *Method,* p. 104.
92. Ibid., p. 36.
93. Ibid., p. 37.
94. Ibid.
95. Ibid.
96. This question is not made explicit by Lonergan, but it seems to accurately express what he means by the exigence to conform decision to judgment. Because judgments of value are not emphasized in *Insight,* and because Lonergan's later stress on questions for deliberation and judgments of value are not placed within the context of *Insight* with a full explicitness, it is necessary to construct some pattern that combines both, as I have done here.
97. Lonergan, *Second Collection,* p. 168.
98. Lonergan, *Method,* pp. 11, 73, 74.
99. Ibid., pp. 11–12, 105.
100. Lonergan, *Subject,* pp. 22–23.
101. Lonergan, *Method,* p. 13.
102. Ibid.
103. Ibid., p. 35.
104. Ibid., p. 34.
105. Lonergan, *Subject,* p. 24.
106. Lonergan, *Insight,* pp. 601–602.
107. Lonergan, *Subject,* p. 23.
108. Lonergan, *Insight,* p. 596.
109. Lonergan, *Subject,* p. 23.
110. Lonergan, *Insight,* p. 601.
111. Lonergan, *Subject,* pp. 23–24.
112. Lonergan, *Insight,* p. 601; Lonergan, *Method,* p. 51.
113. Lonergan, *Insight,* p. 601; Lonergan, *Method,* pp. 48–51.
114. Lonergan, *Insight,* p. 601.
115. Lonergan, *Method,* p. 51.
116. Lonergan, *Subject,* p. 24.
117. Ibid., pp. 25–26.
118. Lonergan, *Method,* pp. 245, 37.
119. Ibid., pp. 66–67, 64.
120. Ibid., pp. 30–31.
121. Ibid., p. 31.
122. Ibid., pp. 31, 38.
123. Ibid., pp. 31–32.
124. Ibid., p. 32.
125. Ibid., pp. 32–33.
126. Ibid., pp. 33–34.
127. Ibid., pp. 37–38.
128. Ibid., p. 38.
129. Ibid., p. 41.
130. Ibid., p. 81.
131. Ibid.
132. Ibid., p. 82; Lonergan, *Collection,* p. 256.
133. Lonergan, *Method,* p. 82.

134. Ibid.
135. Ibid.
136. Ibid., p. 84. See my "The Ontological Status of Theoretical Entities According to Wilfrid Sellars and Bernard Lonergan," *Divus Thomas* 79 (1976): 67–73.
137. See Lonergan, *Insight*, pp. 294–295.
138. Lonergan, *Method*, p. 83.
139. Ibid.
140. Ibid., pp. 247–249.
141. See Lonergan, "Notes on Existentialism," sec. 4, pp. 7–8.
142. Lonergan, *Method*, pp. 40, 237–238.
143. Ibid., p. 238.
144. Ibid.
145. Ibid., pp. 238–239.
146. Ibid., p. 239.
147. Ibid.
148. Ibid., pp. 239–240.
149. Lonergan, *Insight*, p. xxviii.
150. Ibid., pp. xviii, xix.
151. Ibid.
152. Ibid., p. 319.
153. Ibid.
154. Ibid.
155. Ibid., p. 326.
156. Ibid., pp. 326, 327.
157. Ibid.
158. Ibid., pp. 327–328.
159. Ibid., p. 329.
160. Ibid., pp. 329, 330.
161. Ibid., pp. 330–331.
162. Ibid., p. 331.
163. Ibid.
164. Ibid., p. 332.
165. Ibid. As we near the end of this section on intellectual conversion, I would like to emphasize that I understand intellectual conversion as a personally liberating and humbling experience which enables one to appreciate critically the validity and necessity of a variety of viewpoints in the *search* for truth; as such, it is the antithesis of a conceptual *possession* of the truth which one could use as a standard to determine the presence or absence of conversion in another.
166. See *Webster's New World Dictionary*.
167. See Michael Polanyi, *Personal Knowledge: Towards a Post-Critical Philosophy* (Chicago: University of Chicago Press, 1958).
168. Lonergan, *Method*, pp. 262–263.
169. Lonergan, *Insight*, p. 251.
170. Lonergan, *Method*, p. 263; see Lonergan, *Insight*, pp. 250–254.
171. Lonergan, *Method*, pp. 262–263.
172. Ibid., p. 263.
173. Lonergan, *Insight*, p. 253.
174. Ibid.
175. Ibid.
176. Lonergan, *Collection*, pp. 231, 228.
177. See Lonergan, *Insight*, chap. 12, esp. pp. 348–364.
178. Lonergan, *Collection*, p. 228.
179. Ibid., pp. 228, 229.
180. Ibid. To clarify the status of Lonergan's being as intended and thus the issue of

his metaphysical or ontological presuppositions, it may be well to indicate here that the being or reality toward which the subject heads in her or his intentional questions is not merely postulated, hypothesized, or supposed but also verified in fact in each virtually unconditioned of judgment—especially and principally in the affirmation of self as a knower, which in *Insight* functions as the critical link between the realm of hypothesis in pt. 1 and the realm of fact in pt. 2. See Lonergan's important distinction between "analytic propositions" and "analytic principles" (*Insight*, pp. 304–309).

181. Lonergan, *Collection*, pp. 229–230.
182. Ibid., p. 231.
183. Lonergan, *Insight*, pp. 375, 376.
184. Ibid., pp. 376, 377.
185. Ibid., p. 377.
186. Ibid., p. 385.
187. Lonergan, *Method*, pp. 264, 238, 239.
188. Ibid., pp. 264, 265.
189. Ibid., p. 265.
190. Ibid., pp. 262, 265.
191. Ibid., my emphasis.
192. Ibid., p. 351.
193. Ibid., pp. 338, 292.
194. Ibid., pp. 292, 265.
195. Lonergan, *Collection*, pp. 238, 239.
196. Lonergan, *Method*, p. 233.
197. Lonergan, *Insight*, pp. xviii, 613, 599.
198. Lonergan, *Collection*, pp. 224–225.
199. Lonergan, *Method*, pp. 14–15.
200. Lonergan, *Collection*, p. 224.
201. Lonergan, *Method*, p. 15.
202. The language of the second outline is appropriate to its original context within a discussion of transcendental method; in (4), "operate" might well be replaced by "live" in a more existential setting.
203. Lonergan, *Method*, p. 83.
204. Ibid., pp. 240, 35.
205. Bernard Lonergan, "Faith and Beliefs" (mimeographed paper presented at the Annual Meeting of the American Academy of Religion, Newton, MA, October, 1969), p. 6.
206. Ibid.
207. Ibid.
208. Lonergan, *Method*, p. 35.
209. Ibid., p. 241.
210. Ibid., p. 121.
211. Ibid., pp. 121, 240.
212. Lonergan, *Collection*, p. 241.
213. Lonergan, *Insight*, pp. 625, 627.
214. Lonergan, *Method*, pp. 121, 240.
215. Ibid., pp. 240, 51.
216. Lonergan, *Collection*, p. 242.
217. See Lonergan, "Notes on Existentialism," sec. 4, p. 11.
218. Lonergan, *Collection*, p. 242.
219. Lonergan, *Method*, p. 240.
220. See Lonergan, "Notes on Existentialism," sec. 4, pp. 10–11.
221. Lonergan, *Collection*, pp. 242–243.
222. See Lonergan, *Insight*, pp. 619–633.
223. Lonergan, *Method*, p. 240.

224. Ibid., pp. 39-40.

225. Ibid., p. 39; see Abraham Maslow, *Towards a Psychology of Being* (Princeton, NJ: Van Nostrand, 1962), p. 190.

226. Lonergan, *Insight*, p. 627.

227. Lonergan, *Method*, pp. 39-40.

228. Ibid., p. 39.

229. Ibid., pp. 83-84.

230. Ibid., pp. 240-241.

231. Ibid., p. 241.

232. See Karl Rahner, *Hörer des Wortes* (Munich: Kösel, 1963), p. 40.

233. Lonergan, *Method*, p. 241. For the purposes of later argument, I will reproduce here three short passages from *Method in Theology* which express quite straightforwardly Lonergan's understanding of how intellectual, moral, and religious conversions are related to each other by sublation.

... Moral conversion goes beyond the value, truth, to values generally. It promotes the subject from cognitional to moral self-transcendence. It sets him on a new, existential level of consciousness and establishes him as an originating value. But this in no way interferes with or weakens his devotion to truth. He still needs truth, for he must apprehend reality and real potentiality before he can deliberately respond to value. The truth he needs is still the truth attained in accord with the exigences of rational consciousness. But now his pursuit of it is all the more secure because he has been armed against bias, and it is all the more meaningful and significant because it occurs within, and plays an essential role in, the far richer context of the pursuit of all values.

Similarly, religious conversion goes beyond moral. Questions for intelligence, for reflection, for deliberation reveal the eros of the human spirit, its capacity and its desire for self-transcendence. But that capacity meets fulfillment, that desire turns to joy, when religious conversion transforms the existential subject into a subject in love, a subject held, grasped, possessed, owned through a total and so an otherworldly love. Then there is a new basis for all valuing and all doing good. In no way are fruits of intellectual or moral conversion negated or diminished. On the contrary, all human pursuit of the true and the good is included within and furthered by a cosmic context and purpose and, as well, there now accrues to man the power of love to enable him to accept the suffering involved in undoing the effects of decline.

It is not to be thought, however, that religious conversion means no more than a new and more efficacious ground for the pursuit of intellectual and moral ends. Religious loving is without conditions, qualifications, reservations; it is with all one's heart and all one's soul and all one's mind and all one's strength. This lack of limitation, though it corresponds to the unrestricted character of human questioning, does not pertain to this world. Holiness abounds in truth and moral goodness, but it has a distinct dimension of its own. It is other-worldly fulfillment, joy, peace, bliss. In Christian experience these are the fruits of being in love with a mysterious, uncomprehended God (*Method*, pp. 241-242).

234. Lonergan, *Method*, p. 242.

235. Lonergan, "Faith and Beliefs," pp. 9-10.

236. Lonergan, *Method*, p. 240.

237. Ibid., p. 289.

238. Ibid., pp. 243, 267.

239. Ibid., pp. 241, 122-123.

240. Ibid., p. 243.

241. On the other hand, we have also seen that Lonergan identifies religious conversion with *operative* grace (*Method*, p. 241)—indeed, "habitual grace as operative," in "Bernard Lonergan Responds" in P. McShane (ed.), *Foundations of*

Theology: Papers from the International Lonergan Congress 1970 (Notre Dame, IN: University of Notre Dame Press, 1972), pp. 223–234, at 226; but, again, Lonergan has said that by religious conversion he understands both "God's gift and man's acceptance of God's love," in "Bernard Lonergan Responds" in P. McShane (ed.), Language Truth and Meaning: Papers from the International Lonergan Congress 1970 (Dublin: Gill and Macmillan, 1972), pp. 306–312, at 308.

242. Lonergan, Method, pp. 243, 268; my emphasis.
243. See Maslow, Psychology of Being, p. 190; Lonergan, Method, p. 39.
244. Lonergan, "Bernard Lonergan Responds" in Foundations of Theology, p. 234.
245. Lonergan, Method, pp. 241, 267.
246. Ibid., p. 240.
247. Ibid.
248. Lonergan, Insight, pp. 19–25.

4

Conscience: Self-Transcending Subjectivity and Ethical Style

Conscience, in my judgment, and thus from the perspective of this book's thesis, is *the* foundational reality of theological ethics, and so of absolutely central concern to what I have called foundational ethics. Why, then, with so many pages gone and so few to go, have I said so little about conscience up to now? The fact is that all along we have been discussing conscience, while naming it only in passing. Because, as we saw with Paul Lehmann, there is no unanimous view as to exactly what conscience is, despite the common use of the term, we began with the problem of analyzing that aspect, character, or dimension of the human person we call "moral," and we did that in the hope of discovering some intersecting lines which would point to, help us locate and specify, the reality of conscience.

After reviewing the valuable contribution of H. Richard Niebuhr on the responsible personal subject, we worked through the developmental theories of Erik Erikson, Jean Piaget, and Lawrence Kohlberg in order to specify the fundamental elements of an explanatory theory of self-transcendence that would give a "critical edge" to the notion of responsible subjectivity. Finally, in the preceding chapter, we saw how Bernard Lonergan's transcendental method offers the possibility of bringing responsible subjectivity and self-transcendence together in a personally appropriated synthesis. And now, perhaps, after many pages of analysis, we are in a position to suggest a tentative definition of conscience.

A. CONSCIENCE

By keeping the various common sense, psychological, philosophical, and theological meanings of conscience in mind (closer to the back than the front, where they could offer guidance but not steer) as we considered the historical work of Lehmann, the phenomenological

analysis of Niebuhr, the psychological theories of development of
Erikson, Piaget, and Kohlberg, and finally Lonergan's philosophical
analysis of the structure, development, and transformations of the
basic conscious and intentional operations of the human subject, we
have hit upon several lines intersecting at what I think is a critically
sound and methodologically valuable understanding of conscience.
Chief among these lines are: the notions we have seen of the personal
subject; the development of cognitive, affective, and moral structures;
Erikson's normative differentiation between the "moral" and the
"ethical," as well as his concept of basic psychosocial strengths or
virtues; and Lonergan's understanding of consciousness, the structure
of conscious intentionality and its basic operations (especially moral
consciousness and its deliberation, evaluation, decision, and choice),
self-transcendence, objectivity, and conversion; along with my own
variations on affective self-transcendence's conversion to being-in-
love and, especially, the intellectual conversion implicit in moral
conversion or critical self-appropriation. The point at which these
lines intersect, the radical meaning of human conscience, I am
suggesting, is the reality of the authentic personal subject, intellectually, morally, affectively, and religiously converted, operating
on the fourth and highest level of moral, responsible, existential consciousness. Such an understanding, of course, is normative; other
meanings of conscience must be understood in terms of it.

At the end of chapter two I suggested that we need not think that
everyone has a conscience in the fully human sense of conscience we
considered there in terms of developmental psychology. Now that we
have considered the phenomenon of conversion from a philosophical
perspective, that suggestion seems even more to the point. We may
think of mature personal conscience, then, as being either merely
potential (before moral conversion) or actual (after moral conversion). And this actualized (normative) conscience will be critical or
not depending on the nature of the moral conversion, as we have
seen. Within this framework, the term "religious conscience" may
refer to either potential or actual conscience, before or after religious
conversion. In any case, the designation "religious" specifies not the
functional or structural aspect of conscience, but the nature of the
ground which supports and the matrix which shapes one's judgments
and choices of value. Insofar as conversion transforms one's whole
orientation and being, the source and principle from which flow the
judgments, decisions, and actions of the religiously converted person
has little if anything in common with that of the unconverted person.
I must repeat here, however, something we saw earlier with Lonergan,

namely, that *genuine* religious conversion, while giving conscience a new and other-worldly basis, a more efficacious ground, and a cosmic context and purpose, in no way violates or destroys the integrity of human conscience.[1]

For Lonergan, conscience is, as we noted at the beginning of chapter three, a form of consciousness. Specifically, conscience is the consciousness of the fourth level—or, as he variously refers to it, "rational self," moral, responsible, or existential consciousness.[2] But this, I must emphasize again, is the fourth level of consciousness *as distinct* from the other levels taken by themselves, but *not as separated* from the other three levels. For, as I have tried to highlight before, each successive level of consciousness *sublates* the lower level, so that the subject on the fourth level of consciousness is *at once* empirically, intelligently, rationally, *and* morally conscious. Thus, to say that a person is morally or responsibly conscious means that he or she is also empirically, intelligently, and rationally conscious. The higher level complements, presupposes, and includes the lower levels.

Further, to say that conscience is the fourth level of moral consciousness (sublating the lower three levels) means that conscience is the *subject* herself as morally conscious, for, indeed, consciousness, as we have seen, is constitutive of the human person as subject. When this consciousness is moral, responsible, existential, the subject is both constituted and revealed to herself at the peak, the highest intensity of her subjectivity. Most fundamentally, then, this is the critical meaning of my earlier assertion that a person does not have, but *is* a conscience.

To thus identify conscience with moral consciousness, i.e., with the *subject* as morally conscious, is to reject the various attempts that have been made to equate conscience with some particular faculty or power or act of the person.

The continuity and unity of human consciousness as analyzed by Lonergan is, quite simply, directly opposed to a faculty psychology.[3] What is presented to consciousness, he shows, is not a collection of faculties or powers, but a set of interrelated operations, which, in Lonergan's words, together

conspire to achieve both cognitional and real self-transcendence. Such is the basic unity and continuity. No part of the process can be dispensed with, for each has its essential contribution to make. To achieve the good, one has to know the real. To know the real, one has to reach the truth. To reach the truth one has to understand, to grasp the intelligible. To grasp the intelligible, one has to attend to the data. Each successive level of operations presupposes and complements its predecessors. The topmost level is the level of deliberate control and self-control; there consciousness becomes conscience; there operations are authentic in the measure that they are responses to value.[4]

In the same way, it becomes clear that conscience cannot be reduced to any single act or operation, such as decision, choice, or, as has often been the case, judgment of a particular kind. For moral consciousness sublates all the previous levels of intentional operations, and so depends on them. Conscience, then, involves all the subject's conscious and intentional operations insofar as they are practical, heading toward decision and action.

Moral consciousness is highlighted, however, by the manifestation of the personal subject's drive toward self-transcendence in the form of an exigence for consistency between one's knowing and one's doing, for conformity of one's decisions to one's reasonable, objective judgments. And this exigence, standing between knowledge and decision, while concretizing the meaning of freedom, obligation, and responsibility, is, perhaps, the crystallization of the meaning of conscience. In other words, conscience *is* the dynamic thrust toward self-transcendence at the core of a person's very subjectivity revealing itself on the fourth level of consciousness as a demand for responsible decision in accord with reasonable judgment. As such, it points in two directions, to what I have called the two key ethical moments: knowing and deciding. As a drive for self-transcendence, conscience insists on responsible, that is to say, authentic decisions and choices. But, because moral consciousness is itself an enlargement and transformation of the rational consciousness of the third level (whereby rational necessity is transformed into the rational exigence that is obligation), a decision or choice can be responsible and authentic only insofar as it is reasonable, that is, consistent with reasonable judgment. Thus, if decision is to be responsible, judgment itself must be reasonable, truly critical. And most of all, this means *self*-critical. An "easy conscience" is very probably the most personally disastrous way persons fail in their obligation to critical questioning. Human authenticity has no room for complacency, self-satisfaction. The subject who would be authentic must engage himself in a continual process of constantly checking, expanding, and deepening his understanding through a critical exchange with the most informed and sensitive members of his widest community. This self-criticism, of course, must include not only a thorough, ongoing check of one's grasp of human reality and situations, but also, and most significantly, a ruthless critique of one's moral feelings, one's responses to values of various kinds. Only such a critical quest for authentic understanding and feeling can ground the real self-transcendence of a truly human conscience.[5]

Because conscience is intrinsically constituted by a context of understanding and feeling that is developing toward ever greater or lesser authenticity, it is obvious that not only will conscience—in the concrete—mean something quite different from subject to subject (as does, for example, accumulated experience or habitual understanding), but an important aspect of this difference will be varying degrees of authenticity. In other words, even before we get to the question of a subject's authenticity in her attempt to conform decision to judgment—the degree, for example, of her habitual willingness— there is an important question about the authenticity of the subject's conscience, of the entire matrix of understanding, feeling, and judgments which forms the context of each practical judgment of value.

Conscience, in short, is not some given constant of the human person, something which everyone has, period. Rather, human subjects are empirically, intelligently, rationally, and morally conscious, and that consciousness takes endlessly multiple, variant forms in the concrete, each more or less authentic. Therefore there is the need for a *normative* interpretation of conscience. While it may be true that a person must follow his own conscience, and I for one think it is, it will not be enough on that symbolic day of judgment for him to say, simply, "I followed my conscience." For, as we have noted, he will surely be asked not only how faithfully he *followed* his conscience, but also how authentically he *formed* it.

Lonergan has touched upon the normative aspect of conscience in the notion of a "good conscience," the result of conversion. On this point he states, in *Method in Theology*, that "decision is responsible and it is free, but it is the work not of a metaphysical will but of conscience and, indeed, when a conversion, the work of a good conscience."[6] Such a "good conscience," as we have noted, is itself the criterion of judgments of value, for, says Lonergan,

> such judgments are felt to be true or false insofar as they generate a peaceful or uneasy conscience. But they attain their proper context, their clarity and refinement, only through man's historical development and the individual's personal appropriation of his social, cultural, and religious heritage. It is by the transcendental notion of value and its expression in a good and uneasy conscience that man can develop morally. But a rounded moral judgment is ever the work of a fully developed self-transcending subject or, as Aristotle would put it, of a virtuous man.[7]

Such a "good conscience," I am proposing, should be recognized as the only conscience one can appeal to for moral authority. Such a "good conscience," in other words, should be considered as definitive of the primary meaning of conscience. The personal subject's very dynamism for self-transcendence dictates that he or she be defined not in terms common to anyone, but in terms of the person who has achieved the authenticity of normative development. Thus conscience, which is essentially a matter of value—indeed, the criterion of value—should be defined not just as moral consciousness generally, but specifically as the moral consciousness which has transformed itself by shifting the criterion of its decisions and choices from satisfactions to values. It is right that each person should be able to take a stand on his or her own conscience, uncoerced by external force. But everyone who does so should also recognize that appeals to conscience do not automatically or necessarily make one right, that some consciences are more authentic than others, and that one's commitment to his or her "conscience" must always remain critical. Sincerity to what one feels deeply about, or spontaneously "thinks best," in other words, is not enough. Sincerity must be fully and continually self-critical if it is to be authentic. For such self-criticism, of course, a radical openness to other viewpoints is a prerequisite; and such openness seems to have its necessary condition in a deep sense of humility.

While everyone has a "conscience" in the sense that every normal person has some degree of moral sense, some depth of moral consciousness, I am suggesting on the basis of our present analysis that the primary, basic, normative meaning of conscience be understood as at least the consciousness of a morally converted person, and optimally the consciousness of this person as also critically appropriated and affectively or religiously converted. In other words, just as we saw, with Erikson, that conscience is proper to the person with the ethical orientation of the mature adult characterized by fidelity, love, and care (and not the "moral" orientation proper to childhood or the "ideological" orientation proper to adolescence); or, with Kohlberg, that conscience distinguishes the highest level of principled morality from the lower levels of self-interest and conformism; so now I am proposing that we understand conscience in the fully human sense as being proper to and distinguishing the person who has taken possession of her or himself critically as a free and responsible creator and has opted for value over satisfaction as a criterion for decision and choice—the person who is a source of love, a principle of benevolence and beneficence because her or his very being is a being-in-love.

Conscience, then, in a few words, should be understood as the funda-mental, dynamic reality of the personal subject who has committed, dedicated, indeed, surrendered her or himself to the radical demands of the human spirit: be attentive, be intelligent, be reasonable, be responsible, love.[8] Quite simply, conscience is the fullest expression of the personal subject's fundamental exigence for full self-transcendence. A theological ethics capable of accurately interpreting the reality of the human person needs such an understanding of con-science as self-transcending subjectivity.

B. CONCLUSION: NOTES ON ETHICAL STYLE

A proposal for interpreting conscience in terms of self-transcending subjectivity, of course, is not without implications for the very nature of the entire ethical enterprise. In concluding this study, I will men-tion a few of the basic ones.

First of all, the emphasis of an ethics developed from an interpreta-tion of conscience as the drive for self-transcendence will be neither negative, nor minimal, nor legalist, nor deductivist, but positive, maximal, principled, and creative. If, as in the illustration below, one allows a vertical line to represent the moral dimension

Full human development, authenticity;
sensitive and effective responsiveness
to values of concrete situations.

          acceptable, permissible
          not acceptable, not permissible

of human reality and living, two foci of attention immediately appear possible: ethical study may emphasize, or concentrate on locating, identifying, and defining with great clarity and precision, the line between those human actions which are acceptable or permissible, and those which are not. Or, on the other hand, ethics may concen-trate its central attention on clarifying and explicating the meaning of authenticity, of fully human development, and emphasize the manner in which authentic subjects will understand, judge, and make deci-sions and choices in concrete situations—how, in other words, they will attempt to be sensitively and effectively responsive to the values involved in an endless variety of contexts in which they find them-selves faced with decisions and choices. The latter, positive emphasis on human development and response to value will be the focal (though not exclusive) concern of an ethics grounded in an understanding of conscience as self-transcending subjectivity.

Such an ethics, perhaps, can be best compared to literary (or music, art, film) criticism and aesthetics, if one understands the work of the critic not primarily as rendering ultimate judgments on the worth of a particular novel or film, but as the ongoing attempt to illuminate and interpret the meaning and value of a given piece of work, and if one understands the task of aesthetics as the development of the general principles and theory according to which this kind of criticism proceeds.[9] Given this analogue, theological ethics would have a similar twofold division of labor, with the tasks related in the same way. That is to say, there would be a foundational ethics (at the subject-pole) to work out basic philosophical questions and develop fundamental principles of procedure, and there would also be (at the object-pole) the ethical equivalent of criticism, which would attempt to illuminate and interpret (with the help of the human and natural sciences, the humanities and arts, various philosophical and religious perspectives, and the wisdom of personal and communal experience) the meanings and values of more or less typically problematic situations of human life which call for judgments, decisions, and choices.[10] What the world of art is to the critic and aesthetic theorist, then, the entire world of human action—indeed, all of life—is to the ethicist, whether theorist or critic or both. I say "both" because it is important to emphasize that both tasks are necessary, and that they should be done in conjunction and cooperation with each other. In the past, ethics has all too often been divided, separated, split into the two totally different and entirely other worlds of the moral philosopher's theory and the (often Christian) ethicist's cristicism (a "criticism," unhappily, not always of the type I have adumbrated here), with little or no communication between the two realms. Theological ethics needs both theory and criticism, working together. But this working relationship must be understood properly.

The ethical critic, as he or she attempts to understand and shed some light on a problem like abortion, works in light of the theoretical principles of foundational ethics, but does not use these principles as premises from which to deduce answers to particular problems, any more than the literary critic deduces an interpretation of a poem from aesthetic principles. Like the literary critic, the ethical analyst and critic is interested more in deepening understanding than in erecting final certitudes.

Further, because the ethical analyst realizes that decisions are made in particular situations according to the subject's best *creative* understanding of the complex concreteness of the situation, he or she does not regard interpretations of general problem areas like abortion as applicable in a *deductive* way to particular cases, any more than the literary critic pretends to offer the author a formula on how to compose a fine poem or first-rate novel. However, because the members of the ethical critic's audience are all themselves creators in the ethical art of living, the ethical critic functions as the creator's teacher to a much greater degree than does the literary or music critic (whose audience are principally readers and listeners). For the ethical critic attempts to deepen the understanding of the complexities of human reality that each member of his or her audience (of creators) brings to particular situations. Perhaps to some extent, then, the ethical analyst plays not only a role analogous to that of the music critic, but also a teaching role similar to that of the conservatory professor in the formal education of the composer or performer.

The theological ethicist who starts with our understanding of conscience as self-transcending subjectivity, then, is most modest in estimating his or her own role: the ethicist is analyst, critic, theoretician, teacher, but above all student, and especially not legislator. The ethicist tries to deepen and enrich his or her understanding of human life, and attempts to share that understanding of the meaning and value of the personal subject as creator and of the structures of the human world in which he or she creates. But the ethicist never forgets that while each situation the subject faces is not totally different from every other, it is neither entirely the same, and that conscience is authentic in each situation inasmuch as the subject brings to the situation a rich and open matrix of habitual human understanding and sensitive feeling, grasps the particular problem within the widest parameters of its context, and responds in a genuinely *creative* way through critical understanding to the situation's deepest human values. Brian Henderson, the film critic, expresses the creative quality of the subject's response when he says that " . . . it is the power and function of imagination to reveal choices, to raise up options where there was only necessity."[11] Creative human response cannot be predicted or deduced any more than a genuine work of art can be predicted or deduced, and it is in this unpredictability and nondeductibility that the ethical analyst's modesty is rooted. But as painters, writers, and composers must labor many years in the formation of their imaginations before giving birth to their unique creations, so, too, as we have noted, must subjects gradually develop into mature, authentic persons. And in this process of growth, of the education of the sensibilities, understanding, and judgment; of the development of openness, habitual willingness, and genuineness; and, most importantly, of conversion; the theological ethicist, both theorist and critic, can play a crucial role (along with parents, teachers, friends, and other key persons in the subject's world).

Before ending, we might reflect on the following point that Loner-gan makes in *The Subject:*

> Just as the existential subject freely and responsibly makes himself what he is, so too he makes himself good or evil and his actions right or wrong. The good subject, the good choice, the good action are not found in isolation. For the subject is good by his good choices and good actions. Universally prior to any choice or action there is just the transcendental principle of all appraisal and criticism, the intention of the good. That principal gives rise to instances of the good, but those instances are good choices and actions. However, do not ask me to determine them, for their determination in each case is the work of the free and responsible subject producing the first and only edition of himself.
>
> It is because the determination of the good is the work of freedom that ethical systems can catalogue sins in almost endless genera and species yet always remain rather vague about the good. They urge us to do good as well as to avoid evil, but what it is to do good does not get much beyond the golden rule, the precept of universal charity, and the like. Still the shortcomings of system are not an irremediable defect. We come to know the good from the example of those about us, from the stories people tell of the good and evil men and women of old, from the incessant flow of praise and blame that makes up the great part of human conversation, from the elation and from the shame that fill us when our own choices and deeds are our own determination of ourselves as good or evil, praiseworthy or blameworthy.[12]

This passage prompts some final reflections on the relation between art and ethics. First, the centrality of concrete, imaginative, and crea-tive understanding within the moral dimension seems to suggest that ethics, in its attempt to deepen our understanding of concrete human living, has an obligation to involve itself in very detailed analyses of the symbols and stories (past and present, personal and communal) of our culture. This does not mean, however, that ethics itself is to be done within a symbolic pattern (anymore than literary criticism, for example); ethics remains reflective, theoretical, and critical.

Further, it seems to be no merely accidental or superficial resem-blance which relates the task of aesthetics and the criticism of art, music, and literature to the ethical enterprise. For not only does the creative element in human affairs make the ethicist primarily a critic in the manner of the art and literary critic (whose function, of course, has its own creative aspect), but the very concreteness of the reality of the human subject, especially in what we have come to call its moral dimension (the fact, that is, that the deepest human meanings and values are to be found in affect-laden images), suggests that the world of art itself must play a vital and central role in the development of the self-transcending subject's conscience—in the growing autonomy of the authentic human subject. For the education of the imagination and feelings, in which values are apprehended, is as critically important for authentic human living as the development of other (e.g., conceptual) aspects of consciousness.

On this point, George Steiner has questioned, in the aftermath of the Jewish Holocaust, the suppositions of a "world that believed that if people read good books, went to museums, subscribed to the opera, and loved symphonies, certain decencies would follow."[13] He has questioned, to put it simply, the ability of the liberal and fine arts of humanistic education to liberate and humanize men and women, to make them, as he says, "morally responsible."[14] We cannot answer Steiner's questions here. I bring them up only to point out that, in stressing the importance of the arts in the process of personal development and conversion, I do not mean to say that the arts hold a final and complete answer to fully human education. Their importance lies in their integration into a fuller and deeper context of fully human personal development. Not *ars gratia artis*, but *ars gratia hominis*. Without that context, without that substratum of human compassion, kindness, care, and love to penetrate and enlighten, the finest education in the arts can give a person nothing more than a cultural veneer. Perhaps Steiner suggests something like this himself when in *The Death of Tragedy* he says that "great art is not reserved to the specialist or the professional scholar, but that it is best known and loved by those who live most intensely."[15] Another side of this complex of human development is brought out in a striking way by Anne Morrow Lindbergh in her *Hour of Gold, Hour of Lead*, where she affirms: "I do not believe that sheer suffering teaches. If suffering alone taught, all the world would be wise, since everyone suffers. To suffering must be added mourning, understanding, patience, love, openness, and the willingness to remain vulnerable."[16]

This point highlights even more sharply, I think, the emphasis I placed on the significance of love as an ethical reality in our discussion about affective conversion. It also highlights the importance for ethical discussion of the kind of analysis that Erikson has given of psychosocial or affective development. And it is worth noting, I think, as we conclude this study, that the theory of developmental psychology which we have examined is significant not only as a powerful contemporary argument for the truth of the ancient ethical view presented here in the new clothes of self-transcending subjectivity, and not only as a corrective to the misunderstandings that totally identify conscience with a primitive morality of the superego, but also and especially as a distinctively persuasive injection of the themes of affectivity in general and self-transcending human love in particular into the discussion of ethics. For all too often in the past ethical discussion has been exclusively located either within a philosophical context in which justice is normative (and love peripheral or nonexistent), or within a religious context in which love, though central and normative, is principally the supernatural virtue of charity. One of the most significant contributions to ethics of a contemporary psychologist like Erikson,[17] then, is an empirical theory of the development and function of human love as a central reality in a man or woman's life. No longer is the theological ethicist forced to choose between a philosophical concept of justice or the traditional religious concept of charity. Love (and care) as a psychological strength or virtue in Erikson's theory of personal development provides an empirically rooted ethical criterion which moves beyond the concept of justice without involving the metaphysical presuppositions of the supernatural virtue of charity.

It is also worth noting that the interpretation of conscience as the drive for self-transcendence presented here offers a fundamental clarification of what James Gustafson has called a "misplaced debate" between a context-centered ethics and a principle-centered ethics.[18] The issue at stake in this debate has also been phrased in terms of the opposition between absolutism and relativism, or of the distinction between structure and creativity. Taking a merely linguistic cue from Freud's "anatomy is destiny," we may say, perhaps, that for an ethics rooted in an understanding of conscience as self-transcending subjectivity, "structure is authenticity." Authentic living, in other words, is determined neither by absolute principles nor by an arbitrary creativity relative to each situation; authentic living, rather, is defined by a normative structure of consciousness which demands that a person respond to the values in each situation with a creativity that is at once sensitive, critical, responsible and loving. As Lonergan asserts that "method offers not rules to be followed blindly, but a framework for creativity,"[19] so we may consider foundational ethics not as a set of rules but as the explication of a normative, dynamic structure for creative living.

In conclusion, we should note that the understanding of conscience proposed here attacks the so-called "naturalistic fallacy" at its roots by showing that, at the subject-pole, there is no "jump" from "is" to "ought" because one is already there. The fact is that in one stroke transcendental method, by uncovering and revealing the single, fundamental, and radical exigence of the human spirit for full self-transcendence in response to truth, value, and love, shows not only that the human person's genuine *self-realization is self-transcendence*, but also that the *basic human "fact" is a drive for "value,"* that in the most radical sense, *the human person's "is" is an "ought."* Rather than a "naturalistic fallacy," in fact, transcendental method reveals, as Michael Novak has argued, a new and rich meaning of "natural law": not an authoritarian code written on tablets "out there," nor an arbitrary, whimsical standard "in the heart," but a natural law constituted by the radical dynamism of the human spirit, the "first principles" of which are "not verbal, propositional imperatives or judgments, but rather operations of the human person unfolding according to their own inherent exigency."[20]

A final word about the character of a theological ethics rooted in an understanding of conscience as self-transcending subjectivity may be borrowed from some of Lonergan's comments about transcendental method in theology:

> Just as it is one's own self-transcendence that enables one to know others accurately and to judge them fairly, so inversely it is through knowledge and appreciation of others that we come to know ourselves and to fill out and refine our apprehension of values.
> . . . .
> Such an objectification of subjectivity is in the style of the crucial experiment. While it will not be automatically efficacious, it will provide the open-minded, the serious, the sincere with the occasion to ask themselves some basic questions, first, about others but eventually, even about themselves. It will make conversion a topic and thereby promote it. Results will not be sudden or startling, for conversion commonly is a slow process of maturation. It is finding out for oneself and in oneself what it is to be intelligent, to be reasonable, to be responsible, to love. . . . .
> . . . .
> Indeed, the basic idea of the method we are trying to develop takes its stand on discovering what human authenticity is and showing how to appeal to it. It is not an infallible method, for men easily are unauthentic, but it is a powerful method, for man's deepest need and most prized achievement is authenticity.[21]

This study has been psychological and philosophical in method, though theological in purpose and orientation. We began, indeed, with the problem of conscience in the context of Christian ethics as articulated by Paul Lehmann. Since leaving a complex structure by the same door we entered often helps us to get our bearings, we might return to Lehmann's context for a moment on this final page.

In chapter one I argued that the bibilical notion of "heart" which Lehmann finds so illuminating is—though helpful and attractive—radically uncritical as he presents it. We are now in a position to understand the "heart" as a symbol for conscience in a fully critical fashion. We have seen that the personal development necessary for a mature, fully human conscience in the normative sense includes both affective (Erikson) and cognitive (Piaget and Lonergan) aspects. Further, we have seen that while critical, objective, impersonal, and universal (Kohlberg), moral judgment must be sensitively responsive to the values of each concrete human situation as well as imaginatively creative in interpretation. Decision and action, finally, must be responsible and courageous. No symbol seems to capture these various aspects of moral consciousness (as *critically* established through developmental theory and transcendental method) quite as strikingly and persuasively as the "heart." It seems fitting, then, that Lonergan characterizes the fully self-transcending "being-in-love" of affective (at its peak, religious) conversion as Pascal's "reason of the heart that reason does not know."[22]

Notes

1. Lonergan, *Method*, p. 242.
2. See Lonergan, "Faith and Beliefs," p. 9; Lonergan, *Method*, p. 268; Lonergan, *Insight*, pp. 610, 628.
3. See Lonergan, "Faith and Beliefs," pp. 8–9; Lonergan, *Method*, pp. 268–269, 340, 343.
4. Lonergan, "Faith and Beliefs," p. 9.
5. See Lonergan, *Insight*, pp. 599–600, for a discussion of attempts to dodge the moral exigence through the avoidance of self-consciousness, rationalization, and moral renunciation.
6. Lonergan, *Method*, p. 269.
7. Ibid., pp. 40–41.
8. Ibid., pp. 253, 268.
9. See Herbert McCabe, *What is Ethics All About?* (Washington, DC: Corpus Books, 1969), chap. 3.
10. See Johnson, "Lonergan and the Redoing of Ethics," p. 218.
11. Brian Henderson, Review of "Targets," *Film Heritage*, Summer 1969, p. 3.
12. Lonergan, *Subject*, pp. 26–27.
13. Elizabeth Hall, "The Freakish Passion: A Conversation with George Steiner," *Psychology Today*, February 1973, p. 57.
14. Ibid., p. 60.
15. George Steiner, *The Death of Tragedy* (New York: Hill and Wang, 1963), p. viii.

16. Quoted in *Time*, February 5, 1973, p. 35. Also see Sidney Ahlstrom, *A Religious History of the American People* (New Haven: Yale University Press, 1972), pp. 1034–1035.

17. Also see the work of Abraham Maslow, Carl Rogers, Erich Fromm, and Rollo May, to mention only a few of the prominent existential and humanistic psychologists.

18. See James Gustafson, "Context Versus Principles: A Misplaced Debate in Christian Ethics" in Martin Marty and Dean Peerman (eds.), *New Theology No. 3* (New York: Macmillan, 1966), pp. 69–102, esp. at 69–70.

19. Lonergan, *Method*, p. xii.

20. Michael Novak, "Bernard Lonergan: A New Approach to Natural Law," *Proceedings of the American Catholic Philosophical Association* 41 (1967): 246–249, at 248.

21. Lonergan, *Method*, pp. 253–254.

22. Bernard Lonergan, "Natural Knowledge of God," *Proceedings of the Catholic Theological Society of America* 23 (1968): 54–69, at 65.

Acknowledgments

Permission to quote material from the following sources is gratefully acknowledged:

Sincerity and Authenticity by Lionel Trilling, 1972, Harvard University Press; copyright 1971, 1972 by the President and Fellows of Harvard College.

Depth Psychology and a New Ethic by Erich Neumann, 1969, G. P. Putnam's Sons; copyright 1969 by the C. G. Jung Foundation for Analytical Psychology.

Ethics in a Christian Context by Paul Lehmann, 1963, Harper & Row, Publishers; copyright 1963 by Paul L. Lehmann.

The Responsible Self by H. Richard Niebuhr, 1963, Harper & Row, Publishers; copyright 1963, 1978 by Florence M. Niebuhr.

Childhood and Society by Erik H. Erikson, 2nd edition 1963, W. W. Norton & Company, Inc.; copyright 1950, 1963 by W. W. Norton & Company, Inc.

Identity: Youth and Crisis by Erik H. Erikson, 1968, W. W. Norton & Company, Inc.; copyright 1968 by W. W. Norton & Company, Inc.

Insight and Responsibility by Erik H. Erikson, 1964, W. W. Norton & Company, Inc.; copyright 1964 by Erik H. Erikson.

"Life Cycle" by Erik H. Erikson, in *International Encyclopedia of the Social Sciences*, David L. Sills, Editor, Volume 9, 1968, Macmillan and Free Press; copyright 1968 by Crowell Collier and Macmillan, Inc.

Six Psychological Studies by Jean Piaget, translated by Anita Tenzer, edited by David Elkind, 1968, Vintage Books; copyright 1967 by Random House, Inc.

The Psychology of the Child by Jean Piaget and Bärbel Inhelder, 1969, Basic Books; copyright 1969 by Basic Books, Inc.

The Growth of Logical Thinking by Bärbel Inhelder and Jean Piaget, 1958, Basic Books; copyright 1958 by Basic Books, Inc.

"Moral Development" by Lawrence Kohlberg, in *International Encyclopedia of the Social Sciences*, David L. Sills, Editor, Volume 10, 1968, Macmillan and Free Press; copyright 1968 by Crowell Collier and Macmillan, Inc.

"The Adolescent as a Philosopher: The Discovery of the Self in a Postconventional World" by Lawrence Kohlberg and Carol Gilligan, in *Daedalus* 100 (Fall 1971): 1051–1086; copyright 1971 by the American Academy of Arts and Sciences.

Insight: A Study of Human Understanding by Bernard J. F. Lonergan, S.J., 2nd edition 1958, Philosophical Library; copyright 1957, 1958 by Longman Group Limited.

Method in Theology by Bernard J. F. Lonergan, S.J., 1972, Herder and Herder; copyright 1972 by Bernard J. F. Lonergan; by permission of The Seabury Press.

Collection by Bernard Lonergan, S.J., edited by F. E. Crowe, S.J., 1967, Herder and Herder; copyright 1967 by Bernard Lonergan, S.J.; by permission of The Seabury Press.

The Subject by Bernard Lonergan, S.J., S.T.D., 1968, Marquette University Press; copyright 1968 by the Wisconsin-Alpha Chapter of the Phi Sigma Tau Marquette University.

Permission by the editors to publish material which originally appeared in different form in the following journals is gratefully acknowledged:

Thought 51 (March 1976): 82–98; *The Journal of Religious Ethics* 5 (Fall 1977): 249–266; *Journal of Psychology and Theology* 5 (Winter 1977): 34–39; *Dialectica* 30 (1976): 197–221; *Angelicum* 53 (1976): 362–404 and 54 (1977): 67–88; *Lumen Vitae* 30 (1975): 213–230; *American Benedictine Review* 30 (1979): 301–321; *Louvain Studies* 7 (1979): 183–194; *The Modern Schoolman* 54 (March 1977): 215–231; *The Thomist* 40 (April 1976): 243–257.

Index

WESTMAR COLLEGE LIBRARY